AF622277

CENTRAL GRANTS AND STATE AUTONOMY

CENTRAL GRANTS AND STATE AUTONOMY

S.H. PATIL

TLANTIC PUBLISHERS AND DISTRIBUTORS

Published by
ATLANTIC PUBLISHERS AND DISTRIBUTORS
B-2, Vishal Enclave, New Delhi-27
Phones 5413460, 5429987

Sales Office
4346/4C, Ansari Road, Darya Ganj,
New Delhi-110 002
Phones 3273880, 3285873
Fax 91-11-3285873

Copyright © The Publishers, 1995

ISBN 81-7156-532-8

"This research report was financed by the Indian Council of Social Science Research, New Delhi, to the author. The responsibility for facts stated, opinions expressed and conclusions drawn is entirely that of the author and not of the I.C.S.S.R."

No part of this book may be reproduced in any form without permission from the publisher except for the quotation of brief passages in criticism

Typeset at
APD Computer Graphics, Delhi
Printed in India at
Tarun Offset Printers
518/14, Anup Market, Maujpur, Delhi-53

PREFACE

The present work, Central Grants and State Autonomy, is a research project submitted to the Indian Council of Social Science Research, New Delhi and is the result of the financial assistance provided by the latter. I am greatly indebted to the director and other officers of I.C.S.S.R., New Delhi, for their timely financial assistance in completing this research project. I also thank the various authorities of Karnatak University, Dharwad, for their timely correspondence with I.C.S.S.R., New Delhi.

I am grateful to the librarians and other authorities of the following libraries which I had consulted for the present work during 1988-90: (i) Karnatak University Library, Dharwad, (ii) Library of Indian Council of Social Science Research, New Delhi, (iii) Library of Ministry of Finance, Government of India, New Delhi, (iv) Library of Planning Commission, New Delhi, (v) Library of Central Secretariat, New Delhi, (vi) Library of Indian Institute of Public Administration, New Delhi, (vii) Library of Jawaharlal Nehru University, New Delhi, (viii) Library of Karnatak State Legislature, Bangalore, (ix) Library of Institute of Social and Economic Change, Bangalore, (x) Library of Bangalore University, Bangalore, (xi) Library of Madras University, Madras, (xii) Library of Madras Institute of Development Studies, Madras, (xiii) Connemara Public Library, Madras, and (xiv) Office of Zilla Parishad, Dharwad.

DR. S.H. PATIL

CONTENTS

Page Nos.

INTRODUCTION : PROBLEM, OBJECTIVES AND METHODOLOGY

A political system is not a static framework but is an organic living body of men and women who are influenced by various forces like races, religions, castes, regions, economic and political interests, leadership, ideas, ideals, etc. This is particularly true of a federal political system which is subject to centripetal and centrifugal tendencies which are conditioned by various forces from time to time. Consequently in a federal system the centre-state relations are the live relations and equilibrium under such system depends on this centre-state relationship. The centre-state controversy cannot be solved permanently. Issues of controversy shift from generation to generation with changing socio-economic and political conditions, compulsions, etc.

The centre-state relations under the Indian federal system have been a subject of great controversy and debate. Apart from constitutional and legal controversies, there have been political, administrative and financial controversies. Among the various controversies, the centre-state financial controversies have drawn attention of both the academicians and the politicians. These controversies become more pointed and widespread when different political parties are in power at the centre and in the states. Three commissions – Administrative Reforms Commission, Report of the Centre-State Relations Inquiry Committee (Rajamannar Committee) and Report of Commission on Centre-State Relations (Sarkaria Commission) – have devoted sufficient space for discussing centre-state financial relations including central voluntary grants-in-aid.

The centre-state financial relations in Indian federal system are more complex and controversial than in any of the four traditional federations of the world – U.S.A., Switzerland, Canada and Australia. Central planning and welfare programmes in India have made the centre-state relations more complex and controversial. India is committed to the ideology of welfare state. Welfare programmes cannot be carried out by the state governments alone with their meagre resources, nor can they be implemented by the central government without involving the state governments. In order to carry out a joint enterprise, national planning has been adopted to implement the socio-economic programmes for the welfare of the people of India. Though the Constitution of India has divided taxation powers between the centre and the states and has provided for a Financial Commission for readjustment of financial relations between the two, introduction of national planning has upset the constitutional scheme of division of powers and has given rise to the transfer of voluntary grants from the centre to the states for state plans. Voluntary grants are swift, direct, subtle and soft and have penetrated into the state fields with the consent of the state governments which are compelled to accept them to meet their growing plan-needs and welfare programmes. Such central voluntary grants make any one look into their dynamics.

Purpose of Undertaking this Work

The purpose of undertaking this research work is prompted by these considerations : (i) Though the debate has been going on since 1967 about centralizing tendencies of the central voluntary grants, there are no sufficient and independent studies on central voluntary grants alone. (ii) Though there has been increasing demand by the states to minimise the ever growing role of the central voluntary grants and to increase the quantum of statutory grants and shared taxes in order to maintain their state automony, no co-ordinated study has been made so far to find out feasibility of such demands.

Review of the existing literature indicates some aspects of unexplored areas of problem to be investigated.

Overview of Literature

Literature on centre-state relations in India is conditioned by the history of centre-state controversy. As long as one party domination existed at the centre and in many states till 1967, the centre-state relations including financial relations never assumed serious proportion. Any dissatisfaction or protest which arose was removed at the political level. During this period (1950-1967), the centre-state relations were only academic. No serious research on centre-state relations including central voluntary grants was possible. Literature published during this period was more descriptive. "The System of Grants-in-Aid in India" by Shri P.P. Agarwal (1959) was one of the earliest books on grants-in-Aid. It was a general book on grants-in-Aid. No attempt was made to find out centralizing tendencies of the central voluntary grants and the year 1959 was also too early for such attempt. Similar works of this period followed the descriptive nature of general pattern.

After 1967 things changed. With the formation of the non-Congress governments in many states and with the reduced majority of the Congress at the centre, the centre-state controversy became more public and vocal both at the political level and at the academic level. At the instance of the states, the centre adopted Gadgil formula for determining central financial assistance to the states for plan purposes. The centre made attempts to study the centre-state relations by appointing two commissions. The Administrative Reforms Commission (1969) and Sarkaria Commission (1987 and 1988) submitted their reports. Both the commissions recommended greater degree of autonomy for states in some matters. The states also made attempts to study centre-state relations. The Centre-State Inquiry Committee (Rajamannar Committee) appointed by the government of Tamil Nadu submitted its report and demanded more resources for the states on statutory basis. In 1977 the West Bengal government submitted a memorandum to the centre demanding more resources and autonomy for the states. In 1983 the leaders of the opposition parties met at Srinagar and issued a joint statement demanding more state autonomy in legislative, executive and financial fields. In view of the reports of these commissions, memoranda, public debates, etc., the academic literature has come out on centre-state relations including financial relations. The following are some of the books and articles dealing with the centre-state relations including financial relations. "The Union and the States" (1972) edited by S.N. Jain, S.C. Kashyap and N. Srinivas deals with various aspects of centre-state relations. No specific study of central voluntary grants is made. "Federal Fiscal System of Australia and India : A Study in Comparative Relevance" (1976) by G.Thimmaiah has dealt with conditional and unconditional grants but has not touched centralizing tendencies of the central conditional grants. "Centre-State Relations and Co-operative Federalism" (1983) by Dr. Chandra Pal has made only references to the central voluntary grants. "Union-State Relations"

(1984) edited by T.N. Chaturvedi and Datta Abhijit is a collection of research articles by eminent academicians. It does not have a specific section on central voluntary grants. Even its exhaustive bibliography does not reveal any specific work dealing with centralizing tendencies of the central voluntary grants. Though R.K. Sinha's book, "Fiscal Federalism in India" (1987), has exhaustively dealt with the centre-state financial relations, it does not deal with centralizing tendencies of the central voluntary grants. Though some of the articles of the book, "Centre-State Budgetary Transfers" (1987), edited by I.S. Gulati deal with discretionary grants, they do not cover the centralizing tendencies of these grants. Still more research books may be added for review of literature but there is not a single research work dealing with centralizing tendencies of the central voluntary grants and state autonomy.

In view of inadequate research works on centralizing tendencies of central voluntary grants and state autonomy, this research work is taken up. This research work studies the extent of central penetration into state subjects through its budgetary and other financial instruments. Though it is mainly concerned with the central voluntary grants, it also incidently refers to other financial assistance affecting autonomy of the states.

Statement of the Problem

This study focuses on a problem of constitutional theory and practice of federalism with special reference to the centralizing tendencies of the central voluntary grants and the autonomy of the states in India. The problem in this study is to find out relationship between two variables, centralizing tendencies of the central voluntary grants (independent variable) and the autonomy of the states (dependent variable). It is to be investigated how the first variable influences the second variable.

The key questions to be answered in this study are: (i) What are the factors responsible for increase in the central grants? (ii) How is the operational mechanism of grants also responsible for penetration of central grants into state autonomy? (iii) What are the means through which the grants penetrate into state fields? (iv) What are the areas in which centralization has taken place through the voluntary grants? (v) What are the trends in the centralizing tendencies of the voluntary grants? (vi) What are the reactions of the states and others to the centralizing tendencies of the grants and erosion of state autonomy?

The problem of centralizing tendencies of the central voluntary grants and state autonomy is to be studied within the theoretical framework of three federal theories – classical theory of federalism, origin theory of federalism and theory of co-operative federalism. (i) The classical theory supported by A.V. Dicey, Harrison Moore, Jethrow Brown, Robert Garran, K.C. Wheare, etc., is based on the traditional federal systems prevalent in the United States of America, Switzerland and Australia. Under this federal system, powers are divided between centre and states and each of them is independent within its allotted field. The Indian federal system is partially based on classical theory of federalism. An attempt is made in this study to examine to what extent the central voluntary grants have penetrated into limited autonomy of the states under the impact of growing needs of the people, ever expanding programmes of the states and the planning process. (ii) The problem of centralizing tendencies of the central voluntary grants and the autonomy of the states is also to be studied within the another theoretical context of origin theory of federalism. The origin theory of federalism which has been explained by William S. Livingston, Aaron Wildavsky, William H. Riker, etc., takes into account factors responsible for emergence of federal system in a particular country. The origin theory has three components – sociological theory, multiple factor theory and political theory. (A) It is to be examined how centralizing tendencies of the central voluntary grants in India have affected the social balance of the Indian federalism and have penetrated into social autonomy of the states. (B) As Indian federalism is also based on multiple factors in addition to social factors, it is to be analysed how the centralizing tendencies of the central voluntary grants have affected the economic and political autonomy of the states. (C) In addition to multiple factors for establishing Indian federal set up, the Indian political leaders were also responsible for creating two tier political structures – national and regional. These structures are operated by two types of leadership – national and regional. This study also examines how the national party with longer innings at the centre and how the regional parties at the state level with local loyalty react to the centralizing tendencies of the central voluntary grants and to the changing quantum of state autonomy. (iii) Theory of co-operative federalism is supported by Morton Grodzins, Daniel J. Elazar, R.L.Watts, etc. It believes in joint enterprise and aims at common welfare of people with minimum degree of conflicts between centre and states. This study intends to examine to what extent the Indian federalism is developing the spirit of co-operative federalism under the impact of central planning and central voluntary grants.

In terms of conceptual framework, the problem of this study has three dimensions – structural dimension, contextual dimension and operational dimension : (A) Under structural dimension, history and nature of Indian federalism are studied. (B) Under contextual dimension, evolution of voluntary grants is traced. (C) Under operational dimensions, conditions and compulsions for increase in the quantum of central voluntary grants, operational aspects of grants, areas and means of penetration into state fields, centralizing tendencies of central voluntary grants and reactions of the leaders and the groups to the centralizing tendencies are examined.

The problem of the study has three determinants: (1) Constitutional determinants are concerned with distribution of financial powers between the centre and the states and with the nature of state autonomy. (ii) Socio-economic determinants like planning process and welfare measures influence nature and quantity of central voluntary grants. (iii) Political determinants like political parties and political leaders create favourable or adverse reactions to the centralizing tendencies of the central voluntary grants.

The present problem of research is significant in view of present controversy. It is useful to the policy makers, politicians, leaders of public opinion, political parties, certain pressure groups, etc., to know centralizing tendencies of the central voluntary grants and decreasing dimensions of state autonomy and to make changes in the centre-state financial relations. It is also significant to the teachers and the students of Indian federalism to understand theoretical and practical dimensions of federalism. The problem of this research work is theoretically and practically relevant.

The scope of study of this research problem does not cover in detail the whole range of developmental schemes for which the centre provides voluntary grants to the states. However, general references are made to certain popular departments of state governments like education, agriculture, health, community development, etc. These departments are picked up to illustrate how the central voluntary grants have made inroads into state fields. No indept, specific and exhaustive study is made with reference to any department of the state governments. Specific and separate research projects can be taken up to study centralizing tendencies of the central voluntary grants with reference to individual departments of the states. This study emphasizes centralizing tendencies of the central voluntary grants in general. Though this research is mainly confined to the central voluntary grants, it also incidentally or by way of reference and illustration refers to central loans, role of central financial institutions, etc. It does not cover the central voluntary grants provided to non-governmental bodies, boards, institutions, etc., because they do not form a part of the state governments. Thus it concentrates on centralizing tendencies of the central voluntary grants with special reference to the state autonomy. In this study it was not possible to get latest figures for all the topics. Consequently sometimes figures are given to indicate the trends without including latest figures. In terms of period, the study covers the period from 1950-1990 for relevant analysis.

Objectives of the Study

The following are the main objectives of this study: (i) It is to examine how the existing socio-economic conditions complel the states to accept the central voluntary grants. (ii) It is to analyse how the operational aspects of the central voluntary grants have built in mechanism to penetrate into state fields. (iii) It is intended to find out and analyse the central means of penetration into the state fields through central voluntary grants. (iv) It plans to find out areas of state into which the central voluntary grants have made penetration. (v) It wants to critically evaluate trends in centralizing tendencies of these grants. (vi) It desires to measure the reactions of leaders, political parties, reports of the commissions, academicians, civil servants, etc., to the centralizing tendencies of the central voluntary grants.

Contribution of the Study

This study intends to contribute to the federal theory in general and classical theory of federalism, origin theory of federalism and theory of co-operative federalism in particular. Though the federal theory is old, its features and centre-state relations are in the process of change. Thus the study intends to contribute to the changing shades of theory and practice of federalism.

Hypothesis

Some general observations like 'Central voluntary grants have centralizing tendencies' have been made by many economists who have studied centre-state financial relations under the federal system. Such observations have formed the basis of the present hypothesis. 'Central voluntary grants in a federal system have centralizing tendencies' is the hypothesis of this study and is the basis for research investigation. This hypothesis is tested by collecting and analysing the relevant data. 'Central voluntary grants' is an independent variable. 'State autonomy' is a dependent variable. The first variable affects the second variable. Therefore the present hypothesis is a causal hypothesis. The present study intends to establish causal relationship between the first variable and the second variable in the light of collection and analysis of data.

Methodology

The research design adopted in this study is both explanatory and exploratory. It is explanatory because it tries to explain relationship between cause (central voluntary grants – independent variable) and effect (centralizing tendencies of these grants affecting state autonomy – dependent variable). There are also intervening variables which come between independent and dependent variables and help to explain the process. They are: (i) growing socio-economic programmes for increase in the quantum of central grants, (ii) machineries dealing with voluntary grants, (iii) means adopted by the centre to provide voluntary grants to the states, (iv) the areas of the states into which the central grants make penetration, (v) trends towards increase in the quantum of central grants, central supervision, etc., and (vi) reactions of the states, regional parties and others to these grants. These intervening variables influence nature and quantity of state autonomy. The research is also exploratory in the sense that it explores new areas for further research in respect of central voluntary grants and related topics. Such specification of areas for further research helps the scholars in the formulation of hypotheses.

The research design adopts developmental model. All variables (independent, dependent and intervening) are interlinked with one another by some kind of interaction due to developmental process.

This research work adopts four approaches to study the centralizing tendencies of the central voluntary grants and autonomy of the states in a developing federal country like India : (i) Historical approach is adopted to survey Indian federal system and evolution of grants. (ii) Institutional approach describes operational aspects of grants. (iii) Legal approach examines how the state autonomy has been penetrated by the central voluntary grants in various areas of states. It also analyses how the various political parties, the political leaders, the academicians, etc., have reacted to such penetration into state autonomy. (iv) The political approach records how the central voluntary grants have been looked at by the centre and the states at different times. In other words it studies how the political conditions determine operation of the central voluntary grants.

The universe of this study in this context is the whole range of voluntary grants from the centre to the states for various purposes. No specific state subject is taken up for intensive micro study. Only references are made to the various state subjects in general and education, agriculture, health, etc., in particular.

The method of data collection adopted in this study is primarily documentary. It seeks both primary sources like reports, bulletins, memoranda, finance accounts of government of India, guidelines for centrally sponsored schemes, debates of Constitutent Assembly, etc., and secondary sources like books, journals, newspapers etc., pertaining to the problem raised in this study. Research data are collected from the libraries and offices at Dharwad, Delhi, Bangalore and Madras. (Names of various libraries are listed in the preface.)

Definition of Concepts

Various terms and concepts used in this study are to be understood within the framework of federal system. As terms and concepts like federalism, quasi-federalism, co-operative federalism, grants-in-aid, etc., come under nominal definition, there is no need to define them. No term or concept is used in this study under operational definition. Consequently there is no need to define any term or concept for operational purpose. However, only state autonomy in the Indian context is to be understood. In the Indian context autonomy of the state means freedom of initiative and action within constitutionally determined fields. Terms like non-statutory grants, conditional grants and voluntary grants are used synonymously.

Plan of the Study

The problem of this study, the centralizing tendencies of the central voluntary grants and the autonomy of states under Indian federal set up, is examined thrcugh ten chapters.

The first three chapters – A Historical Survey of Indian Federal System, Allocation of Resources, and Grants-in-Aid are – background chapters dealing with nature of federalism in general and of Indian federalism in particular and evolution of allocation of resources between the centre and states. The next six chapters (chapters IV, V, VI, VII, VIII, and IX) deal with intervening variables. The relationship between the independent variable (the central grants) and the dependent variable (the autonomy of the states) is examined in the light of intervening variables in these six chapters. The last chapter (chapter X) deals with conclusions and suggestions based on the analysis of data divided into the above mentioned six chapters.

The first chapter (A Historical Survey of Indian Federal System) tells a historical survey of Indian federal system. It covers meaning and characteristics of federalism in general and evolution of federalism in India from the Mauryan period to the modern period. Further it lists reasons for adopting federal system in India and explains it in theoretical terms by referring to the origin theory of federalism. It also describes the features of Indian federalism, points out how it is different from the classical theory of federalism and gives reasons for such deviation and for adopting a quasi-federal system.

The second chapter (Allocation of Resources) explains allocation of resources between the centre and the states. It examines the principles governing the allocation of resources and traces the evolution of allocation of resources through four stages from 1833 to 1950. It analyses the present constitutional position of allocation of resources and examines the present pattern of transfer of statutory and non-statutory resources. It also discusses the problem of maintaining balance between the resources and functions of the states. It briefly refers to the demand for greater allocation of resources from the centre to the states.

The third chapter (Grants-in-Aid) is concerned with types and characteristics of grants. Evolution of grants-in-aid is traced in order to explain changing pattern of their forumulas in view of changing economic and political conditions and compulsions in India.

The fourth chapter (Conditions and Compulsions for Growing Programmes) describes the conditions and compulsions for increasing programmes to be discharged by the states. It examines how the socialist philosophy, the provisions for welfare state in the Indian Constitution and the comprehensive planning process have immensely increased the programmes of the states. It analyses how specific services like education, social service, health, agriculture, etc., have increased the programmes of the states. It takes into account political compulsions, electoral promises, emergence of new class of elites, etc., which have also caused increase in the programmes of the states. Lastly it examines the imbalance between the growing programmes of the states and their inelastic resources.

The fifth chapter (Operational Aspects of Grants) deals with the machineries like Finance Commission, Planning Commission, National Development Council and Central Ministries which recommend or provide grants to the states. It traces the evolution of pattern/formula for central assistance to the states from schematic assistance to the N.D.C formula. It also explains the pattern of central financial assistance to the centrally sponsored sehemes, centrally assisted schemes, etc.

The sixth chapter (Central Means of Penetration) analyses how the centre penetrates into state fields through various means like planning process, planning commission, advisory boards, finance commission, central financial institutions, article 282, formula for financial assistance, plan grants, non-plan grants, financial inducement, discretionary transfers, centrally sponsored sschemes, centrally assisted schemes, loans, relief measures for natural calamities, central expenditure over state subjects, one party domination, office of P.M., central ministries, central secretariat, conferences, etc.

The seventh chapter (Areas of Penetration by the Centre) examines the various reasons for central penetration into the state fields. Some of these compelling factors are imbalance between resources and functions of the states, planning process, unwillingness of the states to levy additional taxes to meet their growing demands, etc. Certain areas of penetration by the centre are analysed. Some of the areas are education, agriculture, co-operation, village and small scale industries, panchayat raj institutions, etc. These are some of the areas which are taken up for analysis by way of illustration. The present study also examines the impact of central penetration on state autonomy.

The eighth chapter (Centralizing Tendencies of Grants) examines how the centralizing tendencies of the central voluntary grants are revealed through (i) increase in the quantum of central grants to the states for plan and non-plan purposes, (ii) role of the planning commission and central financial institutions in providing financial assistance to the states, (iii) increase in the number of centrally sponsored schemes affecting state fields, (iv) increasing dependence of the states on central voluntary grants, statutory grants and shared taxes for carrying out growing programmes in the state sector, (v) growing dependence of the states on central loans, (vi) central attempts to provide grants to the local self-governing institutions, (vii) common central policy guidelines relating to certain state subjects, (viii) growing central supervision and control over certain state subjects, and (ix) greater emphasis on concurrent list.

The ninth chapter (Reactions to Centralizing Tendencies) examines reactions for and against the centralizing tendencies of the central voluntary grants. When two sets of reactions are taken into consideration, the reactions against the centralizing tendencies of the central voluntary grants outweigh the reactions for them. Such outweighing reactions are influenced by the concepts of classical theory of federalism and origin theory of federalism. Further they are strengthened by religious, ethnic, cultural and linguistic pulls in the various regions of India.

The last chapter (Conclusions and Suggestions) deals with the conclusions drawn on the basis of analysis of data collected. Suggestions are based on theory and practice of fiscal federalism in the Indian context. Contribution made to three federal theories in the Indian context is stated. Areas for further research are also listed.

CHAPTER I

A HISTORICAL SURVEY OF INDIAN FEDERAL SYSTEM

I. FEDERALISM

Federalism is a device by which plural qualities of a society are articulated and protected. It is devised to secure both regional autonomy and national unity. It is a product of historical forces in plural societies. Relation between regional autonomy and national unity has been changing under different conditions. If the forces of regional autonomy are very strong in a plural society, the regional units shall have greater degree of autonomy. If the forces of national unity are very strong in such society, the central government shall have more powers. The strength of these regional and national forces changes from time to time in view of changing social, economic and political conditions and compulsions. Thus federalism has been reflecting these changing historical conditions and compulsions. Nature of small and rudimentary federal systems in ancient Greece reflected those conditions. Similarly the modern Western federal systems of U.S.A., Switzerland, Canada and Australia also reflect the modern conditions and compulsions. These federations are the most successful and prosperous in the world and have influenced new federations. A new set of federations has emerged after the World War II in the third world countries. They are Malaysia (1943), Brazil (1946), Venezuela (1947), Argentina (1949), India (1950), Nigeria (1954), Pakistan (1956), etc. Attempt is made in these countries to secure both regional autonomy and national unity in varying degree in view of their different conditions and compulsions.

Federalism which is a historical product is not a static or a rigid concept. It is a dynamic concept. Birth and development of federalism is a result of various forces which are also dynamic. On account of the inherent dynamic nature of a modern industrial welfare society and of ever growing economic and social needs of people, each federation goes through its pangs of development. Indian federalism is also going through the pangs of socio-economic and political developments. In view of dynamic nature of federal theory, many metaphors are used to indicate different phases of development of federal theory: "Even a glance at the 326 purported federalisms will raise doubts about how so many adjectival modifiers could possibly be consistent with federalism."[1] Numerous models of federalism relate to different stages of social, economic and political developments and complexities in plural societies. Attempts are made to build a federal theory amidst complexities of conditions and compulsions. "The historic federal concept has developed in an extremely programatic fashion. The metaphor represents only a start in the direction of theory-building, but it still may be a legitimate approach."[2] Federal system is designed differently in different plural societies to suit the different conditions. Consequently modern federal system is known by different names: (i) Permissive Federalism (Richard Leach, American Federalism, W.W. Norton and Company INC, New York, 1907), (ii) Contract Federalism (A.J. Davies–Australian Federalism and National Development in the Australian Journal of Politics and History, Vol. XIV, ed. by G. Greenwood, Dept. of History, University of Queensland, 1968), (iii) Creative Federalism (Lyndon B. Johnson, ex-President of U.S.A), (iv) New Federalism (Richard Nixon, ex-President of U.S.A), (v) Co-operative Federalism, etc. All these terms used by academicians and political leaders indicate new developments in the evolution of theory and practice of federalism. These men and others view federalism not as a formal static structure but as a living organism meant for common good. The common good in the modern period is to be achieved not through isolated and separate actions but through the joint efforts of the central and state governments: "In no other field this centre-state relationship is better illustrated than in the field of social services and social welfare in which governments in all the three federations (U.S.A., Australia and India) have become increasingly involved in the past two decades."[3] Among all the terms of federalism, co-operative federalism is becoming more popular in view of demand for joint action by the centre and the states to solve growing socio-economic problems of the people. It is to be observed whether the Indian federalism conforms to the general trend of co-operative federalism in recent years in view of growing regional loyalties based on various considerations.

There is not only evolution in the institution of federalism, but there is also evolution in the meaning of term, federalism. Meaning of federalism has moved from simple meaning of treaty of union of states to complex meanings of various types of federation in the modern period. Etymologically word, federation, has been derived from the Latin word, 'foedus', which means treaty.[4] Historically a federation is meant a union of some states brought about through the instrumentality of treaty. Federation has come to mean a union of two or more states. In such a union there is a central government and there are state governments. Thus there is a dual state authority and powers of the state are divided between the central and regional governments. Both sets of governments are independent within their allotted fields. K.C.Wheare opines that a concept of federation is based on the government of the United States of America: "The modern idea of what federal government is has been determined by the United States of America......nowadays every body regards the United States as an example of federal government. Many consider it the most important and the most successful example. Any definition of federal government which failed to include the United States would be thereby condemned as unreal."[5] This is a classical definition of federalism. The definitions of federalism can be divided into two categories – classical and non-classical. Definitions of federalism given by E.A. Freeman, Sir Robert Garran, A.V. Dicy, Harrison Moore, Jethrow Brown, Lord Bryce, K.C. Wheare, etc., are considered to be classical. These definitions take into account the legal structure of the federal Constitution of the United States of America. E.A. Freeman in his book, History of Federal Government (third edition, 1863) thus described federalism: "On the one hand, each of the members of the union must be wholly independent in those matters which concern each member only. On the other hand, all must be subject to a common power in those matters which concern the whole body of the members collectively..... Each member is perfectly independent within its own sphere."[6] Sir Robert Garran, an Australian scholar (Report of the Royal Commission on Australian Constitution, 1929, p. 230) says that federation is "a form of government in which sovereignty or political power is divided between the federal and the local governments so that each of them, within its own sphere, is independent of the other."[7] A.V. Dicy in his book, *Introduction to the Study of the Law of the Constitution*, defines federalism in these words:

"Federalism means the distribution of the force of the state among a number of co-ordinate bodies each originating in and controlled by the constitution."[8] Among all the classical definitions, a definition given by K.C. Wheare is often quoted. He defines federalism in this way: "By the federal principle I mean the method of dividing powers so that the general and regional governments are each, within a sphere, co-ordinate and independent."[9] All these definitions emphasize two features of federal system: (i) There should be division of powers between the central and state governments, and (ii) each government should be independent within its allotted field.

The critics of classical theory of federalism and champions of non-classical theory of federalism maintain that economic planning, social services, welfare measures, etc., have made the classical theory of federalism outmoded. They insist that non-legal forces should also be taken into consideration while federalism is to be defined or described. William S. Livingston (Federalism and Constitutional Change, 1956), M.C. Vile (The Structure of American Federalism, 1962), R.L. Watts (New Federations: Experiments in Commonwealth, 1966), Morton Grodzins (A New View of Government in the United States, 1966), Aaron Wildavsky (ed. American Federalism in Perspective, 1967), Geoffrey P. Sawer (Modern Federalism, 1969), Daniel J. Elazar (American Federalism : A Working Outline, 1970), M. Venkatrangaiya (Some Theories of Federalism, 1971), Ursula K. Hicks (Federalism : Failure and Success, A Comparative Study, 1978), etc., emphasize non-legal aspects of federalism. Many of them lay emphasis on economic, political, co-operative and functional aspects of federalism. Ursula K. Hicks defines federation in terms of democracy, culture, tradition and rights of the units: "In modern terms a federation is a type of polity operating a constitution which works on two levels of government : as a nation and as a collection of related but self-standing units. The objective of federation is a form of government for the people and by the people. That is to say it is inherently democratic (in the Western sense). It seeks on the one hand to create and maintain a nation, on the other to preserve the integrity of the units, their indentity, culture and tradition. ......But neither level of government can be allowed absolute sovereignty, because this would violate some of the rights of the other level which are guaranteed in the constitution."[10] This definition emphasizes democratic nature of federation, preservation of cultural identity of units, etc.

A large number of non-classical federal governments have been functioning in the third world countries after the World War II. Thus both the classical and the non-classical federations have been working in different parts of the world under different conditions. They differ not only in their structures but also in their functioning. These have created differences in their appearances. Consequently different definitions and names of federalism have come into vogue. Chandra Pal has listed fortyfour types of federal system from the book, Federal Principle : A Journey through Time in Quest of Meaning, written by S. Rufus Devis, an Australian scholar of federalism:[11] Dual Federalism, Orthodox Federalism, Classic Federalism, Polis Federalism, Traditional Federalism, Co-operative Federalism, Bargaining Federalism, Integrated Federalism, Interdependent Federalism, Creative Federalism, New Permissive Federalism, Functional Federalism, Programmatic Federalism, Organic Federalism, Pluralistic Federalism, Monarchic Federalism, Perfect Federalism, Imperfect Federalism, Direct Federalism, Private Federalism, Picket Fence Federalism, Coercive Federalism, Centralised Federalism, Decentralised Federalism, Peripheralized Federalism, Fused Federalism, Corporate Federalism, National Federalism, Social Federalism, Oligarchic Federalism, Unitary Federalism, Constitutional Federalism, International Federalism, Military Federalism, Political Federalism, Monistic Federalism, Partial Federalism, Contrast Federalism, Feudal Federalism, Functional Federalism, Incipient Federalism, etc. These various names indicate that federalism in course of time has acquired different shapes in different countries due to different conditions and compulsions. Yet different federal systems are judged in terms of the federal system of the United States of America which is considered to be the model federal system. In terms of theoretical conception, the Indian federal system is judged on the basis of American model.

Though all the federal constitutions are not the carbon copies of the federal Constitution of the United States of America, yet they are influenced by it in their making. The federal features of the Constitution of U.S.A. are considered to be the features of the classical federalism. The following are the main features of the classical federalism : (i) Powers are distributed between the centre and the states. Subjects which are of national importance are given to the centre and subjects which are of local relevance are entrusted to the states. Division of powers between the centre and the states could be altered only with the consent of both governments. (ii) Both sets of governments are independent within allotted fields and have their own legislative and executive machineries to carry out their functions. They directly deal with citizens. (iii) There is allocation of resources/revenues between these two sets of governments. The revenues are supposed to be sufficient to discharge their respective functions. (iv) There is a written constitution which lists the powers distributed between the two sets of governments. The constitution is supreme and is an ultimate reference to all disputes between the centre and the states. It is rigid because its provisions could be altered only with the consent of both sets of governments. (v) There is an independent judiciary to settle conflicts of jurisdiction between the centre and the states or between two states. It is also the final power to interpret the provisions of the constitution.

These are the institutional characteristics of the classical federalism. Any departure from these oharacteristics is considered to be diviation from the classical model. Many existing federations have deviated from the classical model to smaller or greater extent due to historical legacies, geographical compulsions, separatist tendencies of certain groups, etc. The Indian federalism is also to be examined in terms of classical theory and actual practice in the course of the present study in general and of central voluntary grants in particular.

There is a trend towards federal system of government in plural societies. Even E.C.M. (European Common Market) is moving towards federal system. At present about fifty per cent of the world's population lives in the countries with federal constitutions.[12] India is one of them.

2. EVOLUTION OF FEDERALISM IN INDIA

Even under the Mauryans, the Guptas and the Mughals, India did not have unitary type of government. Under these and other powerful dynasties, small and big princely states accepted overlordship or suzertainty of the emperor and at the same time enjoyed substantial autonomy in certain local matters. After downfall of these powerful dynasties, the regional states used to assert their separate and independent status. Thus a system of regional/local government had been in existence under various empires from the Mauryas to the British. The Indian empires were highly decentralised systems as compared with highly centralised Roman empire. India had feudal federal system rather than the modern constitutional federalism.

The British administration in India underwent two processes – centralization and decentralization. Under the East India Company it was a process of expansion, consolidation and centralization of power from 1773 (Regulating Act) to 1857 (the first War of Independence.) The British who had earlier aimed at centralization were forced to introduce decentralization after the first war of independence (1857). In 1858 John Bright emphasized need for decentralization of power in India: "There could be no successful or efficient government in India unless the fundamental diversities of the country were taken into account and felt that each province be administrated by its own separate government with a minimum interference from outside."[13] The report of the Sarkaria Commission recognised the importance of decentralization of power introduced by the British after 1858: "It is not possible to administer so vast and diverse a country like India without progressive devolution or decentralization of powers to the provinces and local bodies."[14] After the British Crown took over the Indian administration in 1858, the process of decentralization was set in motion for British India. Enlightened public opinion in India also wanted decentralization of power. The British government started the process of decentralization by passing the Indian Councils Act in 1861. The Act provided for participation of non-officials in the legislative council of the governor-general and the legislative councils of the provinces. Process of decentralization of powers was facilitated by decentralization of finances through the Mayo scheme in 1871. A number of socio-economic and political organisations were established in the second part of nineteenth century. Among them the Indian National Congress (1885) was an important organization. Many of these organisations demanded that more Indians should be associated with the governance of the country. In partial recognition of Indian demands, the British passed another Indian Councils Act in 1892. The principle of indirect election to these legislative councils was introduced by this Act. The functions of the legislative councils were also enlarged. Demands of the Congress were increasing year after year for more devolution of powers to the provinces and to the people. The Congress also insisted on federal government for India. In 1904 Sir John Cotton in his presidential address to the twentieth session of the Indian National Congress "spoke of the United States of India comprising of free and separate states."[15] After partition of Bengal in 1905, the Congress became very vocal in its demands. To satisfy the growing demands of the Indian people, the Indian Councils Act (Morley-Minto Reforms) was introduced in 1909. More number of Indians were associated with the central and provincial legislative councils on the basis of separate electorates, narrow franchise and indirect election. The Congress and other public organisations were not happy with this Act. Under the Lucknow Pact of 1916, the Congress and the Muslim League came closer in their demands for political reforms. On 20th August 1917, the British government in England made an important policy statement relating to Indian constitutional reforms. It promised gradual realization of responsible government in India. The Indian leaders and the princes pleaded before Mountagu for federal set up for India. Montagu-Chelmsford report envisaged future India on a federal basis: "Granted the announcement of August 20th, we cannot at the present time envisage its complete fulfilment in any form other than that of a series of self-governing Indian provinces associated for certain purposes under a responsible government of India with possible what are now the Native States of India finally embodied in the same whole, in some relation which we will not now attempt to define. For such an organisation the English language has no word but 'federal'."[16] 1919 Act which was based on the recommendations of Montagu-Chelmsford report contained the seeds of federalism. The Act demarcated the areas of provincial governments in legislative and administrative matters. It also provided rules for devolution of powers. Under these rules in 1920 subjects were distrubuted between the centre and the provinces. The centre got fortyseven subjects while the provinces got fiftyone subjects. Residuary powers were vested with the centre. The central subjects were defence, external affairs, all India communications, posts, telegraphs, shipping, etc. The provincial subjects were medical administration, public health, agriculture, police, prison, education excluding national educational institutions, etc. Dyarchy was introduced in the provinces by separating subjects into two categories – reserved subjects and transferred subjects. Popular ministers were in-charge of transferred subjects. The federal set up under 1919 Act was not really federal system because provincial powers were not derived from the constitution but were grants of the central legislature. Before

1935 Act was passed for providing a federal system for India, political parties, reports of some commissions, Round Table Conferences, etc., recommended federal system for India. In 1920, the Indian National Congress reorganised its Pradesh Congress Committees on linguistic basis and thereby it gave impetus to reorganisation of provinces on linguistic basis and formation of federal system. In 1925 the Commonwealth of India Bill prepared by Annie Besant, Shri B. Shiva Rao and others visualised division of powers between the centre and the provinces of India. On May 17, 1927, demand for federal form of government was made by Shri Motilal Nehru at the Congress session held at Bombay. At the same session of the Congress, Shri Ansari made similar demand in his presidential address. The Nehru Report (1928) envisaged a democratic federal system for India. On Ist January 1929 Muslim League passed a resolution for establishing a federal system with complete autonomy for provinces. According to its resolution, the centre would have limited powers and the residuary powers were to be left to the provinces. The Simon Commission (1930) suggested a federal system with the princely states. It recommended abolition of dyarchy in the provinces. Federal idea was further pursued in the Round Table Conferences (1930-32). All parties and groups at R.T.C. accepted the federal idea but differend on powers of provinces, position of the princely states in the federal set up, etc. At the first R.T.C. 89 delegates were present. 16 represented three political parties of England, 57 represented British India, and 16 represented princely India. Sir Tej Bahadur Sapru proposed all India federation and requested the Indian princes to join it. On behalf of the princes the Maharaja of Bikaner expressed willingness to join the federation. The Federal Structure Sub-Committee of R.T.C. headed by Lord Sankey discussed the various aspects of federal system. In March 1933 White Paper on Indian constitutional reforms contained proposal for federal system. The Joint Select Committee of both Houses of the British Parliament constituted in April 1933 also recommended federal system for India. As a result of the demands of various political parties and groups and of reports of commissions and conferences, the Act was passed in 1935. The Government of India Act, 1935, envisaged an all India federation which was to consist of eleven governor's provinces, six chief commissioner's provinces and such princely states which would agree to join the federation. It constitutionally divided powers between the central list, provincial list and concurrent list. Dyrachy was abolished in the provinces and responsible governments were introduced there. However, the federal provisions (except relating to federal court) at the centre did not come into force for various reasons.

Princely India consisting about five hundred and sixtytwo states had continued with their traditional administration. However, princely states were forced to introduce political reforms and to prepare themselves to join the federation after 1920 under the impact of struggle for freedom carried on by the Congress in British India and of struggle for responsible government carried on by the various Praja Mandals (state people's committees) in these princely states with the moral encouragement from the Congress.

The Cabinet Mission plan of 1946 suggested federation with a weak centre. It had also given option for formation of groups of provinces. Even these proposals of the Cabinet Mission visualizing a weak centre were rejected by the Muslim League which wanted nothing but independent state–Pakistan.

Thus the British, the Indian National Congress, the Muslim League and the princes contributed, in their own way, to the evolution of federalism in India. They looked at federation at different angles : "The British advocated the federal device to placate the Indians so as to avoid the demand for dominion status. The British combined the elements of democracy and autocracy in the fold of federalism. The princely states wanted federalism to safeguard their position *vis-a-vis* the Crown and also thwart the democratic aspirations of the nationalists. The Indian National Congress wanted federalism to achieve the unity and integrity of the country. The Muslims wanted federalism so as to share power in the Muslim majority areas. Thus the concept of federalism suited with the aspirations of all of them."[17] Similar views are expressed by an eminent authority, S.P.Aiyer, on Indian federalism : "Federalism emerged as a means of reconciling conflicting elements in the Indian polity and came to prominence in the nineteen thirties. Federalism then seemed to be the only political device for bringing together the Indian states and the British Indian provinces and for integrating the Hindus and the Muslims – the two major communities of the sub-continent. The native states in particular were being irresistibly driven to search for some sort of union in which they would work together with the provinces of British India without surrendering their independence.''[18]

The objective resolution moved by Pt. Jawaharlal Nehru in the constituent assembly on 13th December 1946 visualized a federation with autonomous units to vested with residuary powers. Before partition of India, the constituent assembly did not stipulate a strong centre with residuary powers because strong centre was not liked by the Muslim League. After the declaration of partition of India, plan for a strong centre in the federal system was revived in the constituent assembly. On June 6, 1947, the Union Constitution Committee headed by Pt. Jawaharlal Nehru favoured a strong centre. Decision to have a strong centre was approved by the joint meeting of the Union Constitution Committee and the Provincial Constitution Committee held on 7th June 1947. The former committee was headed by Pt. Jawaharlal Nehru and the latter committee was headed by Sardar Patel. Thus the idea of strong centre had the support of two strong nationalist stalwarts.

3. REASONS FOR ADOPTING FEDERALISM IN INDIA

Federations are the outcome of historical conditions rather than theoretical devices designed by the learned men. ''Federal governments,'' writes Frankfurt, ''are not the offspring of political science; they are the product of economic and social pressures.''[19] The federal system of the United States of America was not a product of any theory but was a creature of conditions, compulsions, compromise and expediency. The federal constitutions in other countries are also the products of history and are determined by socio-economic and political conditions and compulsions. Consequently features of a federal system of any country indicate the existence of historical legacies, socio-economic and political conditions and compulsions. Therefore the Indian federal system is to be examined under the Indian historical conditions. Shri K. Santhanam, a prominent member of the Indian constituent assembly, emphasizes the importance of historical conditions under which federal constitutions are framed : ''There are many federations in the world, but each federation differs from others owing to the different historical backgrounds. Therefore, it is necessary that we should view our own federation from its historical backgorund.''[20]

Reasons for adopting federal system in India can be explained in terms of concept of one India, origin theory of federalism, centripetal, centrifugal forces, etc.

Federalism in India is the result of concept of one India amidst diversity. Concept of one India in different forms has been entertained by seers, poets, writers, emperors, reformers, etc., from the ancient period to the modern period. The powerful emperors in the past had tried to bring the whole India under one domain. Mauryans, Guptas and Mughals were successful to great extent. Dream of one India was finally realized by Indians during the British rule. The modern Indian leaders during the freedom struggle wanted to organise India as a united democratic federal system statisfying the aspirations of various ethnic, religious, linguistic and cultural groups. Though the majority of Indian political leaders and academicians were in favour of adopting federal system of government for the country, yet there were a few persons who favoured a unitary system of government. Sir P.S. Sivaswamy Aiyer in his book, *Indian Constitutional Problems* (Bombay, 1928) argued for a unitary type of government with a great measure of decentralization in order to avoid separatist tendencies.[21] Earlier Sardar K.M. Panikkar was a champion of unitary type of government. Some members of the constituent assembly of India like Shri Brajeshwar Prasad pleaded for unitary type of government. However, a vast majority of members in the constituent assembly were in favour of federal government with a strong centre.

Why India adopted a federal system can also be explained in theoretical terms with special reference to the origin theory of federalism which takes into account the factors responsible for emergence of federalism. The origin theory of federalism is sustained by three sub-theories – sociological theory, multiple factor theory and political theory.

In terms of sociological theory, India adopted a federal system because Indian society is plural. Indian plurality is marked by differences in race, religion, language, culture, etc. Further these diversities are territorially grouped and have separate identities. They are historical entities and have not been lost in the course of history.

In addition to sociological factors, there are also other multiple factors responsible for establishing a federal system in India. These multiple factors can be divided into two categories : factors promoting unity of India and factors responsible for retaining regional diversities. Compromise between these two forces has given birth to Indian federalism. The following are the forces responsible for promoting unity of India:

(A) There has been a dominant desire to be under a single political system. India as a united land has been in the minds of intellectual elites from the Vedic period to the modern period due to the continuity of Hindu religion, culture, epics, memories, some great emperors, geographical contiguity, beautiful hills, valleys, rivers, historical monuments, etc. Dream of united India was fully realized by Indians under the British rules who consolidated India under a single political system from Kashmir to Kanyakumari and from Sindh to Assam. Before independence, the Indian National Congress became a vehicle to express a long cherished desire for free and united India. The common colonial rule of the British brought the educated Indians together to chalk out a common programme for India. The struggle against the British rule under the leadership of the Indian National Congress in general and of Mahatma Gandhi in particular created a widespread national upsurge which transcended all sectional and regional loyalties. The national movement gave rise to the common national ideals like self-determination, democracy, national unity, federalism, socialism, secularism, etc. The people of British Indian provinces and of the princely states desired to be under a single independent government. The Congress in British India and the Praja Mandals in princely states had worked in that direction for a long period before independence to remain united under a single system. (B) Desire to be under a single system was facilitated by a single administrative system. India became for the first time a single administrative and political entity under the British. The political boundaries of India coincided with the natural boundaries of India. Dream of ancient sages and ancient and medieval emperors about a vast single map of India was realized under the British rule. The Congress wanted to inherit united India and opposed partition of it till 1947. Many members of the constituent assembly who were product of such national movement wanted India with strong centre. (C) Emotional integration brought about by strong desire of Indians to be under a single administrative system, common English language of Indian elites and consolidation of India under one administrative system by the British was sustained and promoted by new mechanised system of transport and communication. Introduction of railways in the Indian transport system linked the different regions of India. It helped development of national markets, facilitated movement of people from one part of country to another part and thus broke regional barriers. Widespread national transport system and national markets continue to be important factors promoting unity of India. (D) The leaders of the Indian national movement and the framers of the Indian Constitution were aware of past fratricidal wars between different regions and communities in India. They did not want repetition of them and planned to control disrputive tendencies inherent in Indian plural society. Shri K.M. Munshi, a prominent member of the constitutent assembly, reminded the members of the constituent assembly that the glorious days of India were only those days under the Mauryas and the Mughals when there was a strong central authority and that the most tragic days were those when the central authority was dismembered by the regions trying to resist the centre.[22] Fears of Shri K.M. Munshi, were shared by many members who later endorsed the need for strong centre. Thus these factors promoted centripetal forces.

If India had only centripetal forces, it would have got unitary type of government instead of federal government. There are many centrifugal forces which want regional autonomy for various reasons : (A) The Indian geography has stood against permanent merger of the regions: "Indian geography and history have always stood out against any permanent merger of the regional units. Big rivers and deep forests, expanding deserts and varying soil conditions have segmented India into many territorial layers, and they have exercised a great and continuing influence upon the meandering course of Indian history."[23] (B) Many regions have been historical units and have historical memories of their sufferings and achievements which have been treasured in regional literature. Tamilians, Telugus, Malayalees, Kannadigas, Marathis, Oriyyas, Bengalis, Assamees, Gujaratis, Kashmiris, Punjabis, etc. have their own past sufferings and glories. "The regional diversities having abiding roots in history reveal the essentially federal nature of Indian society; these constituted the most powerful centrifugal pressures at the time of constitution making."[24] (C) India is very big in size and has nearly 12,59,789 square miles. Administratively it cannot have a unitary system of government. Local conditions do not admit of uniform policies and programmes for divergent regions. Any experiment with unitary type of government under democracy would have been a great failure. Lionel Curtis in his book, *Dyarchy*, advocated a federal system of government for India on the basis of fact that India is a vast country which cannot be ruled democratically from one centre.[25] (D) India has experienced evolution of federal system under the Act of 1909, 1919 and 1935. With the evolution of provincial governments before independence, popular consciousness of provincial authority was gradually developed in British India through these Acts. The 1935 Act of government of India gave a concrete shape to the Indian federal set up and made provisions for accession of princely states to the Indian union. The working of the provincial governments, the movements for linguistic provinces and rise of Praja Mandals in princely states gave birth to the rise of regional leaders who loved to manage regional governments. The people in these provinces and princely states wanted to be under regional governments based on regional considerations. They desired to be united under a single central government for some purposes and also wanted to be under regional governments for some other purposes. On the eve of independence for India, the Negotiating Committee of the constituent assembly negotiated with the rulers and representatives of princely states with a view to secure accession to the Indian Union on federal basis. The former princely states were treated as part 'B' states of the Indian Union. Thus India has undergone the process of evolution of federalism. That evolutionary process cannot be wiped out and India cannot establish a unitary government. (E) Since 1920 the Congress was committed to the creation of linguistic provinces and consequently it reorganised its Pradesh Congress Committees on linguistic basis. According to it, the Indian federation was to consist of linguistic provinces. The report of the Nehru Committee (1928) emphasized the importance of linguistic provinces in new federal set up. Various linguistic movements sprang up during freedom movement and demanded reorganisation of provinces on linguistic basis. (F) Various linguistic, cultural and ethnic groups desired union because democratic federal India would preserve their separate indentities and give constitutional guarantee to them. The present constitution has guaranteed them. For a federal system, common race or religion or language is not necessary. "It is interesting to notice that some factors are unexpectedly absent. Thus commonality of language, of race, of religion or of nationality have not been listed as likely essential prerequisites of the desire for union."[26]

Thus the geographical factors, historical memories, big size of the country, evolution of federal system, desires of various groups, etc., have been responsible for maintaining and preserving regional units.

In addition to sociological and multiple factor sub-theories of origin theory of federalism, there is also a political sub-theory of origin theory of federalism to offer explanation why India adopted federalism. During the freedom movement the Congress had taken a political decision to organise Indian political system on democratic and federal basis. It had dominated the constituent assembly and had made provisions for three types of political structures – national, state and local. They are managed by three types of political leadership. Further the Indian federalism is also the result of political compromise between the national leadership and the regional leadership.

Thus federal system adopted by the framers of the Indian constitution is the result of both centripetal and centrifugal forces. Forces of unity and diversity are politically organised under Indian federal system. The centre represents unifying forces and the states diversities. Balance between these two forces is to be maintained if the Indian federalism intends to have smooth sail. The central voluntary grants are to be examined in this context.

4. FEATURES OF INDIAN FEDERALISM

Before the federal constitution of the United States of America came into existence in 1787, there was no definite concept of federation. The term, federation, was loosely used by the academicians and the practitioners of politics. Later federal constitutions of Canada, Australia, India, etc., were influenced by the American federal constitution. Sri T.T. Krishnamachari, a prominent member of the Indian constituent assembly, said that the Indian Constitution had taken note of both the text of the American federal constitution and the changes that had taken place by judicial decisions, treaty-making powers, taxation power, etc.[27] The federal constitution of the United States of America has been considered as a classical federal constitution. Though the framers of the Indian constitution were aware of theory and practice of classical federalism, they partially adopted classical theory of federalism because of sociological, multiple and political conditions prevalent in India. They introduced federal principle to the extent to which it was possible and desirable under the Indian conditions. Nature of Indian federation has been described as federal, quasi-federal, unitary with some federal features, unique one, etc. K.C.Wheare, an authority on federalism, described it as a quasi-federal constitution.[28]

Indian federalism is organised to a great extent on federal basis but has certain unitary elements. Firstly, it can be examined how for Indian constitution has adopted features of a classical federalism and how for it has been upset in pratice : (A) A classical federation has a written constitution specifying the areas of jurisdiction of the centre and the states. The Indian constitution has written constitution which has distributed powers between the centre and the states through the seventh schedule. The federal constitution should be rigid because distribution of powers between the centre and the states should not be altered unilaterally. The provisions of Indian Constitution dealing with distribution of legislative, administrative and financial powers between the centre and the states and three lists in the seventh schedule cannot be altered unilaterally and are rigid. They can be altered only by amending the constitution which requires the consent of both houses of the central parliament and of a majority of state legislatures. "Thus, in vital matters affecting the powers of the states, the assent of the states is also necessary. Herein lies the substance of federalism and it is not destroyed by weightage given to the union in other matters. The fact that the states of the Indian union did not have any independent status prior to the constitution does not affect their powers under the existing constitution."[29] The centre cannot do away with the existence of the states. Like a classical federal constitution, the constitution of India is written and rigid in vital matters and has guaranteed the existence of the states and of federal system. (B) Division of powers between the centre and the states is an essential feature of a classical federal system. The Constitution of India has distributed powers between the centre and the states. The subjects of national importance are given to the centre and are 97 in number; the subjects of local importance are given to the states and are 66 in number; and subjects of common interest are placed in the concurrent list and are 47 in number. In addition to these, the legislative, executive and financial relations between the centre and the states are regulated under Part XI of the Indian Constitution. Division of legislative and executive powers is supported by division of financial powers. Anticipating gap between state revenues and state functions, the framers of the constitution have provided a comprehensive arrangement of sharing of taxes from the union list by the states and of statutory grants-in-aid from the centre to the states. For this purpose they have provided for the appointment of Finance

Commission at the end of every five years or earlier. The recommendations of the Finance Commission are generally honoured. However, the federal financial arrangements are upset by adoption of socio-economic development of India through centralised planning. "Nowhere is the weakness of its federal character more evident than in the provisions of the constitution relating to financial relations which, except for the provisions relating to the Financial Commission, were largely taken from the Government of India Act, 1935. The weakness derives from the imbalance between the centre and the states in the resource raising powers built into the constitution itself."[30] Though the financial resources are distributed between the centre and the states, the states have come to depend upon the centre for financial assistance due to numerous reasons. Though theoretically the division of powers between the centre and states conforms to the principle of classical federalism, in pratice the financial powers of the states are not in a position to cope with the growing needs of the states. (C) The constitution of a classical federalism is supreme. The Constitution of India is supreme with regard to the centre and the states which derive their authority from the former. None of them is delegate or agent of the other. Consequently the Indian states are not to be treated like the units of local administration in a unitary government. However, the Indian states are subject to the central directions in certain matters. In this respect the Indian federalism has deviated from the classical federalism to some extent. (D) In order to decide disputes arising out of division of powers and jurisdictions between the centre and the states or between the states, an independent judiciary is established in a classical federal system. The independent Supreme Court of India is a custodian of the federal system and is also the final power to interpret the constitution. It performs all the functions of a federal court. Under article 131 it has original jurisdiction in any dispute between the government of India and any state or states or between two or more states. Though the judges of the Supreme Court are appointed by the President of India on the advice of the central council of ministers, yet the independence of the Supreme Court is constitutionally ensured. The judges of the Supreme Court cannot be removed except by impeachment which is a difficult procedure and which results in a nation-wide debate. The classical federal system requires two sets of courts — one for the centre and another for the states but India has a single unified judicial system.

Though the framers of the Indian Constitution have incorporated some basic features of classical federalism into the Indian constitution, yet the constitution has certain provisions which are inconsistent with the federal principles and are unitary in nature. The following are the unitary provisions in the Indian Constitution: (i) Under article 3, the Central parliament can create new states, abolish existing ones, alter their boundaries and change their names. (ii) The constitutional head of the state is appointed and could be removed by the President under articles 155 and 156. (iii) Under article 201 the Governor can reserve a bill passed by the state legislature for consideration of the President. (iv) As per article 213, prior sanction of the President is necessary to issue ordinances by the Governor in respect of certain matters. (v) The central parliament has power to enact laws with respect to matters in the state list under articles 249, 250 and 252. (vi) Under article 254 a law passed by the Parliament overrides a law passed by a state legislature pertaining to an entry in the concurrent list. (vii) Article 256 empowers the union executive to issue directions to the state executive to ensure compliance with the laws passed by the parliament. (viii) The centre can give directions to the states and take action against them for non-compliance with such directions under articles 257, 356 and 365. (ix) Under article 258 the central functions can be entrusted to the states with the consent of the latter. (x) Article 282 empowers the centre to provide discretionary grants to the states. (xi) Under article 356 the President's rule can be imposed in case of failure of constitutional machinery in a state. (xii) Under emergency provisions of the constitution (articles 352-360), the centre has wide powers and can dictate terms to the states. (xiii) All India services are under the control of the centre. (xiv) The Comptroller and Auditor General of India and the Chief Election Commissioner who are the common authorities for the centre and the states are appointed by the President under articles 148 and 324 respectively. (xv) In addition to these constitutional provisions, there are extra-constitutional agencies like Planning Commission, one party domination at the centre, etc., which have strengthened the position of the centre against the states.

All these constitutional provisions, extra constitutional agencies and practices have resulted in centralizing tendencies of the central institutions. Among these various centralizing tendencies, this study focuses its attention on centralizing tendencies of the central voluntary grants.

Though there are many unitary provisions in the Constitution, yet the framers of the Indian Constitution did not adopt a unitary type of government for the following reasons: (A) Under the direct rule of the British Crown, the British India evolved itself into federal system through various Acts passed in 1861, 1892, 1909, 1919 and 1935. The 1935 Act made an attempt to involve the princely states numbering 562 into the federal system. The constituent assembly could not go back to unitary type of government. (B) Diversity in religion, ethnicity, language, culture, region, etc., demanded nothing but some sort of federal system under democratic set up to give functional autonomy to these groups. For example, states like Punjab, Jammu and Kashmir, Nagaland, Mizoram, etc., are organised on the basis of religion and historical legacy. The states like Tamil Nadu, Kerala, Karnataka, Maharashtra, Andhra Pradesh, Orissa, Gujarat, Assam, etc., are organised on the basis of language. Uttar Pradesh, Bihar, Madhya Pradesh, Himachal Pradesh and Rajasthan are organised on the basis of historical legacies and administrative conveniences. The Indian National Congress, the dominant political force in nation-building process, was opposed to the unitary type of government.

There are strong reasons to adopt a modified version of federalism in India : (A) The Indian federalism has evolved out of unitary type of government. Provinces of unitary government were transformed into provinces of federal government under the Government of India Act, 1935. The same federal system with some modifications was adopted by the Constitution of India. The historical legacy is continued. (B) The United States of America and India belong to two different patterns in the formation of their federal system. Thirteen independent states formed a federal union in U.S.A. while in India already politically united India created federal units. In the case of the former, powers flowed from the independent units to the union while in the case of latter powers moved down from the union to the units. Thus the Indian federation is not the result of merger of separate independent sovereign states but the process was in the opposite direction. It was gradual breaking of the unitary system. "Gradually the unitary government accorded progressive autonomy to the provinces by devolution of power and responsibility and finally the Indian political system has been formed as the outcome of this long process of devolution of powers and functions from above."[31] (C) The circumstances which had given rise to the weak centre in the federal set up in the nineteen thirties – the demand of the Muslim League for strong provinces and the problem of associating princely states with the Indian Union – had disappeared after partition of India. Fear of disintegration of the country strongly worked in favour of strong centre in independent India. The separatist forces came as a warning to the members of the constituent assembly. (D) The centralizing forces and the experiences of older federations of U.S.A., Switzerland, Canada and Australia compelled the framers of the Indian Constitution to adopt a federal system with strong centre. Economic, political, social and financial factors have prompted centralizing process in all these countries. Hence a new federal Constitution of India cannot be totally cast in the traditional mould. Therefore the framers of the Indian Constitution were influenced by new centralizing tendencies in the older federations. Dr.B.R.Ambedkar, the chairman of the draft constitution, defended the strong centre and gave these reasons in its favour :[32] It is difficult to prevent the centre from becoming strong. Conditions in the modern world compel the centre to be strong. He gave examples from the federal constitution of U.S.A. However he added that the people should resist the tendency to make the centre stronger. Its strength must be in proportion to its weight and it should not fall due to its overweight. (E) India had tradition of strong centre. The Indian provinces and princely states had been subordinate units during the British rule. They did not enjoy the status of independent self-governing authorities. Shri K.M. Munshi, a prominent member of the constituent assembly, thus wrote: "The units in India were not sovereign states like the American states in the eighteenth century coming together to found a federation."[33] For these historical reasons, the Indian states do not have equal constitutional status with the centre though the former have their own independent legislative, executive and financial jurisdiction. (F) Neither a full federal system nor a full unitary system can meet challenges of situations in India. Consequently Indian Constitution can be federal or unitary to some extent upon circumstances. Such built-in mechanism is provided in the Indian Constitution.

The framers of the Indian Constitution did not purposely establish a model classical federalism with the federal units enjoying real autonomy. They were very much concerned with the national integrity and security. They were fully aware of separatist tendencies of certain regions and took note of experiences of other federal systems and historical legacies and geographical compulsions of India. According to Shri Asok Chand, India has adopted quasi-federal system due to historical legacies and fissiparous tendencies of certain regions backed up by racial, cultural, and religious dissimilarities.[34] In India people are separated by different religions, languages, cultures, races, etc. They want regional autonomy on the basis of religion, language, culture, etc. They are also united by common history, freedom struggle, geographical unity, common goals like secularism, democracy, etc. The framers of the Indian Constitution had tried to bring about a sort of equilibrium between the centrifugal and centripetal forces in the Indian society in the form of quasi-federal constitution. Unity of India can be preserved by maintaining equilibrium between the centripetal and centrifugal forces. This study examines whether the central voluntary grants have encouraged the centripetal forces or the centrifugal forces or both of them in varying degrees.

REFERENCES

1. Stewart William H., *Metaphors, Models and Development of Federal Theory,* The Journal of Federalism, Vol. 12, No. 2, Spring 1982 (Philadelphia, Pennsylvanian: The Centre for the Study of Federalism, Temple University, 1982), p. 5.
2. *Ibid.*, p. 8
3. Rath Sharada, *Centre-State Relations in the Field of Social Services in the United States of America, Australia and India–1950-1970.* Unpublished Thesis (Thesis submitted to the Utkal University for the Degree of Doctor of Philosophy in Political Science, 1975), p. 87.
4. Prasad Anirudh, *Centre and State Powers Under Indian Federalism* (New Delhi : Deep and Deep Publications, 1981), p. 22.
5. Wheare, K.C., *Federal Government* (Third edition; London: Oxford University Press, 1953), p. 1.
6. Quoted by Pal Chandra, *State Autonomy in Indian Federation, Emerging Trends* (New Delhi : Deep and Deep Publications, 1984), p. 17.
7. Quoted by Rath Sharada, "Federatlism : A Conceptual Analysis", *The Indian Journal of Political Science*, Vol XXXIX, No. 4, October-December 1978 (Bhagalpur : The Indian Political Science Association, 1978), p. 574.
8. Quoted by Pal Chandra, *State Autonomy in Indian Federation, Emerging Trends* (New Delhi: Deep and Deep Publications, 1984), p. 18.
9. Wheare, K.C., *Federal Government* (Third edition; London: Oxford University Press, 1953), p. 11.
10. Hicks, Ursula K., *Federalism : Failure and Success, A Comparative Study* (London: The Macmillan Press Ltd., 1978), p. 4.
11. Pal Chandra, *State Autonomy in Indian Federation, Emerging Trends* (New Delhi : Deep and Deep Publications, 1984), p. 39.

12. Doss, Veda, *Impact of Planning on Centre-State Relations in India* (New Delhi : National Publishing House, 1978), p. 2.
13. First Quoted by Strachey, Sir John, *India : Its Administration and Progress* (Third edition; London, 1903), p. 64. Second Quotation by Prasad Anirudh, *Centre-State Relations in India* (New Delhi : Deep and Deep Publications, 1985), p. 35.
14. *Report, Commission on Centre-State Relations,* Part I (Popularly Known as Sarkaria Commission) (Nasik: Printed by the General Manager, Government of India Press, 1988), p. 5.
15. *Indian National Congress* (Madras : S. A. Natesan and Co.), p.773, Quoted by Prasad Anirudh, *Centre-State Relations in India* (New Delhi : Deep and Deep Publications, 1985), p. 35.
16. *Montague-Chelmsford Report* (1918), Para 20, p.78, Quoted by Pandya B.P., *The Federal Idea in India,* Journal of Constitutional and Parliamentary Studies, Vol. 20 (1-4), Jan.-December 1986 (New Delhi : Director, Institute of Constitutional and Parliamentary Studies, 1986), pp. 4 and 5.
17. Pandya, B.P., *The Federal Idea in India,* Journal of Constitutional and Parliamentary Studies, 20 (1-4), Jan.-December 1986, (New Delhi: Director, Institute of Constitutional and Parliamentary Studies, 1986), p. 3.
18. Aiyer, S.P., *The Federal Idea in India* in Aiyar S.P., and Mehta, Usha (ed.), *Essays on Indian Federalism* (Bombay: Allied Publishers Pvt. Ltd., 1965), p. 2.
19. Corry, J.A., *Constitutional Trends and Federalism* in A.R.M. Lower et al., *Evolving Canadian Federalism,* Durham, 1958, p. 96, Quoted by Bombwall, K.R., *Imperatives of Federalism in India* in S.A.H. Haqqi (ed.), *Union-State Relations in India* (Meerut : Meenakshi Prakashan, 1967), p. 4.
20. Santhanam, K., *Union-State Relations in India* (Bombay : Asia Publishing House, 1960), p. 2.
21. Bombwall, K.R., *Imperatives of Federalism in India* in S.A.H. Haqqi (ed.), *Union-State Relations in India* (Meerut : Meenakshi Prakashan, 1967), p. 5.
22. *Constituent Assembly Debates,* Vol. VIII, No. 23 (New Delhi : The Manager of Publications, Government of India, n.d.), p. 921.
23. Ray, Amal, *Inter-Governmental Relations in India: A Study of Indian Federalism* (Bombay : Asia Publishing House, 1966), pp.10 and 11.
24. *Ibid.*, p.11.
25. Lionel Curtis, *Dyarchy* (London : Oxford University Press, 1920), pp.400-409.
26. Wheare, K.C., *Federal Government* (Third edition; London: Oxford University Press, 1953), p. 38.
27. *Constituent Assembly Debates,* Vol. XI, No. 11 (New Delhi : The Manager of Publications, Government of India, n.d.), pp. 51 and 52.
28. Wheare, K.C., *Federal Government* (Third edition; London: Oxford University Press, 1953), p. 28.
29. Chatterji, Amiya, *The Central Financing of State Plan in the Indian Federation* (Calcutta : Firma, K.L. Mukkopadhyaya, 1971), p. 19.
30. George, K.K. and Gulati, I.S., "Centre-State Resource Transfers, 1951-84", *Economic and Political Weekly,* Vol. XX, No. 7, February 16, 1985 (Bombay : A Sameeksha Trust Publication, 1985), p. 287.

31. *Memorandum to the Ninth Finance Commission*; Vol. I, 1988, Submitted by the Government of Karnataka (Bangalore : Government Press, the Government of Karnataka, 1988), p. I.

32. *Constituent Assembly Debates,* Vol. III, No. I (New Delhi : The Manager of Publications, Government of India, n.d.), p. 42.

33. Munshi, K.M., *Indian Law Review,* 1950, Vol. IV, Quoted by Ray, Amal, *Inter-Governmental Relations in India : A Study of Indian Federation* (Bombay : Asia Publishing House, 1966), p. 18.

34. Asok Chanda, *Federalism in India : A Study of Union-State Relations* (London : George Allen and Unwin Ltd., 1965), p. 11.

CHAPTER II

ALLOCATION OF RESOURCES IN HISTORICAL PERSPECTIVE

1. FEDERAL PRINCIPLE IN THE ALLOCATION OF RESOURCES

According to the federal principle, the centre and the states should be independent within their allotted spheres and should not be subordinate to each other but should be co-ordinate with each other. If this principle is to be operative in the financial field, both the central and state governments should have independent sources of revenues to perform their exclusive functions.

Prof. B.P. Adarkar in his book, *Principles and Problems of Federal Finance,* laid down three principles governing allocation of resources between the centre and the states:[1] (i) Independent Sources of Revenues – Both the central and state governments should have independent sources of revenues and the state governments must have sufficient autonomy in matter of collection of revenues. (ii) Adequacy and Elasticity – Revenues of the central and state governments should be sufficient to enable them to discharge their respective functions efficiently and should be capable of expansion to meet the growing needs. (iii) Administrative Economy – There should be economy in collection of taxes by both governments – centre and states.

Allocation of resources between the centre and the states is difficult task. Experience has shown that resources and functions do not expand or contract together. Each does not adjust itself harmoniously to other. In practice it is difficult to achieve such balance between revenues and functions.

Principle or pattern of allocation of resources between the centre and the states is not uniform in all the federations. In older federations like U.S.A. and Australia, taxation is concurrent. Under the constitution of U.S.A., the states are prohibited from imposing import and export duties. Except this restriction, both federal and state governments have full and concurrent powers of taxation. In Australia the power of taxation is concurrent except the customs and excise which exclusively belong to the federal government. Concurrent power of taxation has led to multiple taxation. Since 1942 Australian federal government has been giving compensatory grants to the states for surrendering their rights in the field of income tax. Distribution of taxing power and revenues under the Indian Constitution follows the scheme of 1935 Act which in turn was based on experiences of sixty-five years (since the time of Lord Mayo 1870). However, the Constitution of India has made some deviations in certain respects in the light of experiences of the older federations.

2. EVOLUTION OF ALLOCATION OF RESOURCES

Allocation of resources between the centre and the states in India has evolved from unitary system to federal system. The present allocation of resources between the centre and the states represents that evolution. "The history of the evolution of federal polity in India is in fact the history of process of decentralization of finances which began informally in 1871, which was formalised by the Government of India Act, 1919 and which was finally converted into federal set up by the Government of India Act, 1935. The free India merely took over the set up established by the Government of India Act, 1935 with a hyphen here, with a dot there."[2]

Evolution of allocation of resources between the centre and the states can be divided into five stages : (A) 1833-1871 – unitary financial relations, (B) 1871-1919 – progress decentralization of resources, (C) 1919-1935 – formal decentralization of resources, (D) 1935-1946 – federal allocation of resources, and (E) 1947-1950 – new distribution of resources between the centre and the provinces.

(A) Unitary Financial Relations (1833–1871)

The process of centralization in financial matters began with the Charter Act, 1833. Three presidencies – Madras, Bombay and Bengal – which were independent in financial matters before the Charter Act of 1833, were brought under centralised financial system. The charter introduced a system of centralised administration and finance. It vested the direction and control of the whole civil and military administration and revenues in the Governor-General. The provinces had no financial control over their own affairs. While the centre was responsible for provincial financial administration, the provinces were responsible for provincial administration. As the administrative responsibility in the provinces was not coupled with the financial power, the provincial administration was handicapped in its effective functioning. The provinces were to collect taxes on behalf of the centre and to spend money with the consent of the latter. The centre controlled the smallest details of every branch of expenditure of the provinces. Its previous sanction was necessary for the employment of a person who was to be paid out of public money and for granting funds even for local works like improvement of roads, buildings, etc. The government of India distributed funds to the provinces not on any rational principle but according to the claims of the provincial governments. As the East India Company was interested in expanding and consolidating its empire in India, it followed a policy of excessive centralization.

In 1858 the British Crown took over the Indian administration from the East India Company. The financial control of the financial administration was entrusted to the secretary of state for India. "The Government of India was not given any power to impose any taxes or make any assignments of revenue to the provinces without the prior sanction of the Secretary of State."[3] Thus the financial administration became highly centralised. However, a stage was set for future financial administration with restoration of legislatures to Madras, Bombay and Bengal presidencies. James Wilson, the first Finance Minister of the Crown's Government of India, streamlined the financial administration. Sameul Laing, successor to James Wilson, submitted a scheme for devolution which did not make headway. Another scheme for devolution prepared by Col. Strachy on the federal model of U.S.A. was not accepted. Finance Minister Massey (1866-68) was in favour of devolution of financial powers.

(B) Progressive Decentralization of Resources (1871–1919)

The British Crown had to follow a policy of financial decentralization due to development in infrastructure in transport and communication, pressure from Indian public opinion, political awakening from the people, enlargement of legislative powers of the provincial governments and increasing functions of both the central and provincial governments.

The progressive decentralization of resources goes through five stages : (i) Lord Mayo's scheme in 1870 was the first step towards financial administration. It was prompted by these considerations : (a) Deficit of the central government was to be removed by developing provincial sources of revenue. (b) The provincial governments were to develop sense of responsibility and manage their own finances. (c) Tax administration and appropriation should go together. As per Mayo's scheme, administration of certain departments like education, police, jails, medical service, civil buildings, roads, etc., was entrusted to the provincial governments which were to realize the revenues from these departments. In addition to these revenues, the central government made grants to the provinces from the imperial revenues on the basis of figures of 1869-70. (ii) In course of time it was felt that the departments handed over to the provinces were a few but it was found necessary to hand over to a few more departments to the provinces. Under the settlement of Lord Lytton's Reforms of 1877, the provincial sphere was further widened by entrusting land revenue, stamps, excise, printing and stationery, law and justice, and general administration to the provinces. Certain heads of revenues such as stamps, excise, licence to tax, law and justice, and income derived from minor railways were partly given to the provinces. These were assigned revenues. (iii) The settlements of 1877 were in force till 1882 and new settlements were made in 1882. Under Lord Ripon, the Governor-General of India, the system of assigned revenues was modified and the system of 'divided heads' or 'shared revenues' was introduced. Under the new system, the revenues were classified into three categories: (a) imperial (central) revenues, (b) provincial revenues, and (c) divided revenues. (a) Revenues from customs, salt, opium, post and telegraphs and railways were with the centre for purpose of uniformity. (b) Revenues from law and justice, public works and education were with the provinces. (c) Proceeds from forests, excise, licences, income tax, stamps and registration, irrigation and agricultural land were divided between the centre and the provinces. In respect of divided heads, there was no uniform policy to assign share to the provinces. Each province had a separate arrangement with the centre in accordance with the settlement. Duration of settlement was for five years. After expiry of every five year period, new settlement could be made. The provincial settlements were made in 1887, 1892 and 1897 at the interval of five years. The system of divided heads of revenue was in force till 1919. Lord Ripon's scheme of 1882 paved the way for federal financial system. (iv) As these periodical revisions were found to be inadequate, a scheme of quasi-permanent settlement was introduced in 1904. According to this settlement, the revenues allotted to the provinces were fixed and were not subject to changes by the central government except in special situation. The quasi-permanent settlement gave more independent position and was the first step towards granting financial autonomy to the provinces. (v) On the recommendations of the Decentralization Commission appointed in 1909, Lord Hardinge expanded the quasi-permanent settlement of 1904. Permanent settlements were made in 1912. These settlements continued until the introduction of Montagu-Chelmsford Reforms of 1919 and gave larger share of revenues to the provinces.

Thus the progressive decentralization of resources went through five stages : (i) transfer of departments and revenues (1870), (ii) assigned revenues (1877), (iii) divided head (1882), (iv) quasi-permanent settlements (1904), and (v) permanent settlements (1912).

(C) Formal Decentralization of Resources (1919–1935)

The enlightened public opinion in India was in favour of more financial autonomy and resources to the provinces. The Government of India Act of 1919 (popularly known as Montagu-Chelmsford Reform) was the first step in the goal of gradual transfer of power to the Indian hands in accordance with the announcement made by the British government on 20th August 1917. The Act was designed to give more legislative, administrative and financial powers to the provinces. It abolished the system of 'divided heads' of revenue and expenditure and rearranged the centre-state financial relations. The actual division of subjects and revenues was carried out by the Devolution Rules made under section 45A of the Act and rules were issued in 1920. The central subjects were defence, foreign affairs, railways, post and telegraphs, currency and coinage, commerce, shipping, etc. The provincial subjects were divided into two categories – reserved subjects and transferred subjects. The reserved subjects were law and order, etc. The transferred subjects included local self-government, education, sanitation, public health, public works, agriculture, co-operative societies, development of industries, etc. The Act divided the resources between the centre and the provinces. The central revenues covered these items – customs, non-alcoholic excises including salt, general stamp duties, income tax, receipts from railways posts and telegraphs, etc. The provincial revenues covered these items – land revenue, irrigation charges, alcoholic excises, forest receipts, court fees, stamp duties, registration fees, etc. Further the provinces were free to prepare their own budgets, manage their own finances and borrow from the general public. However, expenditure on reserved subjects continued to be subject to regulation and control by the central government. "Despite this liberation, there was no separation for cash balances of the centre and the provinces. There was a single public account on which both operated."[4]

Abolition of 'divided heads' of revenue and transfer of some revenues to the provinces led to the deficit in the central revenue. A scheme of fixed contributions from the provinces to the centre on the basis of normal surplus of the former was devised and power to levy such contributions was vested with the centre under section 112 of the Government of India Act, 1919. Later on the provinces complained against the contributions to be made by them to the centre. The central government proposed the appointment of a committee to advise on the financial relations between the centre and the provinces. On the basis of this proposal, the Financial Relations Committee under the chairmanship of Lord Meston was constituted in January 1920 to advise on the contributions to be made by the provinces to the centre and to examine the claim of Bombay to a share in the proceeds of income tax. The committee recommended the standard contributions to be made by the provinces to the centre. These contributions were to be abolished when the financial position of the central government would improve.

In course of time four committees had made references to the allocation of resources between the centre and the provinces. In 1924 a high power Taxation Enquiry Committee was appointed to inquire into the whole field of taxation. At the same time another committee, Taxation Enquiry Committee, was constituted with Sir Alexander Muddiman as the chairman to study the defects inherent in the financial working of the Government of India Act, 1919. The recommendations of these two committees were not very important from the point of view of strengthening the financial autonomy of the provinces. The provincial contributions to the centre continued till 1928-29 to meet the central deficit and were abolished in 1928-29. It was soon realised that the central sources of taxation were elastic while the provincial sources of taxation were inelastic. The Simon Commission (1930) and Joint Select Committee of the British Parliament also made references to the allocation of resources between the centre and the provinces.

(D) From Decentralization of Resources to Federal Finances (1935–1946)

The provisions dealing with the allocation of resources between the centre and the provinces under the 1935 Act were the result of recommendations of various commissions/committes/reports. Among these the following are important. They are report of Simon Commission (1930), White Paper (1931), the first report of Peel Committee (1931), the proceedings of R.T.C. (1930-31), report of Percy Committee (1932), the second report of Peel Committee (1932), and report of the Joint Select Committee (1933-34).

Sir Walter Layton who was the financial adviser to the Simon Commission had submitted a report on the allocation of resources between the centre and the provinces which has remained relevant to some extent even today. According to his report, the pattern of distribution of revenues between the centre and the provinces was as follows :

"(i) Wholly centre : collected and spent by the centre;

(ii) Wholly provincial : collected and spent by the provinces;

(iii) Taxes collected by the centre and distributed among the provinces on the basis of origin;

(iv) Taxes collected by the centre and distributed among the provinces on the basis of population."[5]

In the Second Round Table Conference in September 1931, the Federal Structure Committee was constituted. This committee in turn appointed a sub-committee under the chairmanship of Viscount Peel to examine and report about distribution of resources between the centre and the provinces. The first report of the committee recommended that corporation tax should be central tax while income tax should be provincial tax. In order to have uniformity of rates, it was recommended that income tax should be levied by the centre but proceeds should be distributed to the provinces.

In December 1931, the British government brought out a White

Paper containing proposals for the Indian constitutional reforms including financial proposals. The White Paper proposed that proceeds of central taxes should be permanently assigned to the centre. However, proceeds of income tax should be shared between the centre and the provinces for some years and thereafter central share should be reduced to zero. But the centre could impose surcharge on income taxes and use such proceeds exclusively for itself. The corporation tax was to be retained by the centre but after ten years benefits of the tax must be extended to the provinces.

The Percy Committee (1932) recommended that a portion of proceeds of income tax should be retained by the centre and the rest of it should be distributed among the provinces. It opined that if entire proceeds of income tax were to be distributed among the provinces, it would lead to huge deficit in the central budget. Further it recommended that proceeds of corporation tax must be retained by the centre.

The second report of Peel Committee (1932) recommended that the centre should get entire proceeds derived from (i) corporation taxes, (ii) taxes on officers of the central government, (iii) taxes on government securities, and (iv) taxes on income of persons not residents of British India.

As the recommendations of Peel and Percy Committees were contradictory, matter was referred to the Joint Select Committee of the British Parliament. The Joint Select of the British Parliament on Indian constitutional reforms (1933-34) recommended that the share assigned to the provinces should not be more than fifty per cent.

Thus the Government of India Act, 1935 was the result of deliberations of Round Table Conferences, extensive inquiries by the committees and several consultations in the United Kingdom and India. The Act envisaged an all India federation consisting of provinces of British India and states of princely India. Legislative, administrative and financial powers were divided between the centre and the federal units. Allocation of resources between the centre and the federal units was classified into three categories : exclusively central resources, exclusively provincial resources and sharing/assigning resources. (i) The following taxes were levied, collected and utilized by the centre. They were corporation tax, surcharges on income other than agricultural income, surcharges on the items mentioned under article 137, receipts from railways and posts, import and export duties. (ii) The following were the taxes to be levied, collected and utilized by the federal units. They were land revenue, excise duties on alcoholic liquors, taxes on professions and trades, irrigation rates, duties in respect of succession to agricultural land, taxes on animals and boats, taxes on entertainment, amusement, betting and gambling, taxes on sale of goods and advertisement, etc. (iii) (a) The following taxes were levied and collected by the centre but were to be distributed between the centre and the federated units. Duties on salt, federal duties of excise and export duties were to be levied and collected by the centre. If the federal legislature decided to share a part of such revenues with the federated units, they should be paid out of the revenues of the central government. Taxes on income other than agricultural income were to be levied and collected by the centre but were to be distributed among the federated units. A portion of the proceeds might be retained by the centre. (b) Duties in respect of succession to property other than agricultural land, stamp duties mentioned in the federal legislative list, terminal taxes on goods or passengers carried by railway and air, taxes on railway fares and freights were to be levied and collected by the central government but were to be assigned to the federated units. (c) Grants-in-aid were to be given to those federated units whose budgets required assistance to balance them.

The Government of India Act, 1935, prescribed that the allocation of resources between the centre and the federated units was to be determined by an Order-in-Council. In this regard Sir Otto Niemeyer was appointed to make recommendations in respect of (i) allocation of proceeds of income tax to the provinces, (ii) share of jute export duty to the jute growing provinces, and (iii) grants-in-aid to the provinces from the centre etc. The report of Sir Otto Niemeyer was known as Indian Finance Enquiry Report. "In making his report, Sir Otto Niemeyer had two points in mind – the stability of the central finances and equitable basis of distribution."[6] The report recommended various forms of assignments: (i) cash subventions, (ii) fifty per cent of jute duty, (iii) additional 12½ per cent of the jute duty, (iv) benefits from debt cancellation, and shares from income tax proceeds, etc. Recommendations of Sir Otto Niemeyer were accepted and implemented in 1936 and were in operation till 1940. During the World War II, it became necessary to make more resources available to the centre for defence purposes.

(E) Committees of the Constituent Assembly and the Government of India (1947–50)

In January 1947 the constituent assembly set up a union powers committee with twelve members and in April 1947 two members from princely India joined it. The committee recommended the following sources of revenues for the centre : "customs duties including export duties; excise duties; corporation tax; taxes on income other than agricultural income; taxes on capital value of the assets with exclusion of agricultural land, of individuals and companies; taxes on capital of companies; duties in respect of succession to property; estate duty other than agricultural land; and fees in respect of any of the matters in the list of union power but not including fees taken in any court other than the union court."[7] Taxes other than those specially assigned to the centre were supposed to belong to the federated units.

The president of the constituent assembly appointed in 1947 three-man committee under the chairmanship of Shri N.R. Sarkar to examine the federal financial arrangements and to make suggestions. The committee submitted its report in 1948 and made the following recommendations : (i) Entire proceeds of income tax including proceeds from corporation tax and federal emoluments should be brought into divisible pool. (ii) With regard to jute export duty, fixed grants to the provinces of West Bengal, Assam, Orissa and Bihar should be made. (iii) Fifty per cent of excise duty realized on tobacco should be distributed to the provinces on the basis of consumption. (iv) Net proceeds of the following should be wholly retained by the centre. They were duties of customs including export duties, taxes on capital value of assets, taxes on the capital of companies, taxes on railway fares and freights, etc. (v) There should be an independent financial commission to deal periodically with division of shared revenues between the centre and the provinces. The constituent assembly accepted some of the recommendations.

Prior to independence of India the British India was governed by the Government of India Act, 1935, but princely India was unaffected by this Act. After accession of the princely states to the Indian Union, the former were to be financially integrated with the rest of India. In October 1948, the Indian States Finance Inquiry Committee under the chairmanship of Shri V.T. Krishnamachari was appointed to examine the problems of financial integration of the princely states with the rest of India and to make recommendations accordingly. The committee recommended that all assets and liabilities connected with the federal resources should be taken over by the centre and all assets and liabilities associated with provincial functions should remain with the princely states. It also made recommendations for transitory period : The princely states were to be fully compensated "for five years for the gap between the loss due to some tax powers and enterprises having passed over to the union government and the savings in expenditure due to the transfer of certain functions like defence. The grant was to taper off in the next five years."[8] The recommendations of the committee were accepted with some minor modifications. Financial integration was brought about between the former British India and the erstwhile Indian states.

3. CONSTITUTIONAL POSITION OF ALLOCATION OF RESOURCES

Distribution of revenues between the centre and the provinces was influenced by the provisions of 1935 Act, recommendations of the expert committee on the financial provisions of the draft constitution (Sarker Committee), the memoranda submitted by the various provincial governments to the constituent assembly and the experiences of older federations.

After partition of India in 1947, a strong plea for greater autonomy for states received a set back in the constituent assembly. There was concern for unity, integrity and sovereignty of India in the constituent assembly. However, it cannot be said that the members of the constituent assembly lost concern for state autonomy. There were some members in the constituent assembly who demanded state autonomy on a true federal basis. However, overall concern was in favour of unity, integrity and sovereignty of India as a whole.

In the light of working of financial institutions between the centre and the states in many federal systems the framers of the Indian Constitution wanted flexibility in centre-state financial relations and a dominant position for the centre.

Observations of Shri Alladi Krishnaswami Ayyar, a prominent member of the constituent assembly, on the 8th November, 1948 in the constituent assembly clearly indicated the attitude of the important section of the constituent assembly towards centre-state financial relations : "The financial provisions in the Draft Constitution have also come in for strong comment.... While an independent course or sources of revenue are clearly necessary for the proper functioning of a federal government, there is a distinct tendency, however, in the several federations, for the central government to act as the taxing agency, taking care to make adequate provisions for the units sharing the proceeds as also the central or the national government granting subsidies."[9]

The constitutional provisions dealing with the centre-state financial relations are based on the following broad principles : (i) All taxes should be divided between the centre and the states in order to avoid overlapping. (ii) Proceeds of all taxes assigned to the states should exclusively belong to them. (iii) As the central taxes are more elastic, proceeds of certain central taxes are to be shared with the states on the basis of recommendations of the Finance Commission and of the Parliament. Share of the proceeds of income tax is determined by the Finance Commission and share of the proceeds of excise duties is approved by the Parliament. (iv) Certain grants are also made from the centre to the states on the basis of recommendations of the Finance Commission. (v) The centre and the states may raise loans from the public. (vi) Allocation of proceeds of taxes between the centre and the states is intended to enhance financial autonomy of the states and to provide for a periodical and elastic re-adjustment of financial relations in accordance with the changing needs. (vii) Taxes which have inter-state base are entrusted to the centre. Taxes which are to be levied on a uniform basis throughout the country are assigned to the centre. Taxes which can be collected more efficiently and conveniently throughout India are given to the centre. (viii) Taxes which have local base are given to the states. Not many taxes are under the concurrent jurisdiction. Entries 35, 44 and 47 in the concurrent list make provision for concurrent taxation. The residuary taxing power is vested in the centre.

The framers of the Indian Constitution have made their best efforts to distribute taxes and duties between the centre and the states so that both sets of governments could have their independent sources of revenues.

Division of taxes between the centre and the states follows to great extent the pattern prescribed by the Government of India Act, 1935. Taxing powers are not separately indicated but are found along with the legislative powers listed in the seventh schedule of the constitution. However, manner of distribution of certain taxes between the centre and the states is described in Chapter I of the Part XII of the Constitution. Taxes included in this chapter are broadly classified into five categories and are covered under articles from 268 to 281. Further entries from 82 to 92B in the union list under seventh schedule deal with central sources of taxation and entries from 45 to 63 in the state list under the same schedule deal with state sources of taxation but only entries 35, 44 and 47 in the concurrent list under the same schedule deal with common sources of taxation.

Distribution of revenues between the centre and the states is divided into the following five categories and covers articles from 268 to 281: (i) Under article 271 the Parliament can levy surcharges on certain items listed under articles 269 and 270 and can use proceeds from such surcharges exclusively for itself. Such proceeds form a part of the Consolidated Fund of India. (ii) Under article 270 taxes on income other than agricultural income are levied and collected by the centre and proceeds of such taxes are distributed between the centre and the states on the recommendations of the Finance Commission. (iii) Under article 272 the central duties of excise other than such duties of excise on medicinal and toilet preparations as are listed in the central list are levied and collected by the centre. Proceeds from such duties may be shared with the states if the Parliament by law provides for it. (iv) Under article 269 the central government levies and collects taxes on the following items : "(a) duties in respect to succession property other than agricultural land, (b) estate duty in respect of property other than agricultural land, (c) terminal taxes on goods or passengers carried by railway, sea or air, (d) taxes on railway fares and freights, (e) taxes other than stamp duties on transactions in stock exchanges and future markets, (f) taxes on the sale or purchase of newspapers and on the advertisements published therein, (g) taxes on the sale or purchase of goods other than newspapers where such sale or purchase takes place in the course of inter-state trade or commerce."[10] Proceeds from these taxes/duties are exclusively distributed among the states. (v) Under article 268 stamp duties and such duties of excise on medicinal and toilet preparations are levied by the centre but are collected by the states and their proceeds are utilized by the states.

Entries from 82 to 92B in the union list of the seventh schedule deal with taxation power of the centre. Certain taxes are exclusively meant for the centre; proceeds from some other taxes are shared with the states; and in case of some other taxes proceeds from such taxes are assigned to the states: (A) Proceeds from the taxes under the entries 83 (duties of customs including export duties), 85 (corporation tax), and 86 (taxes on capital value of assets excluding agricultural land and taxes on capital of company) are within exclusive jurisdiction of the centre. (B) Proceeds from the taxes under entries 82 (taxes on income other than agricultural income under article 270) and 84 (duties of excise on tobacco under article 272) are to be shared by the centre with the states. (C) Proceeds from the taxes under entries 87 (estate duty in respect of property other than agricultural land), 88 (duties in respect of succession to property other than agricultural land), 89 (terminal taxes on goods or passengers carried by railway, sea or air), 90 (taxes other than stamp duties on transactions in stock exchanges and future markets), 91 (rates of stamp duty in respect of bills of exchange etc.), 92 (taxes on the sale or purchase of newspapers and advertisements published therein), 92A(taxes on sale and purchase of goods other than newspapers in the inter-state trade or commerce) and 92B (taxes on the consignment of goods connected with inter-state trade or commerce) are assigned to the states under article 269.

The items of state taxes are covered under entries from 45 to 63 (19 items) in the seventh schedule. The following are the items of state taxation: land revenue (45), taxes on agricultural income (46), duties in respect of succession to agricultural land (47), estate duty in respect of agricultural land (48), taxes on lands and buildings (49), taxes on mineral rights (50), duties of excise on alcoholic liquors, opium and narcotic drugs (51), taxes on the entry of goods into a local area (52), taxes on the consumption or sale of electricity (53), taxes on the sale or purchase of goods (54), taxes on advertisements other than advertisements in newspapers (55), taxes on goods and passengers carried by road and inland water (56), taxes on vehicles (57), taxes on animals and boats (58), tolls (59), taxes on professions, trades and callings (60), capitation taxes (61), taxes on luxuries and entertainments (62), and rates of stamp duty in respect of documents (63). The state governments are free to levy, collect and utilize the proceeds of these taxes.

The concurrent list contains only three tax entries which are not important and expansive. Entry 35 deals with taxes on mechanically propelled vehicles; entry 44 is concerned with stamp duties; and entry 47 deals with fees in the courts. All these three entries are subject to certain limitations and other entries.

The central taxes are elastic and expanding with economic development of the country. Customs duty has always been an important source of central revenues. Proceeds from income tax has been making a sizable contribution to the central revenue even after giving shares of the states. Corporation tax has made impressive growth on account of higher rate of tax and economic development. Earlier excise duties were negligible source of revenue and now they have become important source of revenue to the centre. In addition to proceeds from the taxes, the centre gets revenues from the commercial undertakings like railways, posts and telegraphs, banking and other public sector undertakings. As the centre has control over currency and coinage, it resorts to large scale deficit financing.

Revenues from the state taxes are not sufficient to meet the growing needs of the states. The states have inelastic sources of revenues but have expanding sources of expenditure.

The distribution of taxes between the centre and the states has been subject to stress and strain and some non-Congress chief ministers in the past have demanded redistribution of taxes between the centre and the states. The constitutional division of functions and resources between the centre and the states has made the former more powerful financially and the latter weak financially and subordinate functionally to the former.

The framers of the Indian Constitution had recognised inadequate resources of the states and had made provisions for statutory transfer of resources from the centre to the states on the recommendations of the Finance Commission. The planning process in the country has upset this mechanism in the form of Finance Commission and strengthened the position of the centre.

Article 282 authorises the central government to make voluntary and discretionary grants to the states. These grants are made mainly on the recommendations of the Planning Commission. The article 282 has come in for great criticism in view of its centralizing tendencies.

Thus the present Constitution has distributed the taxes between the centre and the states, provided for appointment of Finance Commission to overcome the revenue gap of the states and made provision for central voluntary grants to the states under article 282.

4. PRESENT TRANSFER OF RESOURCES

The present pattern of resource transfers from the centre to the states may be placed under three categories : (i) Statutory transfers – Resources are transferred on the recommendations of the Finance Commission under article 275. These are statutory transfers and are unconditional. Further proceeds of certain taxes under articles 269, 270 and 272 are transferred to the states under different formulas. (ii) Non-statutory transfers – Resources are transferred from the centre for execution of state plan targets including centrally sponsored schemes on the recommendations of the Planning Commission. These include voluntary grants (282) and loans (293). These are non-statutory transfer of resources and have centralizing tendencies. (iii) Other transfers – Other transfers consist of small saving loans assistance for natural calamities etc., which are routed through the central Ministry of Finance. These transfers of resources are conditional and contain discretionary element.

5. PROBLEM OF MAINTAINING RESOURCE BALANCE

Constitutional distribution of subjects between the centre and the states have not coincided with the distribution of financial resources. It is easy to allocate functions but it is difficult to allocate resources between the centre and the states. It has not been possible in any federation to provide for allocation of resources to coincide with allocation of functions. Even the so-called balance between the resources and functions at the inception of a federation gets disturbed in course of time due to many factors. This is also the same story of Indian federation. Dr. Chelliah, R.J. opines that this asymmetry in the assignment of tax powers and of expenditure responsibilities has led in all federations to the familiar problem of vertical fiscal imbalance. Expenditure needs of the regional governments are far in excess of their revenues.[11]

Fiscal federalism differs from federation to federation due to many factors including political factors. There are two main problems which confront fiscal federalism:[12] (i) It is a problem of resolving maladjustment of resources and needs between centre and states. (ii) There is problem of harmonising income with needs between states *inter se* the framers of the Indian Constitution tried to solve the problem of maintaining balance between resources and expenditure of states by providing provisions for sharing of taxes and statutory grants. "(1) The main assistance required from the centre would be in the nature of shares in taxes and grants towards the recurring revenue expenditures of the states; and (2) the Finance Commission would be the chief instrument for determining the subventions and grants."[13] But the centralised planning and other factors in India have upset the design of the framers of the Indian Constitution.

In course of time the centre has become financially strong while the states have become financially weak. There has been problem to maintain balance between the resources and expanding expenditure of the states. There are reasons why the centre has become strong financially : As a union government it has all those tax items which have inter-state and all India character and yield great revenue. As international economic relations and balance of payments are central responsibilities, customs and excise are given to the centre. These tax items yield handsome revenue. The process of economic development has also helped the centre to increase its revenues. The central commercial undertakings which are large in size also contribute to the central revenues. These are built-in provisions and conditions which have strengthened the financial position of the centre. Similarly there are also reasons why the states have become financially weak and dependent on the centre : The states are increasingly called upon to spend more money on welfare measures which are unproductive in short term. Consequently they are compelled to spend less on revenue-yielding projects. Thus there has been a problem of maintaining the balance of resources between the centre and the states in India and the balance between the resources and expenditure of the states.

REFERENCES

1. Referred by Ray, Amal, *Inter-Governmental Relations : A Study of Indian Federalism* (Bombay : Asia Publishing House, 1966), pp. 61-62.
2. Diwan, Paras, *Union-State Fiscal Relations : An Overview* (New Delhi : Light and Life Publishers, 1981), p. 22.

3. Chanda, Asok, *Federalism in India : A Study of Union-State Relations* (London : George Allen and Unwin Ltd., 1965), p. 134.
4. *Ibid.*, p.139.
5. Diwan, Paras, *Union-State Fiscal Relations : An Overview* (New Delhi : Light and Life Publishers, 1981), p. 31.
6. Doss, Veda, *Impact of Planning on Centre-State Financial Relations in India* (New Delhi : National Publishing House, 1978), p. 67.
7. *Ibid.*, pp.74 and 75.
8. Lakdawala, D.T., "Evolution of Union-State Financial Relations", *Commerce*, Vol. 125, No. 3198, August 19, 1972.
9. *Constituent Assembly Debates*, Vol. VIII, No. 4 (New Delhi : The Manager of Publications, Government of India, n.d.), p. 336.
10. *The Constitution of India* (Allahabad : Central Law Agency, 1973), p.77.
11. Chelliah, R.J., *The Economic and Equity Aspects of the Distribution of Financial Resources between Centre and States*, Seminar on Centre-State Relations, Bangalore, August 5-7, 1983, organised by The Economic and Planning Council, Government of Karnataka in association with The Institute for Social and Economic Change, Bangalore, and The Centre for Policy Research, New Delhi (Bangalore : Government Press, Government of Karnataka, 1983), p. 61.
12. Reddy, K.N., *Rapporteur's Report, Centre-State Financial Relations*, Papers read at the Indian Economic Conference, Bodh Gaya, 1972 (Bombay : Popular Prakashan, 1974), p. XIV.
13. Sinha, R.K., *Fiscal Federalism in India* (New Delhi : Sterling Publishers Pvt. Ltd., 1987), p. 278.
14. *Constituent Assembly Debates*, Vol. IX, No. 6 (New Delhi : The Manager of Publications, Government of India, n.d.), p. 205.
15. *Constituent Assembly Debates*, Vol. V, No. 4 (New Delhi : The Manager of Publications, Government of India, 1956), p. 82.

CHAPTER III

GRANTS-IN-AID

1. MEANING OF GRANTS

Grants-in-aid, according to Webster's Dictionary, means "a grant or subsidy from public funds paid by a central to a local government in aid of some public undertaking.....usually conditional upon the maintenance of a specified standard or upon similar or proportional appropriations by the grantee."[1] Grants are defined as contributory assistance from government at one level to government at another level.[2] The grants-in-aid are paid by a superior governmental authority to a subordinate one with conditions or without conditions. They cannot be taken back once the conditions are fulfilled. These conditions vary from country to country and from time to time.

Shri P.P. Agarwal makes distinction among grant, compulsory shared tax and loan :[3] A grant is not returnable but the work undertaken is all that remains as a proof of the grant. A shared tax carries with it an element of compulsion on the part of higher authority to share a part of the proceeds of the particular taxes with the subordinate authorities. Loan is to be repaid.

2. PURPOSES OF GRANTS

Purposes of grants-in-aid differ on the basis of types of grants made by the centre to the states. Articles 273, 275 and 282 deal with different purposes of grants.

The centre gives grants under article 273 to compensate the loss of shares of some items of revenue relating to jute which some states like Assam, Orissa, West Bengal, etc., had enjoyed once. These grants are made out of the Consolidated Fund of India and are statutory grants. The centre also provides grants, under article 275, to the states with the approval of the Parliament for promoting welfare of the scheduled tribes or for raising the level of administration of the scheduled areas. The article 275 says: "Such sums as Parliament may by law provide shall be charged on the Consolidated Fund of India in each year as grants-in-aid of the revenues of such states as Parliament may determine to be in need of assistance, and different sums may be fixed for different states.'' The grants under articles 273 and 275 are statutory grants.

The centre makes grants under article 282 to the states to meet the plan expenditure. These grants are voluntary and conditional and are made for any public purpose. The article had been placed under the general heading of 'Miscellaneous Financial Provisions' and not under the head of 'Distribution of Revenues between the Union and the States' under which articles from 268 to 281 are placed.

The statutory grants are made on the basis of recommendations of the Finance Commission and are given for the following purposes: They intend to bring uniform level of economic prosperity among different states. They have to bring about uniform income and services and economic integration among the states.

The voluntary grants are supposed to combine the advantages of national planning with local interest and administration in the matters generally left to the states.[4] Prof. Lakdawala, D.T. says: ''The rationale of conditional grants depends on the presumption that the centre is a better judge of people's interest even in functions which belong to the states.''[5] The voluntary grants with matching contributions from the states are meant to stimulate state expenditure for those schemes in which the states have no spontaneous interest. These voluntary grants made by the centre to the states are generally plan grants and are meant to enable the states to carry on socio-economic developmental activities. The state governments do not possess sufficient resources to undertake developmental activities without financial assistance from the centre which has elastic sources of resources.

Shri Singh, S.S. explains the objectives of voluntary (discretionary) grants : ''The objects of discretionary grants accordingly were argued to be (i) observing the plan priorities and checking diversion of resources from one head of development to another; (ii) continuous co-ordination of the state plans and regulation of the quantum of aid keeping in view the economy with which projects were executed and the central aid matched by the states with their own resources and initiative, and (iii) providing selective pushes to individual programmes in the light of changing conditions to keep the progress of the plan even.''[6] Voluntary grants under article 282 are used to cover all three purposes listed above.

The voluntary grants under article 282 are general and may pertain to any of the three lists. The article states: "The union or a state may make any grants for any public purpose, notwithstanding that the purpose is not one with respect to which Parliament or the state legislature of the state, as the case may be, may make laws." Originally these grants were meant to meet certain special financial needs of the states arising out of natural calamities. Since the Finance Commission is an *ad hoc* body, it cannot foresee assistance for calamities, the article 282 is to be used to provide assistance to the states in need of financial help. But in practice, extensive grants are made by the central government, on the recommendations of the Planning Commission, to the states for implementation of plan programmes. "By the time of the appointment of the Third Finance Commission, the government of India seemed to have come to the firm conclusion that the Finance Commission was not the proper body to recommend plan grants and should only, therefore, concern itself with the non-plan revenue needs of the states."[7] In view of constitutional limitations of the Finance Commission in recommending plan grants, the Planning Commission is given dominant role in providing voluntary grants to the states for plans. Plan grants relate to agriculture, industry, transport, health, education, social service, etc., which fall within the jurisdiction of the states. They are meant to achieve national co-ordination of plan policies and to realize plan goals.

The table on the next page gives a picture how the central and state components can be matched differently for different purposes at different times. Some of the combinations have already been tried in India.

(A) Statutory Grants

Grants under article 275 are statutory grants which are determined by the Parliament on the recommendations of the Finance Commission. They are not variable for a period of five years and are unconditional and need-based. They are given a lumpsum without supervision. They do not interfere with the autonomy of the states and are in keeping with the federal principle. The report of the First Finance Commission states the purposes of the statutory grants : "Unconditional grants should reinforce the general resources of the state governments, which

3. TYPES OF GRANTS

A — Statutory Grants

Grants are made by the centre to the states on recommendations of Finance Commission

B — Non-Statutory Grants (Voluntary/discretionary grants)

I	II	III	IV
100 per cent grants	Matching grants	Partially grants and partially loans	Kinds of grants
(From the centre to the states).	a. More central component in the matching grants. b. More state component in the matching grants. c. Balanced matching grants from the centre and the states.	a. More component of central grants and less component of central loans. b. More component of central loans and less component of central grants. c. Balanced central grants and loans.	a. Plan grants. b. Non-Plan grants. c. Block grants. d. Specific grants. e. General grants.

they should be free to allocate among the competing purposes according to their best judgment, subject to the usual administrative and parliamentary checks. Grants for broad purposes, may be given to stimulate the expansion of particular categories of services rather than specific schemes under those categories."[8] Though the article 275 may authorise the centre through the Parliament to provide conditional grants to the states, the centre has no inclination to do so. The centre intends to provide unconditional grants under article 275 and conditional grants under article 282 for its own reason. Dr. G. Thimmaiah opines that the centre may give conditional grants under article 275 : "However, it should be noted here that article 275(1) empowers the Union Parliament in India to prescribe by law even conditional grants for the states which are in need of such assistance.... But so far the union government has not thought it fit to ask the Union Parliament under article 275 (1) to make any law for the purpose of conditional grants to the states....Only once during the past twenty-two years the President of India prescribed the conditional grants for promotion of primary education by his order on the advice of the First Finance Commission. The latter Finance Commissions have been discouraged by the union government from recommending conditional grants under article 275(1). In fact when the Third Finance Commission recommended conditional grants for the development of road communications in some backward states, the union government did not accept this recommendation....Further he (member secretary of 3rd Finance Commission) rejected the recommendation of such grants by the Finance Commission on the ground that (it) would weaken the position of the Planning Commission in influencing states' development policies over which the union government has no control constitutionally. Thus the union government has rightly bifurcated, by its executive decision, its power to provide unconditional revenue grants under article 275(1) and its power to provide conditional revenue as well as capital grants under article 282."[9]

(B) Non-statutory Grants

Non-statutory/conditional/discretionary grants are those grants which are subject to certain conditions to be fulfilled by the recipient authority. These conditions may change from time to time. The article 282 which enables the centre to make non-statutory grants for any public purpose does not provide for principles governing such grants. When the constitution was framed, grants for plans under article 282 were not visualised. The grants under this article have been extensively used by the central government to provide plan grants to the state governments without passing a parliamentary law. When plan grants were provided before 1968-69, the central government prescribed conditions for various schemes. After adoption of Gadgil formula, certain norms are evolved for providing these grants. However, an element of discretion cannot be ruled out in one form or another.

Non-statutory grants are provided by the centre to the states for various purposes. These purposes also change from time to time. Purposes for which grants are given are listed by the Study Team on Centre-State Relationship:[10] (i) The centre provides grants for schemes which by their very nature have to be implemented by the state governments under the central control or supervision. (ii) Grants are given by the centre to the states to carry out schemes which fall within the executive control of the states. (iii) The centre provides grants to the states to meet large liabilities which are either unforeseen or of an international magnitude. (iv) Grants are given in pursuance of an understanding or an agreement between the centre and the states about some schemes. The report of the First Finance Commission also lists the purposes for which the centre provides grants to the states : "(1) deficiency of the revenues of the states in relation to functions, (2) the concern of the federal government to ensure a national minimum standard of welfare services like education, health and developmental activities, (3) the interest of the federal government in developing certain services which the states themselves would not like to undertake, (4) the possibility of improving the quality of the services provided, and (5) co-ordination of standards."[11]

The following are a few types of non-statutory/voluntary grants based on different matching patterns of contributions between the centre and the states in India : (i) Hundred per cent Grants – Usually some centrally sponsored schemes come under hundred per cent grants from the centre. Report of the Group of Officials on Centrally Sponsored Schemes defines the centrally sponsored schemes : "The group felt that the definition of C.S.S. should cover all schemes fully or partially funded by the centre and implemented by the states or state agencies except those which fell in the centre's sphere of responsibility *i.e.* in the union list.... Only those schemes which were funded directly by central ministries/departments and implemented by states or of their agencies irrespective of their pattern of financing (unless they fell under the centre's sphere of responsibility) would be treated as centrally sponsored.''[12] (ii) Matching Grants – Matching grants can be divided into three categories on the basis of combination of grant components of the centre and the states. (A) Certain schemes may have more central component than the state component. For example, under Jawahar Rozagar Yojana, expenditure is to be shared between the centre and the states, on 80:20 basis in 1990. (B) For some schemes, the state component may be more than the central component. (C) For some other schemes, matching contributions may be equal between the centre and the states. (iii) The centre also provides loans in addition to grants for some schemes. The proportion between the central grants and loans is not uniform. However, they can be classified into three categories : (A) Under the first pattern, the centre provides more grants and less amount of loans to the states for schemes. (B) Under the second pattern, the states get more loans and less grants for some other schemes. (C) Under the third pattern, the centre provides equal grants and loans to the states for some schemes.

One of the reasons for insisting on matching contributions from the states is that demand for central grants from the states should not become insatiable. Sharing of expenditure by the states for schemes ensures interest, responsibility and ability to bear financial burden by the states.

The following are the different kinds of voluntary grants based on the purposes. Voluntary grants are not uniform in all the federations and differ from one federation to another depending on constitutional provisions, historical legacies, customs and conventions. For example, Daniel, J. Elazar classifies grants into five categories : flat grants, proportionate grants, percentage grants, project grants and entitlement grants.[13] Under the Indian conditions grants may be classified on the basis of purposes for which they have been provided by the centre to the states. They are plan grants, non-plan grants, block grants, specific grants and general grants. (A) Plan Grants – Introduction of planning in India has given rise to a new type of financial aid from the centre to the states in the form of plan grants. Plan grant is a new type of financial aid from the centre to the states in the form of plan grants. Plan grant is a new type of federal grant which was not conceived by the framers of the Indian Constitution and which does not exist in any other democratic federal system. Though the Indian plan grants are peculiar to India, yet they resemble other federal grants in respect of conditions attached to the grants. (B) Non-Plan Grants – Discretionary and non-plan transfers can be classified into five categories : (i) scheme-wise transfer, (ii) small savings loans, (iii) assistance for meeting advances, (iv) special accommodation loans, and (v) miscellaneous loans including overdrafts. These transfers are made by the Ministry of Finance, Government of India and not by Finance Commission and the Planning Commission. They cover the items like relief to meet natural calamities, improvement in the scales of college and university teachers, loans for fertilizers, non-plan loans, loans against collection of small savings by the states, etc.[14] (C) Block Grants – Block grant is a categorised grant but not a specific grant. For example, the centre may give block grants to the states for improving education without specifying heads. (D) Specific Grants – Grants are given for specific purposes by the centre to the states, say for example, for construction of staff quarters of university teachers, adult education, etc. Grants are to be spent for these specific purposes. (E) General Grants – General grants are not specified for specific purposes. For example, the centre may give grants to the states to improve their general revenue position.

4. EVOLUTION OF GRANTS-IN-AID

Though the allocation of resources between the centre and the provinces went through evolutionary process from 1833 to 1950, the first statutory provision for grants-in-aid was made under the Government of India Act, 1935. Section 142 of the Government of India Act, 1935, says: "Such sums as may be prescribed by His Majesty-in-Council shall be charged on the revenues of the Federation in each year as grants-in-aid of the revenues of such provinces as His Majesty may determine to be in need of assistance, and different sums may be prescribed for different provinces: Provided that, except in the case of the North West Frontier Province, no grant fixed under this section shall be increased by a subsequent order, unless an address has been presented to the Governor-General by both chambers of the Federal

Legislature for submission to His Majesty praying that the increase may be made.''[15] These grants which were unconditional were given to the provinces in need of assistance. They were prescribed on the basis of recommendations of Niemeyer report. They were provided to meet a part of expenditure on famine and rehabilitation measures. The quantum of grants recommended to the provinces was to cease in 1948. During 1943-44 the centre made several grants to the provincial and some princely states to promote central campaign for higher food production.[16] Besides these grants, several other grants were made by the centre to the provinces to overcome certain problems like famine.

The post-war development grants were related to specific schemes of development and they amounted to 38.32 crores. After independence, the central government continued the post-war development grants to the provinces on population basis. In 1948 it changed over to matching grants from development grants. The matching contribution from the provinces was fifty per cent. Additional grants were made to Assam, Orissa, West Bengal and Punjab for special reasons. The former two provinces were backward and the last two were to solve the problems of refugees.

Under the present Constitution, statutory and non-statutory (voluntary) grants are given by the centre to the states under articles 275 and 282 respectively. In case of article 275, grants are determined by the Parliament on the recommendations of the Finance Commission. Grants under article 282 are made by the central government to the states generally on the advice of the Planning Commision. The grants under article 275 are liable for change only once in five years and cannot be adjusted to changing needs of the states. Grants under article 282 are generally made for purposes of planning and are adjustable. They are provided according to certain formula. They are much larger than the grants provided under article 275.

Until the Fourth Five Year Plan, central voluntary grants to the states for implementation of plan programmes relating to state subjects were provided on the basis of schemes. It was known as schematic pattern of assistance. This pattern of assistance led to rigidities and inequitable distribution of grants. Several states complained against this pattern of assistance. It was discussed in the National Development Council. On the recommendaton of N.D.C., new formula of assistance was adopted in 1968-69. It was modified in 1978-79. New formula of assistance for plan purposes was again modified in 1990. The central assistance is given in the form of voluntary grants and loans.

REFERENCES

1. *Webster's Third New Internationl Dictionary* (Springfield 2, Massachusetts – U.S.A. : G.C. Merrian Company, 1961), p. 989.
2. Rao, N.R., *Union-State Financial Relations in India* (Dharwad : Karnatak University, 1972), p. 117.
3. Agarwal, P.P., *The System of Grants-in-Aid in India* (Bombay : Asia Publishing House, 1959), p. 2.
4. Lakdawala, D.T., *Union-State Financial Relations* (Bombay : Lalvani Publishing House, 1967), p. 13.
5. *Ibid.*, p. 14.
6. Singh, S.P., *Centre-State Relations in Agricultural Development* (New Delhi : Vikas Publishing House Pvt. Ltd., 1973), p. 137.
7. Deole, D.R., *Central Assistance for Planned Economic Development of the States with Special Reference to Madhya Pradesh* (Thesis submitted to Vikram University, Ujjain, for award of Ph.D. Degree in 1973), p. 39.
8. *Report of the Finance Commission* (New Delhi : The Manager of Publications, Government of India, 1953), pp. 95 and 96.
9. Thimmaiah, G., *Federal Fiscal Systems of Australia and India : A Study in Comparative Relevance* (New Delhi : Associated Publishing House, 1976), p. 268.
10. Jha, Prabodh Kumar, *Federal Finance in Developing India* (Delhi : Capital Publishing House, 1983), p. 111.
11. *Report of the Finance Commission* (New Delhi : The Manager of Publications, Government of India, 1953), p. 95, Paraphrased by Chatterji, Amiya, *The Central Financing of State Plan in the Indian Federation* (Calcutta : Firma, K.L. Mukhopadhyaya, 1971), p. 12.
12. *Report of the Group of Officials on Centrally Sponsored Schemes* (New Delhi : Planning Commission, 1987), pp. 6 and 7.
13. Elazer, Daniel J., *American Federalism : A View from the the States* (Third edition; New York : Harper and Row Publishers, 1984), p. 78.
14. Sastry, M.L. and Reddy, G.R., *Centre-State Financial Relations : A Study in Levels of Development of States* (Hyderabad and New Delhi : Centre for Economic and Social Studies and Concept Publishing Company, 1988), p. 43.
15. *The Government of India Act,* 1935 (New Delhi : Manager of Publications, Government of India, 1935), p. 95.
16. Agarwal, P.P., *The System of Grants-in-Aid in India* (Bombay : Asia Publishing House, 1959), p. 10.
17. *Ibid.*, p.11.

CHAPTER IV

CONDITIONS AND COMPULSIONS FOR GROWING PROGRAMMES

1. INTRODUCTION

A modern states is under compulsion to expand its activities. "It is subject to the law of increasing state activities."[1]. Irrespective of form of government, activities of the modern state have been increasing extensively and intensively due to various conditions and compulsions. Expenditure on regulatory, developmental and service sectors has been increasing every year. In his welcome address to the Eighth Finance Commission, the Chief Minister of Karnataka state listed three sectors responsible for increasing programmes of the state government : "They are – first is maintenance, second is development and the third is welfare of the people."[2] Futher he said that the state government has direct and immediate responsibility with regard to all these three fields. So far as welfare of people is concerned, the state government has more direct responsibiltiy than the central government. In a federal system like India it is the state governments which are called upon to render basic economic and social service and to provide infrastrucural facilities to the people. But resources of the states do not increase proportionately with increasing functions. Imbalance between slow expanding resources and past growing services compel the state governments to demand more statutory and voluntary grants from the centre and greater share in the central tax resources.

The various factors like socialist pattern of society, provisions of Indian Constitution dealing with welfare measures, practice of democracy, developing economy, planning process, urbanisation, expanding departments of states like education, health, agriculture, social services, etc., one party dominance at the centre for a long period, electoral compulsions, emergence of new class of elites, etc., have been responsible for tremendous increase in the programmes of the states. These conditions and compulsions have resulted in imbalance between growing programmes and inelastic resources of the states. Such situation has led to the dependence of the states on central voluntary grants.

2. SOCIALIST PATTERN OF SOCIETY

Since the Karachi session in 1931, the resolutions of the Congress had been influenced by the Congress socialists like Pt. Jawaharlal Nehru, Acharya Narendra Dev, Achut Patwardhan, Yusuf Meharally, etc. The Karachi session declared that the state should own or control heavy industries, mineral resources and means of production. Pt. Jawaharlal Nehru in his two presidential addresses in 1929 (at Lahore) and in 1936 (at Lucknow) declared that India should move towards socialist state. After independence the Indian National Congress under the leadership of Pt. Jawaharlal Nehru was wedded to the socialist pattern of society. At Avadi session of the Congress in 1955 the Congress pledged to establish a socialist pattern of society. The Congress at its 68th session at Bhuvaneshwar in 1964 adopted an important resolution on socialism and democracy. The Congress wanted to establish a socialist pattern of society within democratic framework. The political leaders, the political activists, mass media, intellectuals and educated men were influenced by the goals of socialist pattern of society. The concept of socialist pattern of society has generated public demands for various programmes, facilities and services involving huge investments which the state governments cannot meet by themselves out of their own limited resources. The states have to depend upon the centre for voluntary grants. At the same time, the centre has also evolved certain programmes which cannot be implemented without the co-operation of the state machinery. It has been inducing the state governments to take up these programmes with its financial assistance.

3. INDIAN CONSTITUTION AND WELFARE STATE

The framers of the Indian Constitution who were influenced by socialist ideology and concept of welfare state have given positive role to the state in the socio-economic field. Even the Expert Committee on the Financial Provisions of the Constitution appointed by the constituent assembly noted the growing socio-economic programmes to be undertaken by the provinces with their limited resources : "Every province has drawn pointed attention to the urgency of its programme of social service and economic development and to the limited nature of its own resources, both existing and potential.... The needs of the provinces are in contrast (with the centre) almost unlimited, particularly in relation to welfare services and general development."[3] Thus the committee drew the attention of the constituent assembly to the expanding functions and limited resources of the provinces.

The Preamble and the Directive Principles of State Policy of Indian Constitution have influenced both the legislators and enlightened public and have become compelling forces for increasing programmes. The preamble promises to give justice – social, economic and political. In order to provide three dimension justice to the people in general and to the weaker sections in particular, both the centre and the states are compelled to undertake a number of socio-economic welfare measures. The part IV of Indian Constitution dealing with the Directive Principles of State Policy directs the state to secure welfare of the people by providing social, economic and political justice. Article 38 directs the state to secure a social order for promotion of welfare of the people by providing social, economic and political justice. Article 39 insists that (i) citizens should have the right to an adequate means of livelihood; (ii) the ownership and control of material resources of the state are so distributed as best to serve the common good; (iii) the economic system does not result in concentration of wealth; (iv) health of workers, women and children are protected. Article 40 asks the state to organise village panchayats and endow them with sufficient powers to work as units of self-government. Article 41 enjoins the state to guarantee right to work, right to education, and right to public assistance. Article 42 intends that the state shall provide just and human conditions of work for all. Article 43 exhorts that the state shall provide living wages to industrial and agricultural workers. Article 45 insists that the state shall provide free and compulsory education to all children until they complete the age of fourteen years. Article 46 wants that the state should promote educational and economic interests of the weaker sections in general and of scheduled castes and scheduled tribes in particular. Article 47 states that it is the duty of the state to raise the level of nutrition and standard of living of people. Article 48 prescribes that the state should organise agriculture and animal husbandry on modern and scientific lines. In additon to these, many items in the state and concurrent lists contain welfare programmes. Thus the provisions of the Constitution visualise a welfare state.

In consonance with the constitutional obligations, the state have undertaken many welfare measures. Various welfare programmes like old age pensions, widow allowances, allowances for expectant mothers, free supply of school uniforms and text-books to the poor students, concessional bus passes to the students, maintenance of hostels for students of scheduled castes, scheduled tribes and backward classes, maintenance allowances for these students, mid-day meals for school children, various facilities and concessions to farmers, weaker sections, women and slum dwellers, etc., have increased the financial burden and have widened the social responsibility of the state governments. Thus impelemtation of welfare measures under welfare democratic state has revolutionised rising expectations of people in India whose demands before independence were very much limited and who did not expect any welfare measure from the colonial government. Now the people expect many welfare measures from the state governments which are nearest to them. "In India, the state governments are the real governments in the context of public welfare. The central government's role in development administration is primarily that of leadership, consultation and advice. The responsibility for the implementation of programmes rests mainly on the states."[4] The welfare programmes of the states have been increasing year after year and revenues are not coping up with expanding programmes. Shri Kalandaiveln, ex-minister of Tamil Nadu, thus said: "The increase in the gap between revenue and expenditure of the states is towards the gradual shift in emphasis on the administration of welfare measures entrusted to the states....Obviously, the states find themselves in a situation in which they cannot find adequate resources to discharge even their basic responsibilities. The situation, therefore, warrants urgent corrective measures to bring a balance between the resources and responsibilities."[5]

4. DEMOCRACY, PLANNING, ETC.

There are other factors like democracy, developing economy, planning process, urbanisation, matching grants, etc., which are also responsible for increase in the functions and programmes of the states:

(A) *Democracy* – People's demands have increased in independent democratic India. The democratic electorate of India demands from its representatives welfare services and full employment. People's participation in the political process has also increased the developmental activities. As the state governments are not in a position to meet the growing demands of the democratic citizens, they have to depend on the central grants. That is why there is increase in the quantum of central aid over the years.

(B) *Developing Economy* – Underdeveloped economy on the eve of Indian independence is also responsible for increase in the programmes of the states. As India was under the colonial rule of the British for nearly two centuries, it lagged behind the European countries in industrialisation and in securing higher standard of living for its people. Independent India had to cover up the time-lag in industrialisation and modernisation. Consequently both the centre and the states have to undertake numerous socio-economic measures to provide a better quality of life to the people. All socio-economic developmental activities fall within the jurisdiction of the states. These cannot be taken up by the states without developing their economy. Both economic development and welfare measures cannot be undertaken by the states without the financial assistance from the centre. In his welcome address to the Ninth Finance Commission, the Chief Minister of Karnataka state said, "The devolution to the states must be seen in the light of the respective roles of the union and the state governments particularly in the field of social and economic development. The fruits of development can be brought to the people at the grassroots level by the states much more than by the centre. The machinery for the implementation of developmental activities is available with the states."[6] It is the state governments which have to bear the burden of developmental activities in order to improve the quality of life of the people.

(C) *Planning Process* – Planning process is mainly responsible for increasing the programmes of the states. There is a long history of planning process in India. It was in infant stage and covered small areas before independence. After independence it became a comprehensive process covering the areas of the centre and the states and increasing their programmes on unprecedent scale.

Increase in the programmes of the states in independent India can be traced back to the freedom movement. Socialism, planning and concept of welfare state had become a part of socio-economic and political ideology of the Indian National Congress in later part of freedom struggle. After 1930 the Congress gave importance to the planning as a part of democratic socialism. The Congress session held at Karachi in 1931 declared that the state should own or control heavy industries, mineral resources and means of production. In 1937, the Congress secured majority in many provinces. "The formation of Congress governments in these provinces prepared the ground for the acceptance of the ideology of planning and facilitated the formation of a national plan."[7] The Congress ministries introduced several socio-economic reforms. The Congress at the national level decided to have a blueprint of a comprehensive national plan for economic development of India. It appointed a fifteen member National Planning Committee under the chairmanship of Pt. Jawaharlal Nehru. Though the Second World War interrupted the work of the National Planning Committee, its deliberations "had served to infuse a plan consciousness amongst the people."[8] Subsequently the British government could not remain indifferent to the economic development of India.

After independence, the central government established the Planning Commission by a resolution of the cabinet. The Planning Commission was entrusted with the task of formulating a comprehensive planning for both the centre and the states. The terms of reference of the Planning Commission clearly indicate that the programmes of the central and state governments are bound to increase and have increased immensely during the course of forty years. The following are the terms of reference made to the Planning Commission which continue to be guidelines for it in its functioning : (i) It shall make an assessment of the material, capital and human resources of the country. (ii) It shall formulate a plan for the most effective and balanced utilization of the country's resources. (iii) It shall determine priorities, decide stages of plan and allocate resources for completion of each stage of plan. (iv) It shall indicate the factors responsible for the successful implementation of the plan.[9]

The following are the major goals of planning in India and the attainment of these goals has increased the programmes of the states: (i) Rapid economic development – Rapid economic development requires industrialisation of the country. Though the centre plays an important role in industrial development, the states also have to take up some minor industrial projects to supplement the central efforts in industrialisation. (ii) Balanced regional growth – In order to avoid regional disparities, the centre makes more grants to the poor states and consequently the programmes of the poor states also increase. (iii) Establishment of socialist pattern of society – In order to establish a socialist state, the states are called upon to introduce land reforms, improve the economic conditions of marginal farmers and agricultural labourers and to undertake a number of socio-economic welfare measures for weaker sections through planning. The central ministries also induce the state ministries through grants to take up their schemes for implementation. Bulk of the plan grants are provided to the states for agriculture, public health, education, social welfare, etc. The concept that certain basic needs of the people must be provided all over the country has given the central government a mandate to lay down national targets in the state sectors such as agriculture, public health, education, social welfare, etc., and to exercise central authority over them through central voluntary grants. Though the states are directly concerned with people's plan projects, the centre takes interest in some areas of the states through centrally sponsored and centrally assisted schemes. These central schemes have increased the programmes of the states. Thus the planning process has not only increased the programmes of the states but has helped the centre to penetrate into state fields through these central schemes. The central grants and loans are essential ingredients in many central schemes. Inducement of central grants and loans has increased the quantum of state programmes.

Entry 20 in the list III of seventh schedule of Indian Constitution relating to 'socio-economic planning' was adopted by the constituent assembly without much discussion. The framers of the Constitution had not visualised that the successive five year plans would assume such importance and magnitude and would result in massive programmes to be undertaken by the states with the help of central voluntary grants. The centre has found convenient means to provide voluntary grants under article 282 and not statutory grants under article 275. "The Third Finance Commission (1961) recommended grants under article 275 to cover 75 per cent of the states' revenue expenditure on the third plan, but the government of India did not accept this recommendation."[10] The centre has continued to provide voluntary grants under article 282 to the states for various plan programmes. A distinguished economist and a former deputy chairman of the Planning Commission, Shri D.R.

Gadgil, opined that economic planning necessarily results in increase in the programmes of the country and in central direction over the state plans: "The master plan of economic development must be countrywide. In particular respects, the federating units must be left free to control the pace or direction of development and the plan itself would pay proper attention to all sided development of all regions. At the same time, all federating units must accept overall direction imposed by the master plan. The federal government must have adequate powers to evolve the general plan of economic development for the whole country and must have powers to carry out its essential features and to supervise and enforce its implementation by the federating units."[11] Thus the master plan has resulted in increase in the plan programmes and control direction.

(D) *Urbanisation* – Urbanisation is also responsible for increasing programmes of the states. There has been increased pressure on civil services. Consequently the state governments have to demand both statutory and voluntary grants from the centre to meet the growing needs of urbanisation. The Chief Minister of Karnataka state requested the Ninth Finance Commission "to integrate the financial needs of the urban local bodies into the financial needs of the state governments. The Finance Commission has not been able to give enough attention to this aspect partly because they never appreciated the financial problems of the urban civic bodies and partly because they feared that it would be too much of a burden on the central government. This attitude should change and we hope that the normative approach will enable the Finance Commission to integrate at least partially the financial needs of the urban civic bodies into the financial needs of the states."[12]

(E) *Matching Grants* – One of the important reasons why the state governments agree to undertake central schemes for which matching grants are made by the centre is fear of public criticism. The people of the states are more interested in the benefits of programmes rather than in the mode of financing the programmes and control exercised by the centre over such programmes. Undertaking of such programmes by the states puts them in revenue deficit in order to meet a part of matching grants and to continue such programmes after the end of plan period. For example, if U.G.C. pay scales to the teachers of universities and colleges are accepted by the state governments, the centre pays 75% or 80% of additional expenditure for a period of five years. After five years the state governments have to bear the entire expenditure. Thus the matching grants not only result in increase in state'programmes but also in increase in expenditure for the states.

Thus intorduction of democratic system, measures for economic development, comprehensive national planning process, growth in urbanisation, attraction of matching grants, etc., have increased the functions and programmes of the states. These increased programmes can be carried out by the states only with the financial assistance from the centre.

5. SOME SPECIFIC PROGRAMMES

Among the various programmes, education, social service, health and agriculture have immensely contributed to the growth of state programmes.

(A) *Education* – Earlier education was purely concern of parents. Later on it became concern of the state. In early federations, education was placed in the state list. The recent federations have placed education in general in the state list and higher education in both the central and state lists. Indian Parliament, through 42nd amendment to the Constitution in 1976, has placed education in the concurrent list but education continues to be the main concern of the states.

The Planning Commission has considered education not from state angle but from national angle. It stated in its first report: "The Planning Commission is mainly concerned with education as a part of the total national effort, establishing and strengthening its links with other aspects of national life and assigning priorities for the various educational progammes awaiting implementation."[13] Thus the Planning Commission has taken a comprehensive view of education. It has been making assessment of educational system in terms of size of population, overall educational facilities, structure of educational system, service conditions of teachers, examination system, estimation of resources for implementing the educational programmes, etc. In the beginning it has made the point very clear that though education is primarily the concern of the states, the centre shall have "overall responsibility for helping, co-ordinating and guiding the work of the states so that national policies can be evolved and satisfactorily worked."[14] The centre has been providing voluntary grants, on the recommendations of the Planning Commission, to the states to carry out certain educational programmes which are of national importance and relevance. It also suggests adequate and specific machinery to carry out these programmes. The states have to provide their matching contributions to some of the centrally sponsored or assisted schemes in addition to their own expenditure for their own programmes. Thus expanding education has been consuming a lion's share of state revenues. In 1965-66 the states have spent nearly twenty paise on education out of every rupee which they have collected from the tax payers.[15] In recent years number of primary schools, high schools, junior colleges, degree colleges, universities, technical and medical colleges has been increasing by many folds. The states have to spend huge amount on education with the central assistance.

With the passage of time education has been becoming national concern. In 1985 the government of Rajiv Gandhi adopted a national policy of education. It stated: "To achieve the multiple but interdependent goals of personal, economic, social, political and cultural development, it is necessary to make appropriate provision for integrated programmes of education for people who happen to be living at different levels of personal and economic development, possessing different linguistic, social and cultural attributes. Such programmes will have to be a common core curriculum to strengthen unity within diversity and also facilitate mobility from one part of the country to another."[16] Policy document clearly indicates that new education has to be comprehensive and cover various aspects of education and various levels of society. Such educational system is bound to increase the programmes of the states.

(B) *Health Service* – After independence there has been a great increase in the health service. Earlier there were government hospitals only in taluk places. Now government hospitals have come up in the villages. A number of government medical colleges have been established. The state governments have introduced a number of health measures to improve health of the people. At the time of independence, average expectancy of life was 36 years and now it has reached to 58 years. The Planning Commission formulates health programmes from time to time and these programmes are to be carried out by the states with the central financial assistance. On account of all these measures, the health programmes of the state governments have increased by many folds.

(C) *Agricultural Service* – Earlier agriculture was a private enterprise and concern. Later on it became concern of the state governments. The central government's concern for agricultural development has been increasing since the Second World War due to food crises through which India has passed. Scarcity of food has forced the centre to take initiative for modernising agriculture. Though land and agriculture are within the jurisdiction of the states, the centre has taken a leading role in national policy formulation relating to land reforms and modernising agriculture. Since the launching of the First Five Year Plan in 1951, formulation of plan for agricultural development has been a part of national policy. Consequently the centre and the states have taken keen interest in the development of agriculture. Dams have been constructed and hydro-electric projects have been undertaken. Land reforms, irrigation facilities, supply of agricultural implements and fertilizers, marketing of agricultural goods, grant of loans for agricultural purposes, etc., have increased the agricultural activities of the state governments.

(D) *Social Services* – The state governments have undertaken a number of social welfare measures for scheduled castes, scheduled tribes, socially and economically weaker sections, women, children, etc. The centre also provides voluntary grants to the states to carry out these social services. There has been increasing demand from the weaker sections to provide more social services to come out of social inequalities. In developing country like India social services are built with planned efforts. Many states have social welfare ministers.

Socio-economic services are increasingly being performed by both unitary governments and federal governments today. India cannot and should not be an exception to this trend. This trend is observed even in the older federations. "This is true of federations as of unitary states, and is illustrated by the experience of the United States, Canada, Australia and other federations. In these countries in spite of jealous safeguarding of "states' rights", federal aid and direction have increased in recent times..... Education, public health, agriculture and industries are primarily provincial subjects, but, if these important nation-building agencies are to produce the greatest possible benefits in service to the public, suitable policies must be formulated in many respects on a more or less all India basis."[17] Social service has been becoming world-wide phenomenon. The world organisations have been insisting on the member countries to implement certain socio-economic programmes. The resolutions and measures of the Economic and Social Council, International Labour Organisation, World Health Organisation, UNESCO, etc., call upon member governments to implement certain social services and welfare measures. The central government in India cannot implement these socio-economic measures without the co-operation of the state governments. The state governments in turn cannot implement them without the financial assistance from the centre. Consequently the socio-economic programmes of the states and the central assistance to the states have been increasing.

6. POLITICAL COMPULSIONS

Some political compulstions like one party rule at the centre for a longer period, electoral promises, emergence of new class of elites, etc., are also responsible for increase in the programmes of the states and for dependence of the states on the centre for central voluntary grants.

One party rule by the Congress at the centre and in many states for a long period is responsible for increase in the programmes of the states. The Congress leaders at the centre and in the states have been very particular for economic development of the country as a whole and have not given much attention to state autonomy. The Congress attitude continued in milder manner even when the non-Congress parties were in power at the centre.

In order to win the votes of the people, all political parties in India have been promising many reforms, programmes, projects and concessions. Manifestoes of all the national parties, on the eve of general elections, mainly deal with the state subjects but references to the central subjects are very much limited. It is the state subjects which immediately involve the interests of the voters. The comparative chart of the manifestoes of the four national parties/national fronts given by *The Hindu*, on the eve of ninth Lok Sabha elections in 1989, clearly indicates how the national parties/national fronts are more concerned with the state subjects than with the central subjects in order to win over the voters.[18]

The state subjects have immediate concern for the people. Expectations of the people have been revolutionised by rosy promises of the political parties, increasing political awareness among them and greater political participation by them. When the national parties come into power at the centre, they try to implement some of their promises by inducing the state governments including those state governments whose ruling parties are different. Such inducement is carried out through the central voluntary grants. The people are generally interested in those central projects from which they derive benefit. They are not concerned with state autonomy nor with centre-state controversy so far as socio-economic welfare measures are concerned. They criticise the state governments if the latter do not make use of central programmes meant for them. Therefore, the parties in power in the states are compelled to accept the central programmes along with the central voluntary grants. They do not want to lose the support and sympathy of the people for the sake of centre-state controversy. However, they carry on centre-state controversy at political level but accept the central programmes which carry central aid and guidelines.

Economic development and irrigation facilities have led to the growth of an affluent community of farmers who are now new elites. These elites want all sorts of facilities and services from both the centre and the states. The political parties, in order to win over rural elites, have been promising a number of facilities and reforms. When they come to power, they are forced to undertake measures to implement their promises. Consequently the functions of the state governments have increased.

In addition to rural development, there is also urban development. Urbanisation has compelled the state governments to increase transport services, housing facilities, water supply, etc., to meet the demands of growing population, gushing influx of immigrants and expanding slum areas. New elites have come up from both well-developed and slum areas of the urban centres. They have been pressurising the state governments to provide services to these groups. The state governments have been compelled to undertake various socio-economic measures for these groups.

Metropolitan cities with high degree of industrialisation have become multilingual and multireligious islands. They are also centres of haves and have-nots whose life styles are mutually hostile. Though these groups live in the same city, they do not share in common social life.

CHART

Congress (I)	National Front	BJP	Left Parties
Agriculture			
Already invested Rs. 5.500 crores annually in agriculture and irrigation since 1985, compared to Rs. 3,500 crores a year during earlier five years. Reduced interest rate on crop loans from 12.5% in 1984 to 10% in 1989. Increased support prices for paddy, wheat, groundnut. Doubled credit supply to farmers over last 5 years. Proposed National Agri. Credit Relief Fund.	Review existing laws on land reforms for equitable distribution of land, to make tiller owner of land. Surplus land to be distributed among landless SC/ST farmers. Remunerative prices to cultivators, provision of inputs at fair price fixed on basis of real cost of farming by Agricultural Prices and Cost Commn. Guarantee that no rural lands will be acquired at deferred prices for profiteering by private coloniser or the State. Crop Insurance against natural and man-made disasters. Loans up to Rs.10,000 of small, marginal landless cultivators and artisans to be written off.	Write off debts of farmers, agricultural labourers and rural artisans, ensure remunerative prices to farmers; minimum wages to farm labour, restructure the Agriculture Cost and Price Commission so that 2/3rd of its members are from farm sector and maintain parity between agricultural and industrial produce.	Implementation of land reforms and distribution of land, enactment of central legislation to protect rights of agricultural workers, cancellation of rural debt, remunerative prices for peasants produce.

SC/ST			
To consolidate the initiatives already taken such as reservation and welfare schemes. Scavenging to be eradicated in five years, training of SC/ST in modern skills and technology to be strengthened.	Special efforts to provede free and compulsory education to SC/ST and other backward classes, hand over to SC/ST land already allotted to them, statutory powers for SC/ST commission. Special courts to try cases of atrocities.	Mobile or speical courts to try cases of atrocities against SC/ST, speical agency to meet the credit needs of SC/ST, remove impediments in development of tribal and hill areas.	Protection of the life and property of SC/ST and giving social and economic justice to them.
Women			
30% representation in local self-government through schemes to ensure distribution of assets and house-sites to women, quick implementation of Indira Mahila Yojna.	Appointment of statutory all-India Commn. on women to monitor and accelerate the process of equal representation, a review of all social legislation concerning marriage, divorce, maintenance, custody, inheritance, etc. Strict action to check harassment and violence against women	Ban sex tests, make wife co-sharer in husband's income and assets. Special drive to improve educational status of women; reserve 30% of jobs in certain areas.	Social and economic reforms against oppression of women.
Youth			
A youth club in every village to initiate social change; awards to recognise the contribution of youth in constructive work.	Special scheme of soft loan of up to Rs. 50,000 for self-employment of youth, launch "earn-while-you-learn" scheme.	Ensure youth participation in programmes of poverty alleviation, literacy and conservation of environment.	Right to work and unemployment benefit for youth.

Congress (I)	National Front	BJP	Left Parties
Backward Classes			
Special programmes for employment, scholarships and other schemes for academic improvement.	Enforce constitutional guarantees about education and employment etc, scholarships for education, "pucca" houses and credit facilities for self-employment.		
Industry, Labour			
To consolidate the gains of past 4 years and accelerate the rate of industrial growth; special thrust to agro-based industries to provide market-linkages between the process of agricultural diversity on the one hand and growing urban markets on the other; priority to export development; introduction of pension scheme for workers in the organised sector; a family pension for the widow or the dependents of the workers in case of death in service; stocks of public sector companies to be sold to workers on preferential basis.	To provide industrial development so as to maximise employment, emphasis on producing wage goods and services; to encourage agro-processing industries; workers to be made effective partners in management at plant and shop levels; recognition of union on the basis of secret ballots; regularisation of casual labour; to activate Indian Labour Conference.	To keep multinationals out of consumer industry, emphasis on self-reliance in external economic relations. Primacy for agricultural and agro-based industry; to encourage healthy trade unionisms; simplify labour laws; recognition of trade unions on the basis of secret ballots.	Work for self-reliance economy, generate employment.

Employment			
To make the Eighth Plan a "Plan for productive employment". public investment will be reoriented to catalysing the growth and expansion of employment-intensive economic activities; to provide adequate funds for Jawahar Rozgar Yojanas.	To recognise the right to work as a fundamental right; generate socially productive employment.	To recognise the right to work as constitutional guarantee; work guarantee scheme.	Employment-oriented economic policies.
Housing			
To increase access of low income groups to institutional finance for housing; urban poor to be given adequate funds to repair, redevelop or augment their homes.	Develop slums into livable shelters; emphasis on urban development to shift from major cities to small and medium towns; to levy cess on urban rich to develop slums, focus on rural housing.	Evolve a housing policy based on minimum housing standards for urban and rural poor; decongesting metro towns by developing small and medium towns.	Housing to be recognised as a basic right.

These have provided scope for unscrupulous elements to whip up antagonism based on religion, language, region, etc. It is again the state governments which have to deal with them. These are not mere law and order problems. They have socio-economic and political roots and call for socio-economic and political measures to solve them. Consequently there is increase in the functions and programmes of the states.

7. GROWING PROGRAMMES AND INELASTIC RESOURCES

On account of introduction of democratic system, nature of developing economy, planning process, urbanisation, expansion in socio-economic services, political compulsions, etc., there has been a substantial expansion in the programmes of the states. Consequently there has been tremendous increase in the expenditure of the states. For example, between 1951 and 1971 the expenditure of the state governments had increased by eight-fold from Rs. 409 crores to Rs. 3,438 crores while the revenues during the same period has increased only by six-fold – from Rs. 330 crores to Rs. 2,073 crores. Therefore the grants-in-aid under articles 275 and 282 from the centre to the states have become inevitable. The same trends in the disproportionate increase in the expenditure and revenues of the state governments continued during the last twenty years (1971–1991). Consequently the quantum of the central grants has also increased during this period.

The centre has elastic sources of revenues. Its taxes have a good degree of elasticity. Income tax, corporation tax, custom duties, etc., are very elastic. In addition to these, it has full control over currency and banking. It can resort to issue of more currency notes. It has more financial resources than its normal requirements. But the states have inelastic sources of revenues and further they have been compelled to undertake more developmental and service oriented activities for social and economic upliftment of the people. Therefore they are compelled to seek central grants and aids to meet their growing needs.

REFERENCES

1. Wagner Adolph, *Finazwissenschaff,* Leipzig, Quoted in *Centre-State Financial Relations in India,* prepared by Birla Institute of Scientific Research and Economic Research Division (New Delhi : Abhinav Publications, 1979), p. 16.
2. *Proceedings of the Meeting with the Eighth Finance Commission,* held on 10th August, 1983 (Bangalore : Government Press, Government of Karnataka, 1983), p. 4.

3. *The Expert Committee on the Financial Provisions of the Constitution* (appointed by the Constituent Assembly), paras 23 and 28; Quoted by Markandon, K.C., Centre-State Relations, The Perspective (Jalandhar : ABS Publications, 1986), p. 88.

4. Fadia Babulal, *State Politics in India*, Vol. I (New Delhi : Radiant Publishers, 1984), p. 3.

5. Kolandaiveln, P., *Financial and Economic Issues in Centre-State Relations,* a paper presented at Seminar on Centre-State Relations, 5-8 January, 1984, organised by Tamil Nadu Academy of Political Science, Madras, p. 2 (Papers are in cyclostyled form and are available in Madras Institute of Development Studies, Madras).

6. *Speech of Shri S.R. Bommai, Chief Minister, at the Discussions with the Ninth Finance Commission* during their visit to Karnataka on 13th January, 1989 (Bangalore: Government Press, Government of Karnataka, 1989), pp. 6. and 7.

7. Chanda Asok, *Federalism in India : A Study of Union-State Relations* (London : George Allen and Unwin Ltd., 1965), p. 260.

8. *Ibid.*, p. 261.

9. *Ibid.*, p. 266.

10. *Report of the Fourth Finance Commission,* 1965 (New Delhi : The Manager of Publications, Governments of India, 1965), p. 8.

11. Gadgil, D.R., *Federating India* (Poona : Gokhale Institute of Politics and Economics, 1945), p. 44, quoted by P.R. Dubhashi, *Unitary Trends in Federal System,* Indian Journal of Public Administration, Vol. VI, No. 3, July-September, 1960 (New Delhi : I.I.P.A., 1960), p. 244.

12. *Speech of Shri S.R. Bommai, Chief Minister of Karnataka State, at the Discussion with the Ninth Finance Commission* during their visit to Karnataka on 13th January, 1989 (Bangalore : The Government Press, Government of Karnataka, 1989), p. 22.

13. *The First Five Years Plan* (New Delhi : Planning Commission, Government of India, n.d.), p. 525.

14. *Ibid.*, p. 532.

15. Baker, Abu M., *The Union and the States – A Study in Educational Finance and Planning* (New Delhi : Shabd Sanchar, 1976), p.105.

16. *Challenge of Education – A Policy Perspective* (New Delhi : Ministry of Education, Government of India, 1985), p. 4.

17. Thomas, P.J., *The Growth of Federal Finance in India,* Oxford University Press, 1939, pp. 408-409, quoted by P.R. Dubhashi, *Unitary Trends in a Federal System,* Indian Journal of Public Administration, Vol. VII, No. 3, July-September, 1960 (New Delhi : I.I.P.A., 1960), p. 243.

18. *The Hindu,* A National Daily Newspaper, 21.11.1989 (Madras : S. Rangarajan, 1989).

CHAPTER V

OPERATIONAL ASPECTS OF GRANTS

1. MACHINERIES FOR PROVIDING GRANTS

The central agencies connected with central grants and loans to the states are (i) Finance Commission, (ii) Planning Commission, (iii) National Development Council, (iv) Central ministeries, and (v) Some central financial institutions. The Finance Commission recommends share in central taxes like income tax, central excise, etc., and grants to cover revenue gaps of the states. The Planning Commission recommends grants and loans to the states for implementation of plan projects according to formula evolved from time to time. National Development Council is concerned with review of socio-economic policies affecting national development and planning process in a broad manner and with formulation of formula for providing central assistance to the state plans. The central ministries also provide financial assistance to the states to carry out certain programmes. The central financial institutions like banks and others provide loans to the states to carry out certain projects.

(A) Finance Commission: In the centre-state financial relations the Finance Commission occupies a unique position. It is appointed by the President of India under article 280 and is entrusted with the task of determining the shares of the centre and the states in the taxes (income tax, excise duty, etc.) and grants-in-aid for non-plan purposes to the states. It intends to reduce inequalities between different states by filling budgetary needs and by taking into account the social service capabilities and disabilities of each state.

The following figures indicate statutory transfers of tax-shares and grants-in-aid from the centre to the states on the recommendations of the Finance Commission from 1951–79.[1]

Finance Commission	Share of Taxes	Grants	Total (Rs. in crores)
First Finance Commission (1952–57)	371.3	50.0	421.3
Second Finance Commission (1957–62)	822.4	197.2	1019.6
Third Finance Commission (1962–66)	1067.5	250.4	1317.9
Fourth Finance Commission (1966–69)	1328.0	421.8	1749.9
Fifth Finance Commission (1969–74)	4643.0	710.7	5353.7
Sixth Finance Commission (1974–79)	8250.6	2509.6	10760.2

The following tables (1 and 2) give the break up of share in divisible taxes and duties and statutory and other grants provided by the centre to the states between 1951-52 and 1978-79 on the recommendations of the Finance Commissions.[2]

With the introduction of planning in India, less importance came to be attached to the budgetary needs of the states. The fiscal needs of the states which are reflected in the formulation of plans have taken precedence over the budgetary needs.

TABLE 1

Transfers to the States on the basis of the recommendations of the Finance Commision during 1951-52 to 1978-79

	Share in Divisible Taxes & Duties					Statutory and other grants			Grand Total
	Income Tax	Union duties of excise		Estate Duty	Total	Art. 275 grants	Other grants**	Total	
		Basic.	Addl.						
1	2	3	4	5	6	7	8	9	10
1st Five Year Plan									
1951-52	53	-	-	-	53	1	16	17	70
1952-53	57	17	-	-	74	5	14	19	93
1953-54	57	15	-	-	72	7	14	21	93
1954-55	56	15	-	-	71	7	15	22	93
1955-56	55	17	-	2	74	7	17	24	98
Total	278	64	-	2	344	27	76	103	447
2nd Five Year Plan									
1956-57	59	18	-	2	79*	8	12	20	99
1957-58	74	29	11	2	116*	36	12	48	164
1958-59	76	33	40	2	151*	36	21	57	208
1959-60	79	36	39	3	157*	36	26	62	219
1960-61	87	37	33	3	165*	37	26	63	228
Total	375	153	128	12	668	153	97	250	918

3rd Five-Year Plan									
1961-62	94	41	40	4	179	40	16	56	235
1962-63	95	79	46	4	224	61	19	80	304
1963-64	119	92	44	4	259	62	20	82	341
1964-65	124	86	41	7	253	65	23	88	346
1665-66	123	100	46	7	276	64	24	88	364
Total	555	398	217	26	1196	292	102	394	1590
Three Annual Plans									
1966-67	137	184	47	5	373	141	28	169	542
1967-68	175	203	32	7	417	141	24	165	582
1968-69	195	241	50	6	492	141	25	166	658
Total	507	628	129	18	1282	423	77	500	1782
4th Five-Year Plan									
1969-70	293	266	56	7	622	153	26	179	801
1970-71	359	318	72	6	755	142	29	171	926
1971-72	462	369	106	7	944	141	27	168	1112
1972-73	492	432	135	8	1067	146	31	177	1244
1973-74	532	465	166	11	1174	131	33	164	1338
Total	2138	1850	535	39	4562	713	146	859	5421

—Contd

	Share in Divisible Taxes & Duties					Statutory and other grants			Grand Total
	Income Tax	Union duties of excise		Estate Duty	Total	Art. 275 grants	Other grants**	Total	
		Basic.	Addl.						
1	2	3	4	5	6	7	8	9	10
5th Five-Year Plan									
1974-75	512	524	178	10	1224	482	24	506	1730
1975-76	734	646	211	8	1599	503	16	519	2118
1976-77	652	774	254	10	1690	500	16	516	2206
1977-78 (RE)	675	812	302	10	1799	583	18	601	2400
1978-79 (BE)	737	916	317	10	2025	672	17	689	2714
Total	3310	3717	1262	48	8337	2740	91	2831	11168

* Does not take into account States 'share' in tax on railway passenger fares. These transfers are shown under other grants.

** Other grants : The break-up is shown in next table.

TABLE 2

(Rs. crores)

	Art. 275	Provisors to Art. 275	Art. 278	States' reorga-nisa-tion grants	Railway passenger fares Tax/ grant	Wealth tax on agricul-tural property	Total
1951-52	2	1	13	-	-	-	16
1952-53	3	2	9	-	-	-	14
1953-54	3	2	9	-	-	-	14
1954-55	3	3	9	-	-	-	15
1955-56	3	5	9	-	-	-	17
1956-57	3	5	-	4	-	-	12
1957-58	3	3	-	1	5	-	12
1958-59	3	6	-	1	11	-	21
1959-60	4	8	-	1	13	-	26
1960-61	-	12	-	-	14	-	26
1961-62	-	4	-	-	12	--	16
1962-63	-	7	-	-	12	-	19
1963-64	-	7	-	-	13	-	20
1964-65	-	10	-	-	13	-	23
1965-66	--	11	--	-	13	--	24
1966-67	-	12	-	-	16	-	28
1967-68	-	8	-	-	16	-	24
1968-69	-	9	-	-	16	-	25
1969-70	--	10	-	-	16	-	26
1970-71		10	-	-	16	3	29
1971-72	-	11	-	-	16	-	27
1972-73	-	14	-	-	16	1	31
1973-74	-	16	-	-	16	1	33
1974-75	-	8	-	-	16	-	24
1975-76	-	-	-	-	16	-	16
1976-77	-	-	-	-	16	-	16
1977-78 (RE)	-	-	-	-	16	2	18
1978-79 (BE)	-	-	-	-	16	1	17

(B) Planning Commission: Nature of composition of the Planning Commission has its impact on nature and direction of planning process and on nature and magnitude of voluntary grants to be made by the centre to the states. Strength and qualifications of members of the Planning Commission are not prescribed. Its chairman is the Prime Minister; deputy chairman is a cabinet minister or an academician; and its other members include some central ministers and academicians. It is a quasi-political body and is greatly influenced by personality and style of functioning of the Prime Minister. It is open to pulls and pressures of politics. Though it is an advisory body, it has come to play a dominant role in the national planning process and socio-economic development of the country. Vast plan grants are made available to the states by the centre at the instance of this advisory body. The states have come to depend on it for a number of purposes. Though the recommendations of the Planning Commission in regard to voluntary grants to the state plans are not binding on the central government, yet the latter accepts them as a matter of routine. Functioning of the Planning Commission is facilitated through the exercise of article 282 by the centre.

After completion of framework for the national plan, the Planning Commission indicates to each state the guidelines and financial magnitude of the state plans. After discussion between the members of the Planning Commission and the representatives of the states, the financial aspects of the state plans including the quantum of central assistance are determined. Thus the Planning Commission prepares a national plan with sectoral allocations broken into central plan and state plans. The states have to fall in line with the Planning Commission because the centre holds the financial strings.

The central assistance for state plans is determined by the Planning Commission in consultation with the Ministry of Finance: "The same is approved by the National Development Council along with the pattern of financing of the five year plan. For the annual plans, however, the size of the central assistance is left to be determined by the Planning Commission in consultation with the Ministry of Finance in the light of the approved five year plan. For the five year plan period, the central assistance actually given is observed to be more than what was initially approved by the National Development Council."[3]

The following table gives the central financial assistance to the states for state plans and for centrally sponsored schemes between

1951-52 and 1978-79 in the form of grants and loans on the recommendations of the Planning Commission.[4]

TABLE 3

Central Transfers to the States for the Plan during 1951-52 to 1978-79

	Assistance for State Plans			Central/Centrally Sponsored Schemes			Grand Total
	Grants	Loans	Total	Grants	Loans	Total	
1	2	3	4	5	6	7	8
First Five-Year Plan							
1951-52	*	*	29	*	*	*	*
1952-53	*	*	35	*	*	*	*
1953-54	*	*	58	*	*	*	*
1954-55	*	*	100	*	*	*	*
1955-56	*	*	128	*	*	*	*
Total	*	*	350	*	*	530	880
Second Five-Yar Plan							
1956-57	33	126	159	*	*	*	*
1957-58	40	182	222	*	*	*	*
1958-59	48	161	209	*	*	*	*
1959-60	62	154	216	*	*	*	*
1960-61	71	181	252	*	*	*	*
Total	254	804	1058	*	*	*	*
Third Five-Year Plan							
1961-62	*	*	354	20	5	25	379
1962-63	*	*	412	26	4	30	442
1963-64	*	*	457	36	14	50	507
1964-65	*	*	606	44	11	55	661
1965-66	*	*	686	49	14	63	749
Total	*	*	2515	175	48	223	2738

	Assistance for State Plans			Central/Centrally Sponsored Schemes			Grand Total
	Grants	Loans	Total	Grants	Loans	Total	
Three Annual Plans							
1966-67	*	*	568	*	*	*	*
1967-68	91	489	580	*	*	*	*
1968-69	124	495	619	*	*	*	*
Total	*	*	1767	*	*	150	1917
Fourth Five-Year Plan							
1969-70	189	446	635	69	1	70	705
1970-71	200	456	656	66	13	79	735
1971-72	227	498	725	144	18	162	887
1972-73	236	529	765	352	170	522	1287
1973-74	225	529	754	338	25	363	1117
Total	1077	2458	3535	969	227	1196	4731
Fifth Five-Year Plan							
1974-75	269	569	838	197	77	274	1112
1975-76	371	720	1091	252	85	337	1428
1976-77	530	783	1313	340	103	443	1756
1977-78(RE)	730	1191	1921	484	171	655	2576
1978-79(BE)	914	1680	2594	685	202	887	3481
Total	2814	4943	7757	1958	638	2596	10353

* Break-up not available.

(C) National Development Council: Another institution connected with operational aspect of central finance assistance is National Development Council established in 1952. It consists of the Prime

Minister (chairman), the central cabinet ministers, the members of the Planning Commission and the chief ministers of all the states and the union territories. The secretary of the Planning Commission acts as secretary to National Development Council. The following are the important functions of National Development Council : (i) It reviews the working of the national plan from time to time. (ii) It considers important questions of social and economic policies affecting national development. (iii) It recommends measures for achieving aims and targets of the national plan. (iv) It also prescribes guidelines for formulation of the national plan including assessment of resources for the plan.

Though National Development Council is an informal federal structure, it has no effective voice in determining quantity of central voluntary grants to the states. It is the central government which decides it. However, National Development Council plays an important role in determining formula for central assistance to the states.

(D) Central Ministeries and Others : On the recommendations of the Planning Commission, plan grants under article 282 are made by the Ministry of Finance. All grants are to be issued through the central ministries. For example, the central ministry of education provides grants to the state ministries of education.

The central ministries and the departments are concerned with transfer of voluntary grants from the centre to the states. They have their own planning cells for preparation of plans and participate in the process of planning state plan schemes.

(E) Central Institutions : In addition to the central ministries and departments, the central agencies like Reserve Bank of India, Life Insurance Corporation of India and other central financial institutions are also concerned with the central assistance to the states.

The following tables give a picture of central transfers to the states other than those of the Finance Commission and the Planning Commission during 1951-52 and 1978-79.[5]

The following Table (No. 4) gives a comprehensive and comparative picture of transfer of resources from the centre to the states on the recommendations of the Finance Commission, the Planning Commission and the central ministries from the first five year plan to the sixth five year plan.[6]

TABLE 4

Central Transfers to the States – Other than those the Finance Commission and the Planning Commission during 1951-52 to 1978-79

	Grants	Loans	Total
First Five-Year Plan			
1951-52	*	*	*
1952-53	*	*	*
1953-54	*	*	*
1954-55	*	*	*
1955-56	*	*	*
Total	*	*	104
Second Five-Year Plan			
1956-57	*	*	*
1957-58	*	*	*
1958-59	*	*	*
1959-60	*	*	*
1960-61	*	*	*
Total	*	*	892
Third Five-Year Plan			
1961-62	*	*	234
1962-63	*	*	224
1963-64	*	*	266
1964-65	*	*	216
1965-66	*	*	332
Total	*	*	1272

	Grants	Loans	Total
Three Annual Plans			
1966-67	*	*	*
1967-68	*	*	*
1968-69	*	*	*
Total	*	*	1648
Fourth Five-Year Plan			
1969-70	94	582	676
1970-71	107	533	640
1971-72	315	675	990
1972-73	179	1227	1406
1973-74	231	1006	1237
Total	926	4023	4949
Fifth Five-Year Plan**			
1974-75	48	430	478
1975-76	77	469	546
1976-77	163	574	737
1977-78(RE)	133	610	743
1978-79(BE)	111	1146	1257
Total	532	3229	3761

* Break-up not available.

** The details of the grants and loans for the period 1974-75 to 1978-79 are given in the next table.

TABLE 5

	1974-75	1975-76	1976-77	1978-79 (RE)	1978-79 (BE)
I. GRANTS					
1. Relief and Rehabilitation	7	8	8	7	7
2. Improvement of roads and subversions from Central Road Fund	17	27	31	35	36
3. Incentive Bonus for procurement of food	10	24	90	30	1
4. To Rajasthan to cover additional interest liability on reallocated Beas loans	–	–	9	–	–
5. Relief on account of natural calamities	–	–	–	27	10
6. Education	3	8	10	12	19
7. Non-Plan grant to Sikkim	–	–	3	4	5
8. Police	1	3	4	3	7
9. Others	10	7	8	15	26
Total	48	77	163	133	111

II. LOANS					
1. Small Savings Loans	269	249	293	290	300
2. Ways and Means advances	77	96	150	200	300
3. Short-term loans for fertilizers etc.	55	110	100	100	100
4. Loans to cover gap in resources for the Plan	–	–	–	–	427
5. Others	29	14	31	20	19
Total	430	469	574	610	1146

TABLE 6

Financial Transfers from the Union Government to the State Governments Under the Instrumentalities of the Finance Commission, Planning Commission and at the Discretion of the Union Ministries

(Rs. crores)

Plan Period	Finance Commission Transfers			Planning Commission Transfers				Directionary Transfers	Transfers of all
	Tax Share	Grants	Total	Per cent to total financial transfers	Total	Per cent to total financial transfers	Total	Per cnt to total financial transfers	Total of all financial transfers
First Plan (1951-56)	344	103	447	31.24	350	24.46	634	44.30	1,431
Second Plan (1956-61)	668	250	918	32.00	1,058	36.89	829	31.11	2,868
Third Plan (1961-66)	1,196	394	1,590	28.39	2,515	44.91	1,495	26.70	5,600
Fourth Plan (1969-74)	1,152	500	1,782	33.33	1,767	30.05	1,798	36.62	5,317
Fifth Plan (1974-79)	8,275	2,773	11,048	43.01	7,722	30.55	6,683	26.44	25,453
Sixth Plan (1979-84)	21,335	1,711	23,046	41.00	16,099	29.34	16,267	29.65	55,412

Notes :

1. Finance Commission transfers include tax shares, all grants-in-aid under Article 275 and grants in lieu of tax on railway fare.
2. Planning Commission transfers include plan grants under Article 282 and loans under Article 293 for state sector plans only under Gadgil formula.
3. Discretionary transfers include grants under Article 282 and loans under Article 293 for Centrally-sponsored and Central sector schemes, plus small savings loans, loans for clearing overdrafts and other *ad hoc* assistance.

2. FORMULA FOR ASSISTANCE

Three types of grants are provided by the centre to the states : (i) statutory grants for non-plan purposes, (ii) non-statutory grants for plan purposes, and (iii) non-statutory grants for non-plan purposes. (a) Statutory Resource Transfers : Resources are transferred in the form of divisible taxes, grants-in-aid, etc., on the recommendations of the Finance Commission which takes two types of formula into consideration – one for division of taxes between the centre and the states and another for providing grants-in-aid. (b) Non-Statutory Resource Transfers : The central government provides financial assistance in the form of grants and loans to the states to implement state plans including centrally sponsored schemes on the recommendations of the Planning Commission. Some formulas have been adopted in this connection. (c) Non-Statutory Resource Transfers : The central government gives grants and loans to the states for natural calamities, improvement of roads, upgradation of salaries of teachers, relief and rehabilitation of displaced persons, etc.

Out of these three types of transfers of resources, this study is mainly concerned with the last two. Grants and loans for the last two categories are made under articles 282 and 293. The plan grants are given by the centre to the states according to certain formulas which have been evolved from time to time in the light of changing economic and political conditions and compulsions.

Pattern of Assistance Prior to Gadgil Formula: Before the introduction of the First Five-Year Plan, the states were receiving development grants from the centre under the post-war reconstruction programme. Though some of these grants were stopped by 1950-51, yet grants for "Grow More Food" scheme continued for some time.

During the First Five-Year Plan, grants and loans were given by the centre to the states on the basis of individual schemes. Volume of voluntary grants and loans from the centre to the states for the period of First Five Year-Plan and for early period of Second Five-Year Plan varied from scheme to scheme and also from year to year. A definite pattern of central assistance was not formulated in the First Five-Year Plan because the states' first five-year plans included projects and programmes which were in progress before the commencement of the planning : "A broad view was taken of the development efforts that were envisaged in the different states, and after assessing the resources to be raised by individual states, the quantum of central assistance was fixed for each year."[7]

Under the Second Five-Year Plan, the schemes which were to receive central voluntary grants and loans were classified into groups. The states were free to divert funds from one scheme to another within the same group if there was need for such diversion. Further transfer of funds was also permitted from one group to another within the same head of development only with the approval of the central ministry concerned and with information to the Planning Commission. However, river valley projects were not subject to the changed procedure. Though the system of specific purpose grants continued, two important changes were brought into the system: (i) The rate of grant-in-aid was fixed for the whole plan period instead of year-wise. (ii) Group of schemes became a unit of aid instead of individual scheme as a unit of aid. Though the rate of grant-in-aid was fixed, quantum of central assistance was not predetermined. "It (quantum of central assistance) continued to change from year to year in the light of financial position of states and the centre and the requirements of projects undertaken in both the state as well as the central sectors."[8]

In 1961-62 procedure of payment and utilization of grants for grouping of projects were simplified on the basis of suggestions made by the states. Each sub-head of development was divided into pattern and non-pattern schemes and reappropriation from one to another could be made only after a reference to the central ministry concerned. In course of time this condition was relaxed. Observance of the pattern within the composite groups was entrusted to the state planning boards and the state finance ministries. "The broad patterns of centre-state shares during the third plan were 50:50, 75:25, 25:75."[9]

Thus for the first three plans the central assistance was given on the basis of schematic pattern. Such assistance aimed not only at stimulating activities of the states in particular directions but at overall national plan. It intended to achieve certain national priorities.

Plan grants, during the first three five year plans, were provided by the centre to the states on the basis of financial needs of the states in relation to their plan outlays. They were provided to the states to fill the gap between the plan outlays of the states as approved by the Planning Commission and the resources available to the states for plan purposes. Though they were to be given on the basis of population, area, extent of development already made, on-going development projects, etc., yet there was political bargaining between the centre and the states.

No uniformity and fixed pattern of assistance from the centre to the states were developed during the course of the first three plans because the Congress was the ruling party at the centre and in many states and because the towering personality of Pt. Jawaharlal Nehru, the first Prime Minister of India, commanded unquestioned support from the states. With the death of Pt. Nehru in 1964, with the emergence of the non-Congress governments in many states and with the reduced majority of the Congress party at the centre in 1967, political situation changed significantly. The non-Congress state governments were in favour of some pattern for central assistance to the states. The Administrative Reforms Commission had completed its work and its views on centre-state relations were made known to the public. In the light of these developments, the National Development Council appointed a sub-committee in May 1968 to study and recommend the criteria for central assistance to the state plans. The sub-committee submitted its report. In the light of this report, a new pattern was evolved and was popularly known as Gadgil Formula. According to the new pattern, central assistance was to be given in the form of block grants and loans for state plans. The formula was based on PFN (Population, Financial ability and Need).

Gadgil Formula (1969-1980) : The new formula for central assistance was accepted by the National Development Council in 1969. With the exception of states like Assam, Nagaland and Jammu and Kashmir (for whom specific assistance was set apart), the assistance was given in the following five factor formula : "According to this formula the central government's assistance in the form of plan grants for the first category of states' plan schemes was distributed 60 per cent on the basis of population, 10 per cent on per capita income, as on October 1, 1966 (only to those states whose per capita incomes were below the national average), 10 per cent on tax effort in relation to per capita income, 10 per cent on commitments in respect of major continuing irrigation and power projects (each costing Rs. 20 crores and above), and 10 per cent on special problems (such as floods, chronically drought

TABLE 7

Central Assistance to States (Revised Allocation for 1974–79)

(Rs. crores)

	State	Total allocation	Population 60%	Per capita income 10%	Per capita tax effort 10%	I & P projects 10%	Special problems 10%
1.	Andhra Pradesh	412.38	250.19	60.26	37.70	73.23	–
2.	Assam	289.36	–	–	–	–	–
3.	Bihar	542.04	324.13	110.91	25.20	33.63	48.17
4.	Gujarat	240.80	153.57	–	37.65	46.14	3.44
5.	Haryana	113.88	57.76	–	40.86	14.11	1.15
6.	Himachal Pradesh	156.97	–	–	–	–	–
7.	Jammu & Kashmir	494.64	–	–	–	–	–
8.	Karnataka	266.63	168.57	–	38.54	59.52	–
9.	Kerala	272.77	122.80	29.58	36.83	14.75	68.81
10.	Madhya Pradesh	374.19	239.58	71.14	30.13	33.34	–
11.	Maharashtra	383.56	289.98	–	49.82	43.76	–
12.	Manipur	67.08	–	–	–	–	–

13. Meghalaya	70.95	–	–	–	–	–
14. Nagaland	66.58	–	–	–	–	–
15. Orissa	262.81	126.23	35.59	14.66	7.40	79.13
16. Punjab	151.84	77.94	–	43.52	30.38	–
17. Rajasthan	313.58	148.20	39.81	30.97	37.24	57.36
18. Sikkim	40.06	–	–	–	–	–
19. Tamil Nadu	340.11	236.98	–	53.26	51.14	44.73
20. Tripura	58.29	–	–	–	–	–
21. Uttar Pradesh	902.42	508.15	146.07	25.16	80.83	142.21
22. West Bengal	345.57	254.06	–	28.86	13.69	48.16
Total	6184.61*	2958.94	493.16	493.16	493.16	493.16

*Excluding assistance for IDA Financed Projects.

Source : Planning Commission.

affected areas and tribal areas) of individual states. The total amount of plan grants for each state as determined on the basis of this formula is provided by the central government, 30 per cent in outright grants and 70 per cent in loans."[10] The entire plan grants for Assam, Nagaland and Jammu and Kashmir states were outright grants from the centre. The formula was applicable to the central assistance to the state plans only. The centrally sponsored schemes continued to receive hundred per cent grants from the centre.

The table 7 gives a picture of pattern and amount of central assistance (grants and loans) to the two categories of states on the basis of the Gadgil formula.[11]

Modified Gadgil Formula (1980-1990) : The Gadgil formula in its original form continued to be in existence from 1969 to 1979. In 1979 Shri Morarji Desai, the Prime Minister, gave an award for distribution of plan grants among the states. The new award came into existence in 1980 and was known as Desai formula. It took two factors into consideration – population and inverse per capita income – for distributing Rs. two thousand crores among the states. As the Desai formula was only *ad hoc*, the Gadgil formula was modified by N.D.C. in 1980. The modified Gadgil formula abolished the weightage of 10 per cent assistance to on-going irrigation and power schemes and doubled the weightage from 10 per cent to 20 per cent for backwardness as measured by per capita income. The table 8 gives a comparative picture of original Gadgil formula and modified Gadgil formula:[12]

N.D.C. Formula (1990): In October 1990, the National Development Council replaced Gadgil formula by its own formula.[13] This formula is meant for distribution of central budgetary support to the states' plan expenditure during the eighth plan period. This formula gives higher weightage for backwardness as well as extra allocation for special problems faced by certain states and weightage to population has been slightly reduced. In spite of opposition from other states, Assam and Jammu and Kashmir states have been included among the special category states. These states shall receive 90% plan grants and 10% loans.

Out of the total funds available for distribution to the states, 30% of funds would be for centrally sponsored schemes. Out of the remaining amount, separate amounts would be provided for three special area

TABLE 8

	Criteria	Weights (Per cent)	
		In the original formula	As modified by N.D.C. in 1980
1.	Population	60	60
2.	Per capita income below the national average	10	20
3.	Per capita tax effort	10	10
4.	Outlay on continuing irrigation and power projects	10	–
5.	Special problems	10	10

programmes pertaining to (i) hill areas, (ii) tribal areas, and (iii) border areas. Out of the remaining balance, 30% of funds would be earmarked for special category states including the North-Eastern Council. The rest of the resources would be distributed among the non-special category states on this basis : (A) Weightage to population – 55%, (B) per capita income of a state – 25%, (C) tax efforts – 5% and (D) special development problems of a state – 15%. None of the non-special category states neither loses nor gains more than seven per cent of what it was getting earlier.

The following is a comparative table of central assistance to the non-special category states according to three formulas:

TABLE 9

	Criteria	Original Gadgil Formula 1969–1980	Modified Gadgil Formula 1980–1990	N.D.C. Formula Since 1990
1.	Weightage to population	60	60	55
2.	Per capita income	10	20	25
3.	Per capita tax efforts	10	10	5
4.	Outlay on continuing irrigation and power projects .	10	–	–
5.	Special Problems	10	10	15

The special problems include coastal areas, environment, flood, drought, sparsely or thickly populated areas, deserts, slums, etc.

Non-pattern Assistance

Grants and loans are also provided by the centre to the states outside Gadgil formula : (A) Schematic Transfers – The centre provides assistance to the states for centrally sponsored schemes and non-plan schemes. (B) Relief for Natural Calamities – Another component of discretionary transfers of grants and loans by the centre to the states is relief assistance for flood, famine, etc. The central assistance for relief in connection with natural calamities is over and above the provisions for famine relief recommended by the Finance Commission. For allotment of relief, clear guidelines have not beeen laid down by the centre. Consequently there is considerable scope for exercise of discretion by the centre. Many states have been demanding assistance on a liberal scale. Whenever there is a demand for such non-plan assistance from the states, the central government usually sends teams to inspect the extent of calamities on the spot and estimate the quantum of central assistance. Such assistance is usually in the form of grants and loans. When the different parties are ruling in the centre and in some states, the quantum of central assistance becomes a political issue. (C) Special Assistance for Tribal Areas – The central government provides special assistance to the tribal areas outside the formula. "Special central assistance for the tribal sub-plans is done on the basis of a three factor formula, *viz.*, total scheduled tribes population in the state (50 per cent weightage), area occupied by scheduled tribes population (30 per cent weightage), and inverse proportion of state domestic product (20 per cent weightage)."[14] (D) Special Assistance to Hill Area – Special central assistance is given for sub-plans of hill areas of Assam, Uttar Pradesh, West Bengal, Maharashtra, Karnataka, Kerala, Tamil Nadu and Goa. "The special central assistance is allocated with 75 per cent weightage to area and 25 per cent (weightage) to population."[15] (E) In addition to these, the centre provides assistance in the form of various types of loans and advances – loans towards share in small savings, loans for clearance of overdrafts, loans for meeting gaps in resources, special accommodation loans, etc. All these involve central discretionary powers. Through these, the centre influences policies of state governments and penetrates into state autonomy.

3. ADMINISTRATION OF CERTAIN PROJECTS/SCHEMES

The pattern of central assistance to the states outside the recommendations of the Finance Commission is a complex process. These grants achieved prominence through the five-year plans.

The schemes that are fully or partially implemented by the states can be divided into three categories : (i) State schemes, (ii-a) Centrally sponsored schemes, (ii-b) Centrally assisted schemes, (ii-c) Centrally sector schemes, and (iii) Financial assistance to some departments of states.

(i) *State Schemes:* The state schemes are those schemes which are initiated by the state governments and which are approved by the Planning Commission. They are exclusively in the state sector of the state plans and cover subjects like irrigation, agriculture, health, etc. They also receive central grants and loans. The central assistance has been given for these schemes according to some formulas like schematic formula, Gadgil formula, modified Gadgil formula and N.D.C. formula.

(ii-a) *Centrally Sponsored Schemes:* Centrally sponsored schemes are initiated by the central ministries in consultation with the Planning Commission and the state governments. They are outside the state plans and are taken up in those areas where the initiative of the states is lacking for paucity of funds or for some other reasons. They are financed by the centre mostly on hundred per cent basis. Sometimes certain components of the schemes such as cost of the staff, etc., might be shared with the state governments on some basis. Ratio between the central share and state share depends on nature of scheme. The central share of expenditure is shown in the central plan and budget and the share of the states is shown in the state plans. The schemes are to be implemented by the states. At the end of the plan period, these schemes become a part of committed expenditure of the state governments.

The centrally sponsored schemes present a variety in respect of their nature and coverage : (a) Some are pilot projects relating to agriculture, education, research, training, extension, statistics, etc. They are entirely funded by the centre. (b) Some programmes like family welfare programmes which are of all India importance also receive hundred per cent assistance from the centre. (c) Certain schemes like eradication of unemployment, poverty, rural development and agricultural production carry from matching contribution to hundred per cent contribution from the centre.

The Expert Committee appointed in 1984 under the direction of the National Development Council classified the centrally sponsored schemes into two : (i) Some are very general and comprehensive such as I.R.D.P, N.R.E.P, E.G.P., Rural Water Supply, Health and Family Welfare, etc.; (ii) Some are very specific and involve small outlays.

The A.R.C. Study Team on Financial Administration first suggested criteria for schemes to be included in the centrally sponsored schemes. The position of the centrally sponsored schemes was also reviewed by the Planning Commission in consultation with the central and state governments in the light of changed political conditions after 1967 general elections. The National Development Council, at the beginning of the Fourth Five-Year Plan, laid down criteria for centrally sponsored schemes : (i) Centrally sponsored schemes should relate to demonstration, pilot projects, survey and research. (ii) They have regional or inter-state character. (iii) They should require lumsum provisions until they could be broken down territorially. (iv) They should have an overall relevance to the country as a whole.

According to the Report of the Group of Officials on centrally sponsored schemes, the total number of these schemes was 262 on 1.4.1985.[16] Out of these 262, 24 schemes are being implemented by autonomous bodies. The group recommended transfer of 113 schemes to the states and retention only 125 schemes by the centre.

As assistance given to the centrally sponsored schemes is direct, the centre has direct interest in them. As the central share is liberal, degree of central supervision is detailed and uniformity is insisted.

(ii-b) *Centrally Assisted Schemes:* Until the end of third plan, centrally sponsored schemes and centrally assisted schemes existed distinctly. This distrinction has now disappeared. The centrally assisted schemes were those schemes for which the centre provided financial assistance to the plan projects of the states. They were exclusively in the state plans and were initiated by the states. The Planning Commission in consultation with the central government determined the grants for the centrally assisted schemes which were included in the state plans. The central government participated in the promotion of these schemes under state plans on an agreed basis. Until 1969-70, it generally provided grants to these schemes on the following pattern: 25 per cent of the cost of each such scheme was to be paid by the centre in the form of conditional block grants; 50 per cent of it was to be paid in the form of loans by the centre to the states; and the remaining 25 per cent of the cost of it was to be borne by the state governments in the form of matching contribution. Plan grants earmarked for each individual scheme were not to be diverted by the state government to another scheme. Percentage of grants and loans from the centre to the states varied from scheme to scheme and from time to time. The pattern of central assistance indicated the relative priority which the centre attached to the schemes to which it agreed to finance. The following table gives a picture of central assistance to the centrally assisted schemes during 1966-67.[17]

TABLE 10

Assistance to State Plans, 1966-67

(in crores of rupees)

	Head of Development	Tentative Plan Outlay	Central Assistance Loan	Grant	Total
I.	Agricultural Programme	225.68	100.90	35.74	136.64
II.	Community Development and Cooperation	53.85	16.63	19.82	36.45
III.	Irrigation and Power	394.65	97.99	–	97.99
IV.	Industries and Mining	45.83	8.01	4.19	12.20
V.	Transport	65.17	–	–	–
VI.	Social Services	133.66	24.33	38.77	63.10
VII.	Miscellaneous	12.62	3.52	8.82	12.34
	Loans for Development	–	150.68	–	150.68
		931.46	402.06	107.34	509.40

(ii-c) *Central Sector Schemes* : During the fourth plan period, a new scheme emerged. It was central sector scheme. The central sector schemes suggested by the Planning Commission are sponsored by the central ministries. They are entirely financed by the central government and are included in the central sector plan. The programmes under these schemes cover employment, drought prone area development, agency for small and marginal farmers, etc. "The only task left to the states is the implementation."[18]

(iii) *Financial Assistance to Some Departments* : The centre gives financial assistance in the form of grants and loans to certain state departments like education, agriculture, health, etc., to achieve plan priorities :

(A) *Education* : In 1957 the central ministry of education had six groups for purpose of financial assistance to the states. They were (i) elementary education, (ii) secondary education, (iii) university education, (iv) other education schemes, (v) welfare projects, and (vi) state social welfare schemes. There were eighteen schemes covering these groups for central financial assistance to the states. Eight of them were under the category of centrally assisted schemes and ten were under centrally sponsored schemes. In most cases central grants were on matching basis and in many cases they were tapering.

The centre, through the New Education Policy, adopted in the recent years, provides financial assistance in the form of grants and loans to the various educational schemes including operation black board in the state plan sectors.

The central financial assistance to the various educational schemes and matching ratio vary from plan to plan. The same schemes do not get central assistance in all the plans. Each plan has its own set of schemes receiving central financial assistance.

The table 11 indicates how education has become joint venture of centre and states and also points out how there has been steady increase in the expenditure on education.[19]

(B) *Agriculture* : The centre has been providing financial assistance in the form of grants and loans to the states for various agricultural schemes like minor irrigation, land improvement, fertlizers, manures, quality seeds, fisheries, soil conservation, etc., and for co-operative schemes like primary credit societies, land mortage banks, co-operative marketing, co-operative processing, training of co-operative personnel, etc. The central assistance to schemes relating to agriculture and co-operative sectors varies from plan to plan. Quantum of central assistance and matching ratio also vary from plan to plan. Different schemes are evolved in each plan for central financial assistance.

(C) *Health* : The centre has been providing financial assistance in the form of grants and loans to the various health schemes of states like water supply and sanitation, medical education and training, family

TABLE 11

Plan-wise Sub-head Expenditure on Education Combined Centre, States and Union Territories

Sl. No.	Sub-head	First Plan	Second Plan	Third Plan	Annual Plans 1966-67	Annual Plans 1967-68	Annual Plans 1968-69	Fourth Plan	Fifth Plan (Revised Outlay)	1978–83 Plan Outlay
1.	Elementary Education	85	95	201	15	26	33	239	410	900
		(58)	(35)	(34)	(17)	(25)	(26)	(30)	(32)	(45)
2.	Secondary Education	20	51	103	13	16	23	140	250	268
		(13)	(19)	(18)	(15)	(16)	(18)	(18)	(19)	(14)
3.	University Education	14	48	87	27	25	26	195	292	265
		(9)	(18)	(15)	(30)	(24)	(20)	(25)	(23)	(13)
4.	Adult Education	5	4	2	neg.	1	1	5	18	200
		(3)	(1)	neg.	neg.	(1)	(1)	(1)	(1)	(10)
5.	Other Programmes	9	23	64	7	8	15	90	122	118
		(6)	(8)	(11)	(8)	(8)	(11)	(11)	(9)	(6)
6.	Sub-total General Education	133	221	457	63	76	98	668	1092	1751
		(87)	(81)	(78)	(70)	(74)	(76)	(85)	(85)	(88)
7.	Art and Culture	Included in	3	7	1	1	2	12	37	65
		Sl. No. 5	(1)	(1)	(1)	(1)	(1)	(2)	(3)	(3)
8.	Technical Education	20	49	125	25	26	29	106	156	170
		(13	(18)	(21)	(29)	(25)	(23)	(13)	(12)	(9)
9.	Total Education	153	273	589	89	103	129	786	1285	1986
		(100)	(100)	(100)	(100)	(100)	(100)	(100)	(100)	(100)

(Figures in parenthesis indicate percentage to the total outlay/expenditure Sl. No. 1).

planning, etc. The central financial assistance and matching ratio for various health schemes differ from plan to plan. Different health schemes receive different ratio of financial assistance.

4. CENTRAL ASSISTANCE TO STATE PLANS

A budget of the state can be divided into two parts : (i) non-plan budget, and (ii) plan budget. Revenue gap of non-plan budget of the state is generally balanced by devolution of taxes and grants recommended by the Finance Commission. Revenue gap of plan budget has to take these factors into consideration: (a) amount of additional resources to be raised by the state itself, and (b) amount of central aid available to the state. As the central assistance is mainly on matching basis, the state has to raise additional resources to receive matching grants from the centre. Plan grants are provided by the centre to the states to enable the latter to undertake development schemes which have been given priority in the five-year plans. Quantum of plan grants is determined by the central ministries in consultation with the Planning Commission.

A state plan has two components – state plan schemes and centrally initiated schemes. (A) The state plan schemes initiated by the state governments and approved by the Planning Commission belong exclusively to the state subjects. (B) Some plan schemes which are initiated and sponsored by the central government in consultation with the Planning Commission and the state governments relate to state subjects like education, agriculture, health, etc. These received central assistance in the form of grants and loans. Earlier they were divided into two categories – centrally sponsored schemes and centrally assisted schemes. At the end of Third Five-Year Plan, the distinction between these two disappeared. During the Fourth Five-Year Plan period another central scheme was introduced and was known as 'central sector' scheme. The central sector schemes are entirely financed by the centre and the state governments are entrusted with the task of implementing these schemes.

Thus total revenue expenditure of state plan is shared by the state and the centre. Usually a share of the state in revenue expenditure of the state plan is more than that of the centre. "The share of the states in the total revenue expenditure is more than half."[20] The remaining plan expenditure has been borne by the centre through grants and loans on the basis of schematic pattern (till the end of third plan),

TABLE 12

Federal Fiscal Transfers from the Centre to the States During the Period 1951–79

Plan periods	Statutory transfers on the recommendations of the Finance Commission (tax shares + grants-in-aid)	Discretionary transfers on the recommendations of the Planning Commission (Plan Grants and Central loans)	Discretionary transfers at the discretion of the Central Ministries (loans+grants)	Total federal fiscal transfers
First Plan (1951–56)	447 (31.2)	800 (61.5)	104 (7.3)	1,431 (100.00)
Second Plan (1956–61)	918 (32.0)	1,058 (36.9)	892 (31.1)	2,868 (100.00)
Third Plan (1961–66)	1,590 (28.4)	2,738 (48.9)	1,272 (22.7)	5,600 (100.00)
Three Annual Plans (1966–69)	1,782 (33.3)	1,917(35.9)	1,648 (30.8)	5,347 (100.00)
Fourth Plan (1969–74)	5,421 (35.9)	4,731 (31.3)	4,949 (32.8)	15,101 (100.00)
Fifth Plan (1974–79)	11,048(44.2)	10,353 (40.9)	3,761 (14.9)	25,282 (100.00)
Sixth Plan (1980–85)	20,845 (61.14)	13,245 (38.86)	—	34,090 (100.00)

Note: Figures shown in brackets are percentages.

Source: Report of the Eighth Finance Commission, Government of India, New Delhi, 1984 Appendix IV.1 (ii), (iii), (iv), pp. 174-177.

Gadgil formula (since the beginning of fourth plan), modified Gadgil formula (1980–1990) and N.D.C. formula (since 1990).

The table 12 gives a picture of resources transferred to the states from the centre to meet revenue gap of non-plan budgets of the states on the recommendations of the Finance Commission and to meet resources gap of plan budgets of the states on the recommendations of the planning commission and the central ministries.[21]

REFERENCES

1. *Centre-State Financial Relations in India* prepared by Birla Institute of Scientific Research and Economic Research Division (New Delhi : Abhinav Publications, 1979), p.127.
2. *Report of the Finance Commission,* 1978 (Delhi : The Controller of Publications, Government of India, 1979), pp. 215 and 216.
3. *Report, Commission on Centre-State Relations* (Popularly Known as Sarkaria Commission) (Nasik : Printed by the General Manager, Government of India Press, 1988), p. 374.
4. *Report of the Finance Commission,* 1978 (Delhi : The Controller of Publications, Government of India, 1979), pp. 216 and 217.
5. *Ibid.,* pp. 217 and 218.
6. Source: *Reserve Bank of India Bulletins,* Quoted by Memorandum to the Ninth Finance Commission, Vol. I, 1988, Submitted by the Government of Karnataka (Bangalore : Government Press, Government of Karnataka, 1988), p. 5.
7. *Summary of Record of the Twenty-fourth Meeting of the National Development Council,* December 18-20, 1967, p. 37. Government of India, Planning Commission, referred by Sinha R.K., Fiscal Federalism in India (New Delhi : South Asian Publishers, Pvt. Ltd., 1980), pp. 84 and 85.
8. *Ibid.,* pp. 84-85.
9. Singh, S.P., *Centre-State Relations in Agricultural Development* (Delhi : Vikas Publishing House Pvt. Ltd., 1973), p. 143.
10. Thimmaiah G., *Burning Issues in Centre-State Relations* (New Delhi : Ashish Publishing House, 1985), p. 102.
11. *Ibid.,* p. 106.
12. *Report, Commission on Centre-State Relations,* Part I (Popularly Known as Sarkaria Commission) (Nasik : Printed by the General Manager, Government of India Press, 1988), p. 277.
13. *The Hindu,* a National Daily English Newspaper, 12.10.1990 (Madras : S. Rangarajan, 1990).
14. Source : *Government of India, Ministry of Home Affairs, Report of the Working Group on Tribal Development during the Sixth Plan (1980),* p. 24, referred by Report, Commission on Centre-State Relations, Part I (Popularly Known as Sarkaria Commission) (Nasik : Printed by the General Manager, Government of India Press, 1988), p. 373.

15. Source : *Government of India, Planning Commission, Seventh Five-Year Plan, 1985–90,* Vol. II, p. 338, referred by Report, Commission on Centre-State Relations, Part I (Popularly Known as Sarkaria Commission) (Nasik : Printed by the General Manager, Government of India Press, 1988), p. 373.
16. *Report of Officials on Centrally Sponsored Schemes* (New Delhi : Planning Commission, 1987), p. I.
17. Lakdawala, D.T., *Union-State Financial Relations* (Bombay : Lalvani Publishing House, 1967), p. 98.
18. Reddy, Balwant, *The Impact of Planning on Centre-State Relations* in Maheshwari, B. L. (ed), *Centre-State Relations in the Seventies* (Calcutta : Minerva Associates, 1973), p. 284.
19. *Draft Sixth Five-Year Plan* (New Delhi : Planning Commission, Government of India, n.d.), p. 429.
20. Lakdawala, D.T., *Planning and Centre-State Relations,* Seminar on Centre-State Relations, Bangalore, August 5-7, 1983 (Bangalore : Government Press, Government of Karnataka, 1983), p. 137.
21. *Report of the Eighth Finance Commission* (New Delhi : Printed by the Ministry of Finance, Government of India, 1984), pp.174-177, referred by Thimmaiah, G., *Burning Issues in Centre-State Relations* (New Delhi : Ashish Publishing House, 1985), p. 6.

CHAPTER VI

CENTRAL MEANS OF PENETRATION

1. Introduction

When the centre provides financial assistance to the states for planning and non-planning purposes, it does so through various means. It penetrates into state fields through these means – planning process, Planning Commission, advisory boards, Finance Commission, central financial institutions, article 282, formula for financial assistance, plan grants, non-plan grants, financial inducement, discretionary transfer of resources, centrally sponsored schemes, centrally assisted schemes, loans, relief measures for natural calamities, control over expenditure, increased percentage of central expenditure on state subjects, one party domination at the centre for a longer period, office of Prime Minister, central ministries, central secretariat, conferences, seminars, etc. These are the financial, political and administrative means through which the centre penetrates into state fields when the centre provides grants and loans to the states for various purposes.

2. PLANNING PROCESS

The members of the Indian constituent assembly did not deliberately discuss about socio-economic planning for India. Though socio-economic planning was not forgotten, it was placed as an item No. 20 in the concurrent list. Shri K. Santhanam, a prominent member of the constituent assembly, has thus to say: "It may be asked whether planning was not contemplated by the constituent assembly and what steps that assembly took to promote planning. I am afraid that planning did not figure largely in the discussions of the constituent assembly but it was not altogether forgotten. It was put down as item No. 20 in the concurrent list which reads as 'social and economic planning'. But when the Planning Commission was set up in 1950, it was not done under this item."[1] Though the framers of the Indian Constitution had thus visualised socio-economic planning, they had not anticipated that planning would be on the present scale. At the time of framing the Indian Constitution, no democratic federal country had planning process on a massive scale. That is why the framers of the Indian Constitution did not make provisions for transfer of plan grants from the centre to the states. They made detailed provisions for the Finance Commission for distribution of revenues between the centre and the states.

Indian socio-economic planning is direct imitation of socio-economic planning of Soviet Union. It is an important strategy for social change and economic development. The states are drawn into this strategy through central financial assistance in the form of grants and loans. They are supplementary planners and eager recipients of plan grants. Ursula K. Hicks says that the Indian planning process has led to centralization by the centre and loss of autonomy by the states: "The Indian experiment in national planning in a federation is of great international and constitutional interest. The net effects on Indian federalism have unquestionably been a substantial increase in centralization and loss of autonomy by the states."[2] Indian planning has been characterised as the most centralised system of planning among the democratic countries. The all India targets are fixed by the Planning Commission and are accepted by the states. The states consider planning to be mainly central concern and are at the receiving end.

Indian planning is very comprehensive and covers vast areas of both the centre and the states. "Planning in India embraces all branches of economic and social life, ranging from industry, agriculture and power to family planning, community development and slum clearance. The direct participation of the central and state governments is an accepted feature of the economic philosophy followed in the country. As a result, the scope of economic planning in India is more comprehensive than is usually the case in free enterprise economies."[3] The comprehensive national planning under the present set-up continues to have central direction, financing and determination of national targets even though socio-economic planning is placed in the concurrent list. It transcends the barriers of division of powers between the centre and the states. In this process of planning, both the Planning Commission and the central government have acquired a voice in matters of states' jurisdiction. The state plans are prepared in conformity with the objectives set by the Planning Commission. This conformity is secured through the process of consultation with the states and through the central financial assistance in the form of grants and loans. However, "the states feel aggrieved that their autonomy is being unduly frustrated by the national plans in the shaping of which they have little or no hand."[4] The planning process in India is towards centralization. The centre and its various agencies including Planning Commission have greater share in the formulation of five year plans. The states play secondary role in the formulation of five year plans and are expected to conform to the central guidelines and targets. Vast resources to finance planning process are with the centre while many subjects to be planned are under the state list. Consequently the centre has taken over bigger role in the formulation of five year plans and the states are to implement them. Planning has affected states' spheres even more than the centre's spheres : "As a matter of fact, planning affected the state's spheres even more than the central sphere. About 70% of the total expenditure of planning in the First Five-Year Plan and about 65% in the Second Five-Year Plan relate to matters which have been exclusively assigned to the states, like education, health, forests, agriculture, irrigation, electricity, etc."[5] Shri K. Santhanam, a promiment member of the constituent assembly, concludes that planning process has superseded the federal constitution through consent and agreement : "What I want to suggest is that planning for purpose of economic development practically superseded the federal constitution so far as states are concerned but this supersession was not legal or constitutional but was by agreement and consent."[6] Such consent and agreement is based partly on central voluntary grants and loans to the states for plan purposes and partly on dominant position of the ruling party at the centre.

3. PLANNING COMMISSION

The Planning Commission is not a creation of the constitution and does not suffer from any constitutional limitations to its power. It is appointed by the central government and is its organ. From the point of view of its objectives and style of functioning, it is more unitary than federal. It has penetrated into state fields by various means like (a) process of plan formulation, (b) role in state plan formulation, (c) control over state plan outlays, (d) control over state plan in implementation, (e) transferring grants from the centre to the states, (f) compelling the states to levy more taxes for plan purposes, (g) controlling non-surplus revenues of the states, (h) influence over state subjects, etc. It has become an economic cabinet for the whole country.

(a) *Process of Plan Formulation* : The Planning Commission deals not only with the central subjects but also with the state subjects. It is entrusted with the task of formulating a plan for the whole country. It prepares the basic documents and its working groups work out most of the details. The working groups on central subjects are mostly manned by the experts from the Planning Commission and the central ministries and by a few outside experts. The working groups on state subjects are manned by the experts from the Planning Commission and the representatives of the states. However, the role of the states in formulating their plans is subject to the targets fixed by the Planning Commission and quantum of central assistance in the form of grants and loans available to them. Shri A.N. Jha opines that process of plan formulation "gives the Planning Commission and the central cabinet greater control over the formulation of policy in the state sphere than the constitution warranted."[7] Though there is a National Development Council to give its approval, its role is limited and its deliberations are very brief and general. The states accept the plan targets and the guidelines of the Planning Commission due to the attraction of central voluntary grants and loans.

A detailed plan formulation process indicates the extent of centre's control over annual plans of the states. The programmes of the five year plan are broken into annual plans for implementation. The states have to approach the Planning Commission in advance for the approval of their next year's plans. Since they have to depend on the centre for central voluntary grants and loans, they cannot bypass the Planning Commission. Annual plans of the states are prepared for the coming year in the light of the Planning Commission's review of the budgetary needs, available resources of the states and magnitude of central financial assistance. Financial dependence of the states on the Planning Commission has curtailed the autonomy of the states in respect of plan policy formulation and plan priorities. Shri G. Ramachandran, a former central administrator, says thus : "The fact that these grants are conditional and are canalized through a maze of patterns is further calculated to deprive the states of all initiative and flexibility in formulation as well as implementation of plans."[8] Formulation of five year plans or annual plans is mainly done in the light of accepted policies and decisions of the central government. Consequently the five year plans reflect mainly the mind of the centre. Thus centralized planning in India has introduced a powerful centralizing tendency in the centre-state financial relations.

(b) *Role of P.C. in State Plan Formulation* : The Planning Commission plays an important role in the preparation of state plans. Though the state governments are responsible for their plan programmes and projects to their state legislatures, yet their plan budgets are expected to conform to the central pattern of allocation of resources and plan targets. Thus the state plans are not totally the product of state initiative and innovation. They are scrutinised, adjusted and approved by the Planning Commission which is backed up by the political will of the central government. Dispersal of industries, weightage in welfare programmes, choice of projects; location of industries, financial inducement to industries established in backward areas, special programmes, etc., are determined by the central government and are pushed through the Planning Commission. Submission of state plans to the Planning Commission has led "to central guidance, interference and control over the economic and social development even in the spheres especially allotted to the states in the constitution as their developmental responsibility for which they are accountable to their legislatures and electorates."[9] Thus opined an eminent economist, Dr. V.K.R.V. Rao, in 1983. Even a decade earlier, the same views were forcefully expressed by the Rajamannar Report: "The centre is able to impose its will on the states in the formulation and execution of the plans by virtue of the non-statutory grants under article 282, which are dependent on the absolute discretion of the centre. It will thus be seen that the process of planning and the activities of the Planning Commission have a very deleterious effect on the autonomy of the states particularly in spheres exclusively allotted to the states by the constitution."[10]

(c) *Control of P.C. Over State Plan Outlays* : The following two tables (table 1 and table 2) give clear picture of the control exercised by the Planning Commission over the state plan outlays.

Table 1 Indicates how the various central agencies including the Planning Commission look at the plan outlays proposed by the state government.

Table 2 gives a comparative picture of wide gap between the annual plan outlays proposed by the government of Andhra Pradesh and the annual plan outlays approved by the Planning Commission between 1983 and 1989.

TABLE 1

The Plan Outlays of Seventeen States[11] : Fourth Five Year Plan, 1969–74

(Rs. in crores)

	States	Outlays Indicated by Planning Commission	Outlays Proposed by States	Col. 4 as % to Col. 3	Recommended by Working Groups	Recommended by Adviser (PA)	Outlays Approved in the Draft Plan (April 1969)	Col. (8) as % to Col. 4	Final Outlays on the basis of Resources (Mar. 1970)	Col. 10 as % to Col. 4
(1)	(2)	(3)	(4)	(5)	(6)	(7)	(8)	(9)	(10)	(11)
1.	Andhra Pradesh	522.00	660.64	127	651.17	360.00	360.55	54.5	420.50	64
2.	Assam	190.00	394.81	208	260.28	225.53	225.50	57.1	261.75	66
3.	Bihar	545.00	493.74	91	597.60	441.00	441.61	89.4	531.28	108
4.	Gujarat	446.00	565.90	126	562.58	390.00	450.22	79.5	455.00	80
5.	Haryana	168.40	262.00	155	293.59	190.00	190.49	72.7	225.00	86
6.	Jammu & Kashmir	126.00	225.46	179	184.36	145.00	145.00	64.3	158.40	70
7.	Kerala	293.00	466.75	159	400.21	257.37	258.40	55.3	258.35	55
8.	Madhya Pradesh	458.00	552.80	121	554.34	355.00	355.96	64.3	383.00	69
9.	Maharashtra	951.00	1000.22	105	1030.88	810.97	811.80	81.2	898.12	90
10.	Mysore	421.00	440.00	106	446.15	355.00	327.10	74.3	350.00	80
11.	Nagaland	30.00	58.66	196	42.88	34.00	35.00	59.6	40.00	68
12.	Orissa	300.00	321.49	107	303.22	179.16	180.50	56.1	222.60	69

(1)	(2)	(3)	(4)	(5)	(6)	(7)	(8)	(9)	(10)	(11)
13.	Punjab	280.00	325.00	116	401.28	250.00	271.40	83.5	293.56	90
14.	Rajasthan	313.00	313.00	100	349.73	236.70	238.96	76.3	302.00	96
15.	Tamil Nadu	564.32	623.68	111	604.82	501.00	502.00	80.5	519.36	83
16.	Uttar Pradesh	926.00	1350.00	146	1235.80	950.00	951.00	70.4	965.00	71
17.	West Bengal	492.51	654.74	133	639.41	324.00	320.51	48.9	322.50	49
	Total	7,026.23	8,708.89	124	8,558.31	6,004.73	6,066.00	69.6	6,606.42	76

*The State Governments were requested not to exceed to outlay which had emerged in old Fourth Plan (1966–70).

Source : Programme Administration Division, Planning Commission.

The control of the Planning Commission over the state plan outlays is maintained through the lure of voluntary grants and loans from the centre to the states. The states complain about cut in their plan outlays by the Planning Commision but continue to accept the decisions of the Planning Commission in this regard.

TABLE 2

State Plan Outlays of Andhra Pradesh[12]

(Rs. in crores)

Year	Plan Outlays Proposed by Andhra Pradesh	Plan Outlays Approved by the Planning Commission
1983-84	909	825
1984-85	–	981.31
1985-86	1170	810
1986-87	1218.98	1090
1987-88	1363	1200
1988-89	1550.40	1250

(d) *Control Over Implementation* : The Planning Commission supervises the work of plan implementation in the states through its advisers.

(e) *Role of P.C. in Transfer of Grants* : The Planning Commission has to come to play an important role in transfer of grants from the centre to the states. About sixty per cent of the funds have been transferred through the budgets from the centre to the states during the last thirty-four years (1951–1984) in the form of discretionary grants on the advice of Planning Commission.

(f) *P.C. Compelling States to Levy More Taxes* : The Planning Commission has occasionally asked the states to levy more taxes to bear extra financial burden on account of plan projects. In March 1969 it had asked six states -- Andhra Pradesh, Haryana, Tamil Nadu, Mysore, Punjab and Uttar Pradesh -- to revise their water rates in order to mobilize resources for plans.[13] It takes non-plan surplus of the states into consideration for plan purposes and asks the latter to make special efforts to mobilize more taxes for plan purposes. Prof. Lakdawala, D.T., an eminent Indian economist, explains how the Planning Commission has interferred in the tax field of the states : "Since the non-plan surplus is regarded as an item of plan resources, the Finance Commission's tax-sharing also comes indirectly within the purview of the Planning Commission. Whereas the Finance Commission only compares, if at all, the tax system of different states with a view to guage the adequacy of tax effort, the Planning Commission's thrust is on additional resource mobilization so that the states are pressed to tax more and obtain greater non-tax revenues. This goes counter to the orthodox concept of federalism where states with varying tax systems and services offer the people the choice of residence and place of business."[14]

(g) *P.C. Controls Non-Surplus Revenues of States* : Prof. V.M. Dandekar, a noted economist, also opines that the Planning Commission tries to control non-surplus revenues of the states in the name of planning and interferes with the autonomy of the states : "The Finance Commission strives to leave as many states as possible with a surplus in their non-plan revenue accounts hoping that the states may then be free to use this surplus to finance planned development of their own conception. This does not happen. A state has no freedom to use its non-plan revenue surplus any more than it has to use the plan assistance from the union. The two are put together along with any additional finance resources it may be expected to raise and the expenditure of it all is subject to an overall plan approved by the Planning Commission. That is it. A state may have a non-plan surplus. It may be willing to raise additional resources. It will accept plan assistance of which a large part is in the form of loans which must be repaid. But it has no freedom, no autonomy in deciding the pattern of its development."[15]

(h) *Centre Controls State Subjects through P.C.* : The centre controls the state subjects through the Planning Commission. With the assistance of the Planning Commission, it has assumed the responsibility of planning the state development in state spheres like education, agriculture, health, social welfare, etc. The Planning Commission not only indicates broad national priorities and guidelines for programmes in the state spheres but also lays down standard in these spheres.

The Planning Commission is supposed to be an advisory body. But with the Prime Minister as the chairman and a few central ministers as members, it has not remained merely as an advisory body. Now it has assumed a role of the economic cabinet for the whole country. It has overshadowed the role of the statutory body like the Finance Commission.

The Finance Commission and the Planning Commission have been working in different directions in respect to state autonomy. The latter has brought the state plans into a national plan framework and does not leave sufficient spheres to the states to plan in their own way. It has thus curtailed state autonomy through plan formulation, plan targets and plan grants. On the other hand, the Finance Commission have tried to ensure financial autonomy of the states. As terms of references to the Finance Commission are limited to non-plan expenditure only, it has no say in plan expenditure. Recommendations of the Finance Commission relate to tax-sharing and statutory grants for the states. Tax-sharing is regarded as a matter of right for the states. Grants under article 275 are limited to non-plan deficits but can be conditional but generally are not. Thus the Finance Commissions have tried to ensure financial autonomy of the states.

Recommendations for distribution of plan grants and loans to the states have enabled the Planning Commission to retain its control over priorities and targets of state plans and their implementation. The Planning Commission has altered the profile of centre-state financial relations and has penetrated into state fields through plan assistance. It has given the position of donor to the centre and the position of recipient to the states.

Report of the Commission on Centre-State Relations (popularly known as Sarkaria Commission) has summarised the complaints of the states against penetration into state fields in general and decision-making process in particular by the Planning Commission: "A general complaint of the state governments is that they are required to adhere to unduly rigid and detailed union directives mainly because of their dependence on the union government for plan funds. The perceptions on these matters, however, vary. The views of the sate governments may be summed up as under : (i) Most of the states have maintained that they are not given due opportunity to participate in national planning.

The present process of consultation involving the states commences after the broad features of the five year plan are already cast. (ii) While most of the state governments agree that the Planning Commission should lay down broad national priorities and targets, they have urged that they should have greater freedom and flexibility in formulating the details of the schemes concerning their spheres. They complain that their initiative in this regard is restricted by (a) the procedure of detailed scrutiny and finalisation of state plans; (b) the mechanism of central assistance and earmarking of outlays; and (c) the control exercised by the union ministries through the centrally sponsored schemes.''[16]

4. ADVISORY BOARDS

The various central advisory boards also penetrate into state fields through their technical advice and clearance.

The states have to submit their plan proposals to the Planning Commission for latter's approval. The working groups in the Planning Commission make detailed scrutiny of state plan proposals. They also suggest modifications in the plan outlays of the states in accordance with the sectoral priorities and financial resources available for state plans. They also suggest cuts in the plan outlays which the states accept grudgingly.

The state governments have to get prior technical scrutiny and clearance from central technical boards for certain projects. Only after such clearance from the technical boards, the states can get central grants for their projects like irrigation, power projects, etc.

Major irrigation projects and those irrigation projects involving inter-state interests are to be cleared by the Directorate of Central Water Commission, Department of Environment and Ministry of Irrigation before they are submitted to the Central Advisory Committee of the Planning Commission. These central agencies take lot of time for detailed study of these irrigation and power projects. Such delay also amounts to interference with the state autonomy.

Prior clearance from the central Ministry of Works, Housing and Supply is necessary for schemes relating to industrial housing and slum clearance. There are also other boards whose clearance is necessary for other projects in the state sectors.

5. FINANCE COMMISSION

Though the Finance Commission is a statutory body, it is not totally independent in its composition, terms of reference and acceptance of its recommendations. Its members are appointed by the President of India on the advice of the central cabinet. Its member secretary is usually a senior central government officer. Its terms of reference are determined by the central government. The terms of reference exclude reference to plan expenditure (other than committed expenditure under the previous plans) and capital expenditure. Sometimes the central government has turned down the recommendations of the Finance Commission relating to loans, plan expenditure and special grants for specific fields of development.[17] In order to achieve plan targets, the centre has bypassed the Finance Commission in respect to developmental grants but has relied upon the Planning Commission for discretionary grants to the states.

6. CENTRAL FINANCIAL INSTITUTIONS

Banking and insurance subjects are placed in the central list. With the nationalisation of major banking and insurance institutions, the centre exercises immense control over the use of all financial savings. The states depend on these financial institutions for their internal debt and market borrowings. By controlling lending policies of these institutions, the centre can influence the programmes and projects in the state sector.

The table 3 gives a comparative picture of financial assistance made by the central financial institutions including Reserve Bank of India to the various state programmes and projects during 1978-79 and 1979-80.[18]

In addition to banking and insurance, a large number of central institutions like National Co-operative Development Corporation, the Central Social Welfare Board, Indian Dairy Corporation, etc., have come up under various central ministries. These institutions also exercise considerable influence over the choice of priorities of the states. Report of the Administrative Reforms Commission notes the increasing influence of these institutions on the choice of priorities of the states.[19]

TABLE 3

S. No.	Name of subject/service	Amount in Lakhs
1.	Housing	22,002
2.	Co-operatives	1,54,551
3.	Agriculture and Allied Services	2,66,619
4.	Dairy Development	8,027
5.	Fisheries	2,458
6.	Minor Irrigation	23,489
7.	Area Development	2,191
8.	Forestry	100
9.	Small Scale Industries	50,113
10.	Large Scale Industries and Minerals	1,58,241
11.	Electricity Generation and Transmission	1,33,940

7. ARTICLE 282

The financial arrangements envisaged in chapter I of part XII of the Indian Constitution are based on two assumptions : (a) The main assistance required by the states from the centre would be in the form of shares in central taxes and grants towards the recurring revenue expenditure of the states. (b) The Finance Commission would be the main instrument in determining tax-shares and grants under article 275. The grants under article 282 would be occasionally used for emergencies arising out of certain natural calamities like famine and flood.

Both assumptions have been relagated to the background by adoption of national Planning Commission and by extensive use of article 282 for transfer of plan grants from the centre to the states. There has been increase in the grants under article 282 as compared with the grants under article 275. Article 282 was not intended to be an important article in the centre-state financial relations. Shri K. Santhanam, a prominent member of the constituent assembly, explains how this article was viewed in the constituent assembly: "This was not intended to be one of the major provisions for making readjustments between the union and the states. If that was the idea, then there was no purpose in evolving such a complicated set of relations of shares, assignments and grants.... Therefore, in my view, this article was a residuary or reserve article to enable the union to deal with unforeseen contingencies. That was how this article was used both by the British government, and after transfer of power, before the first year of the First Five-Year Plan.... But this has now become a crucial article for the plan.''[20]

Now grants under article 282 have been extensively used for plan purposes without reference to the Finance Commission or passing a relevant statute. Practically there is no limit for making any quantity of grants from the centre to the states for plan purposes under the phrase 'public purpose' of article 282. The centre has been able to impose its will on the states in the formulation and execution of the plans by virtue of non-statutory grants under article 282. In his note to the Report of the Fourth Finance Commission, Dr.P.V. Rajamannar, a member of the Commission, opined that the use of article 282 for giving conditional grants to the states by the centre was not legitimate. Further he said that it was well recognised principle that the spending power of the states as well as of the centre in a federation is co-existence with their legislative powers and it is improper for the centre to spend for the purposes which are not covered by the union list.[21]

The table 4 indicates increasing trends in the quantity of grants under article 282 from the centre to the states.[22]

The trend continues to be the same even now with some variations.

8. FORMULA FOR FINANCIAL ASSISTANCE

Formulas for financial assistance have gone through four stages : (i) schematic transfer (1951–1969), (ii) Gadgil formula (1969–1980), (iii) modified Gadgil formula (1980–1990), and new formula of N.D.C (since 1990).

Plan projects under different heads had their own patterns of assistance from 1951 to 1969. The states were to get their grants and loans accordingly. Such funds could not be diverted to other heads of development without the approval from the centre. The central assistance was tied to heads and sub-heads of development as well as individual schemes. Central discretion was more in this schematic assistance.

TABLE 4

Conditional Grants Provided under Article 282 by the Union Government to the States in India

(Rs. in million)

States	1961-62	1962-63	1963-64	1964-65 (R)	1965-66 (B)
Andhra Pradesh	69.8	65.1	97.9	151.9	204.3
Assam	34.5	—	67.3	80.4	84.7
Bihar	94.6	114.1	105.7	134.4	170.6
Gujarat	35.3	41.4	37.2	58.0	70.0
Jammu & Kashmir	16.1	13.3	15.8	32.9	47.4
Kerala	45.5	48.6	17.6	69.0	84.6
Madhya Pradesh	112.0	105.6	106.1	168.5	169.8
Madras	N.A.	N.A.	N.A.	N.A.	N.A.
Maharashtra	N.A.	N.A.	N.A.	N.A.	N.A.
Mysore	64.0	49.8	61.2	62.4	133.3
Orissa	39.8	53.3	76.8	95.5	129.0
Punjab	54.9	65.8	78.8	112.2	156.0
Rajasthan	59.7	47.6	74.7	92.6	103.5
Uttar Pradesh	137.6	172.2	166.3	275.8	337.5
West Bengal	62.7	68.8	88.5	155.8	171.5
Total	826.5	845.6	1035.9	1588.5	1862.2

Note: (R) Revised Estimates.
(B) Budget Estimates.
N.A. Not available.

Source: Report of the Fourth Finance Commission, Government of India (New Delhi : 1965), pp.192-95.

Plan assistance has been given according to the formulas since 1969 until today. The three formulas have been in existence since 1969. Though central assistance is not tied to any individual schemes and projects, an element of discretion is still left with the centre. The central financial assistance is generally given in the form of grants (30%) and loans (70%) in order to ensure that overall priorities of the plans are adhered to. The centre has used grants as a weapon to influence priorities in the state sectors and the decisions of the state governments. Though the grants and loans are given by the centre to the states for plan purposes, according to the formulas, priorities, targets, outlays and total quantum of the state plans are subject to the approval of the central Planning Commission.

9. PLAN AND NON-PLAN GRANTS AND LOANS

(i) *Plan Grants*: Plan grants are meant, among other things, to execute programmes of national importance through state machinery. "This is a new type of federal financial assistance because it was not conceived by the framers of the Indian Constitution and also because this type of federal financial aid is not generally prevalent in other federations."[23] These plan grants are conditional, close ended and are provided under article 282. No legislative enactment is required to provide conditional grants under article 282 while legislative enactment is required to provide conditional grants under article 275. Consequently the centre has decided to provide all conditional grants under article 282 because procedure is flexible and simple and requires only executive action. As these grants have been provided for developmental purposes under five year plans and have assumed discretionary nature, they have penetrated into state fields and have influenced budgetary policies of the state governments much against their will.

There has been substantial increase in the quantum of plan grants from the centre to the states : "This is evident from the fact that plan grants which amounted to only Rs.7.8 crores in 1951-52 increased to Rs. 52.32 crores in 1955-56, to Rs. 82.08 crores in 1960-61, to Rs. 186.22 crores in 1965-66, to Rs. 269.4 crores in 1970-71 and further to Rs. 411.68 crores in 1973-74. During the fifth plan period (1974—79), plan grants amounted to Rs. 6361.44 crores. What is more, during the sixth plan period, plan grants further increased to Rs. 2964 crores in 1979-80....to Rs. 5099 crores in 1983-84."[24]

While the centre has sufficient resources, it has no socio-economic spheres for spending. While socio-economic welfare activities are within the jurisdiction of the states, the states have no adequate resources to carry out these developing programmes. Consequently the states are compelled to accept the central voluntary grants and loans. But the centre has successfully used financial assistance to dictate national programmes and policies to the states through the five year plans. "The effective use of this financial string has been openly admitted by the member-secretary to the third Finance Commission in the following words : 'Under the constitution, economic and social planning is a concurrent subject. But many functions undertaken in furtherance of the plan are entirely in the state field in respect of which the centre has no constitutional authority to require the states to execute the programme in any particular manner. The only way it can do so is by providing that at least for that part of the programme, which is considered to be of national importance, the states are given a financial inducement in the shape of tied grants to undertake and implement these schemes."[25]

(ii) *Non-Plan Grants*: Non-plan discretionary grants are not governed by objective criteria.

(iii) *Plan and Non-Plan Discretionary Grants* : Plan and non-plan discretionary grants have undermined the autonomy of the states by encroaching upon the state subjects through fiscal means. In spite of the formulas, there is an element of discretion in providing grants and loans. "Large scale discretionary transfers leave the area of fiscal transfers open for political bargaining and horse-trading."[26] In its replies to the questionnaires sent by the Sarkaria Commission, the government of Andhra Pradesh complained that the quantum of central voluntary grants and loans has made the states subservient : "It is seen that statutory transfers account for 40% while discretionary transfers 60% of total transfers. It is this preponderance of discretionary transfers (which are mostly in the form of loans) that negated the principle of viability of state unit and made states vulnerable in their relations with the union government."[27]

The table 5 gives a comparative picture of transfers through statutory body (Finance Commission) and non-statutory bodies (Planning Commission and central ministries) to the states from 1951–1984. The table clearly indicates the increasing quantum of central voluntary financial assistance to the states.[28]

TABLE 5

Resource Transfers (Gross) through Various Agencies, 1951–84

(Rs. in crores)

Plan Periods	Statutory Transfers	Plan Transfers	Directionary Transfers	Total
First Plan (1951–56)	447 (31.2)	350 (24.0)	634 (44.3)	1431
Second Plan (1956–61)	918 (32.0)	1058 (36.9)	892 (31.1)	2868
Third Plan (1961–66)	1590 (28.4)	2515 (44.9)	1495 (26.7)	5600
Three Annual Plans (1966–69)	1782 (33.3)	1767 (33.1)	1798 (33.6)	5347
Fourth Plan (1969–74)	5421 (35.9)	3535 (23.4)	6145 (40.7)	15101
Fifth Plan (1974–79)	10873 (43.0)	7722 (30.5)	6683 (26.4)	25278
Sixth Plan (1979–84)	22496 (41.0)	16055 (29.3)	16267 (29.7)	54818
Total (1951–84)	43527 (39.4)	33002 (29.9)	33914 (30.7)	110443

Note: Fifth and Sixth Plan periods taken for this study are different from the actual periods. This has been done so as to coincide with the award periods of the Sixth and Seventh Finance Commissions.

Source: Report of the Seventh Finance Commission (1978) for data on all plans other than the Sixth. For the Sixth Plan, Annual Studies of State Finance published in the R.B.I. Bulletin, various issues.

(iv) *Loans* : Under article 293(2), the centre provides short term loans to the states in the form of ways and means advances. Medium and long term loans are given by the centre to the states mainly from the Consolidated Fund of India. Loans are also given from the Special Developments built with the funds received in the form of foreign aid. In regard to schemes involving an element of foreign exchange the states are completely dependent on the centre. The Reserve Bank of India, a central financial institution, also provides ways and means advances to the state governments. A major chunk of central loans has been provided to the states on the advice of the Planning Commission. The states cannot raise loans in the open market without the consent of the centre if they are already indebted to the latter.

The centre determines terms and conditions of loans and does not consult the states about the rate of interest to be charged and repayment period of loans. Thus it regulates borrowing programmes of the states. The states are compelled to accept the priorities, strategies and mode of implementation of the schemes for which the centre provides loans.

There has been steady increase in the flow of loans from the centre to the states over the years. Consequently indebtedness of the states to the centre has also increased enormously. "Till the year ending 1983-84 the amount of loans on the state governments was Rs.3512 crores."[29]

10. RELIEF ASSISTANCE

The centre provides financial assistance to the states, under article 282, for drought relief, flood relief, etc. Political considerations enter into the decisions regarding relief assistance for natural calamities. The Telgu Desham government of Andhra Pradesh had complained that the centre discriminated against it in providing assistance for flood relief. The following table gives a comparative picture of estimated loss, assistance asked and assistance provided.[30]

TABLE 6

Central Assistance for Flood Relief to A.P.

(Rs. in crores)

Month/Year	Estimated Loss	Assistance asked by the State	Assistance given by the Centre
August 1983	520	260	19.25
October 1983	900	520	94.02
November 1984	200	114.86	37.08
August 1986	1,680	1,196.47	132
July 1989	530	450	--

Similar complaints have been made by other state governments against the central discretion in providing relief assistance from time to time. Such complaints have become frequent and vocal in recent years.

11. CENTRALLY SPONSORED SCHEMES

The centrally sponsored schemes give the central ministries concerned a great deal of influence over state subjects. The central ministries prescribe certain conditions with respect to coverage, methodology and staffing pattern of these schemes. The states which accept these schemes have to implement them in accordance with the outlines prepared by the central ministries. Further they have to make commitment that they would maintain staff and infrastructure even after completion of the schemes. The schemes are executed by the state governments under the technical guidance and supervision of the central ministries concerned. Funds are provided to these schemes on the basis of some norms and procedure. "Funds are released once in a quarter on the basis of expenditure in the previous quarter."[31] Many of these schemes relate to agriculture, health, family planning, welfare of backward classes, education, etc. Shri R.C.S. Sarkar, formerly Law Secretary, Government of India and former Chairman of the Union Public Service Commission, explains how the centrally sponsored schemes penetrate into the state autonomy by central supervision and control in the name of uniformity: "The assistance given to centrally sponsored plans is slightly different.

The centre has a more direct interest in them, and the central expenditure on them is a part of the central plan. As a logical corollary, the central share is liberal, the degree of supervision and control is detailed and uniformity is insisted on.''[32]

Though there has been demand for reduction in the number of centrally sponsored schemes from time to time, yet their number has not been declining consistently. The quantum of funds transferred through these schemes is massive. The booklet published by the government of Karnataka opines that the centrally sponsored schemes have penetrated into the state fields and have eroded the autonomy of the states: ''Most of the centrally sponsored schemes are beneficial to the state economy, but it is nevertheless necessary to limit the total quantum of central resources for funding these schemes for the following reasons: (a) The autonomy envisaged for state governments in the constitution is being increasingly eroded through resource transfer of such magnitude under such schemes. For Karnataka, the central resources-transfer under such schemes now is almost equal to the resources transfer under normal central plan assistance. Resources transferred by the centre under centrally sponsored schemes are akin to tied transfers where normal central plan assistance is in the nature of untied transfer. Unless the former category of transfers is more strictly limited, the division of powers between the union and the states contained in the seventh schedule of the constitution becomes increasingly notional; and (b) state governments perceive a number of organisational irritants in obtaining the clearance of centrally sponsored schemes from the ministries of the Government of India, as such clearance are often contingent on the ministries' satisfaction of minute details of schemes.''[33]

The central expenditure on centrally sponsored schemes has been increasing.[34] The table at next page (Table 7) gives a picture of growing investment in the centrally sponsored schemes.

The money invested in centrally sponsored schemes amounts to 40% of central plan assistance to the states during 1966–1984.[35] The central and centrally sponsored schemes continue to dominate the central plan assistance to the states even in recent years : ''In 1986-87, according to revised budget estimates, the central and centrally sponsored schemes accounted for 30.88 per cent of the total plan assistance to the states amounting to Rs. 9977.78 crores. If we confine our attention to plan grants only, the central and centrally sponsored schemes accounted for

TABLE 7

Period	Amount (Rs. in crores)
3rd Five Year Plan	223
4th Five Year Plan	1,332
5th Five Year Plan	1,639
6th Five Year Plan	3,350
1982-83	1,100
1983-84	1,746

50.27 only, the central and centrally sponsored schemes accounted for 50.27 per cent of the total plan grants amounting to Rs. 5,801.08 crores. According to the budget estimates for 1987-88, the central and centrally sponsored schemes account for 32.5 per cent in total plan assistance and 51.46 per cent in plan grants.''[36]

The table 8 gives a picture of distribution of central assistance to the centrally sponsored schemes and to the state plan according to the modified Gadgil formula during the period 1980–85.[37]

Though the centrally sponsored schemes penetrate into state fields, yet the states accept them with murmur because the schemes carry handsome central grants.

12. CENTRAL EXPENDITURE ON STATE SUBJECTS

The centre spends huge amount on certain state subjects through its own departments directly and through plan and non-plan schemes indirectly. By referring to the figures of the sixth plan outlays for the centre, the states and the union territories, Sarkaria Commission points out growing percentage of central expenditure on state subjects.[38] About 43 per cent of outlay on agriculture and rural development was in the central sector plan. In the sphere of village and small industries, the central plan outlay accounts for about 52 per cent of the total outlay. Under health, housing, urban development and water supply the outlay in the central sector plan is quite sizable.

Growing central expenditure on state subjects through these means clearly indicates that the centre has penetrated into state fields.

13. POLITICAL AND ADMINISTRATIVE MEANS OF PENETRATION

One party domination, office of the Prime Minister, central ministries, central secretariat, national conferences and seminars influence policies and programmes of the states. They also facilitate flow of central assistance to the states and thus help the process of central penetration into state spheres.

(a) *One Party Domination* : The Congress party has ruled at the centre and in many states for longest period in independent India. The centralized character of the Congress party has compelled the Congress ruled states to accept both central political direction and central financial assistance without murmur in public. Only non-Congress ruled states make public protest against central penetration but silently accept financial assistance from the centre.

Policies are determined by the central Congress leaders and are implemented by the central and state governments. Grants are provided by the centre to implement such policies. Deviation from the centrally decided policies and programmes are looked with disfavour by the party high command and the central government. Policies relating to state subjects like agriculture, health, education, social welfare, etc., are determined by the central Congress leadership and the state governments are asked to formulate their policies in conformity with the national policies. Implementation of these policies is ensured through joint conferences of central and state ministries and administrators.

The non-Congress rule at the centre has been very short and has tried to follow the Congress pattern with an element of democratic participation by the states.

(b) *Office of the Prime Minister* : The Prime Minister plays an importance role in influencing the states to accept the central grants and loans to carry out centrally determined schemes. Pt. Jawaharlal Nehru's charismatic personality was responsible for acceptance of central grants by the states to execute plan programmes. Assertive Prime Minister like Smt. Indira Gandhi would threaten the states by withholding or delaying financial assistance to them. *The Tribune* reported : "The Prime Minister, Mrs. Gandhi, is reported to have recently made in a speech in which she threatened that if the centre wanted, it could make a state government fall in less than half an hour by stopping all financial aid to it."[39]

TABLE 8

Assistance for Centrally Sponsored Schemes and Central Assistance for the State Plans in the Sixth Plan 1980—85

State	Assistance for C.S.S.* (Actuals) (Rs. crores)	Assistance for C.S.S.* % to Total	Assistance for C.S.S.* distributed as per Gadgil Formula (Rs. crores)	% to Total	Col. 2—Col. 3 Rs. crores	Per Capita assistance for C.S.S.* on the basis of Col. 2 Rs.	Per Capita assistance for C.S.S.* on the basis of Col. 3 Rs.	Total C.A.** for State Plans under Gadgil Formula (Rs. crores)	% to Total	Per Capita for C.A.** under Gadgil Formula (Rs. crores)
(1)	(2)	(3)	(4)	(5)	(6)	(7)	(8)	(9)	(10)	(11)
I. **General Category States**										
A. *Developed States*										
1. Gujarat	510.44	5.87	365.36	4.20	+145.08	191.20	136.85	443.11	4.09	165.98
2. Haryana	215.18	2.47	189.64	2.18	+25.24	214.39	188.94	218.63	2.02	217.82
3. Karnataka	450.69	5.18	384.50	4.42	+66.19	153.82	131.23	482.72	4.45	164.76
4. Maharashtra	808.13	9.29	589.80	6.78	+218.33	160.31	117.00	765.27	7.06	151.80
5. Punjab	233.54	2.68	236.62	2.72	—3.08	172.34	174.61	272.44	2.51	201.05
6. West Bengal	499.31	5.74	526.30	6.05	—26.99	112.68	118.77	678.62	6.26	153.15

– *Contd.*

(1)	(2)	(3)	(4)	(5)	(6)	(7)	(8)	(9)	(10)	(11)
B. *Backward States*										
7. Andhra Pradesh	855.88	9.84	766.39	8.81	+89.49	196.74	176.17	935.98	8.63	215.15
8. Bihar	850.96	9.78	1116.97	12.84	—266.01	151.01	198.21	1415.14	13.05	251.12
9. Kerala	291.87	3.36	360.14	4.14	—68.29	136.73	168.71	442.34	4.08	207.21
10. Madhya Pradesh	861.70	9.91	806.41	9.27	+55.29	206.87	193.60	996.61	9.19	239.26
11. Orissa	509.00	5.85	577.62	6.64	—68.62	231.94	263.21	676.52	6.24	308.28
12. Rajasthan	488.22	5.61	547.18	6.29	—58.96	189.48	212.37	694.78	6.41	269.65
13. Tamil Nadu	655.87	7.54	549.79	6.32	+106.08	159.20	133.45	698.82	6.45	169.62
14. Uttar Pradesh	1468.34	16.88	1682.41	19.34	—214.07	166.21	190.44	2119.36	19.56	239.91
Total A+B (I)	8699.13	100.00	8699.13	100.00	—	169.11	169.11	10840.34	100.00	210.73

C.S.S.* = Centrally Sponsored Scheme. C.A.** = Central Assistance.

N.B.: Per capita central assistance has been worked out on the basis of 1981 population.

(c) *Central Ministries* : The Planning Commission recommends matching grants for various schemes. On the basis of recommendations, the central ministries provide grants to the state ministries concerned. For example, the central agriculture ministry provides grants to the agriculture ministries of the states. Through these grants the central ministries penetrate into state fields. Though the constitution has established a territorial federation, the matching grants have created a vertical federation.[40]

Some of the central ministries spend huge amount on state subjects. The West Bengal government has pointed out in its memorandum to the third Finance Commission that there has been more increase in the central expenditure on state subjects than on the central subjects. Table 9 gives a comparative pictutre of central expenditure on state and central subjects.[41]

The central ministries which release the grants are in a position to exercise some sort of control over corresponding ministries in the states. Referring to the control of the Central Ministry of Community Development over its counterpart in the states, Shri P.R. Dubhashi, an ex-I.A.S. Officer, who had worked in both the centre and the states,

TABLE 9

(Rs. in millions)

Subjects State/Central	1957-58	1960-61	Percentage Increase
State Subjects			
1. Education	210	454	116
2. Medical	45	88	95
3. Public Health	87	120	38
4. Agriculture	113	155	36
5. Animal Husbandry	95	—	—
6. Co-operation	10	35	250
Central Subjects			
1. External Affairs	70	104	48
2. Defence Services	2740	2930	07

thus says : "Over the years the union and state organisations have worked in such great unison that the union ministry has found it possible to use the state organisation as almost its direct operational instrument rather than as a distinct administration of an autonomous unit of a federal structure."[42] In 1984 Shri P. Kolandaivelu, ex-minister of Tamil Nadu, has questioned the existence of certain central ministries corresponding to the state ministries and has criticised penetration of these central ministries into state fields: "The Government of India is maintaining vast administrative hierarchy even in areas like agriculture, education, health and many other related economic and social fields which are essentially the responsibility of the states. Even in matters in which the states should have been encouraged to take significant initiative, the central ministries tend to impose on the states. The continuation of central jurisdiction over quite a number of subjects can only cause delay and waste. There is no point in having vast control establishments in the subjects like agriculture, education and health."[43]

(d) *Central Secretariat* : An ex-secretary of the central government, Shri A.N. Jha, explains how the central secretariats are also responsible for central penetration into the state fields: "The secretariats including that of the Planning Commission have tended to think out problems..... on an all India scale and have tended to assume that deviations from their way of thinking are acts of sacrilege.... In practice, however, we secretaries and our advisers insist on laying down the policy even for subjects that concern the states alone."[44] The central secretariats have weight in relation to the states due to the central financial assistance to the states for plan and non-plan purposes.

(e) *Conferences* : It has become practice to hold the conferences of ministers, secretaries and heads of departments relating to every state subject. These conferences are intended to secure co-operation of the states. But they also provide convenient means to enforce central direction which is backed up by central financial assistance. The states which are in need of financial assistance to implement a number of plan and no-plan projects are compelled to accept both central direction and central financial assistance. The agenda of these conferences would indicate thinking of the central ministries.[45] Important decisions relating to state subjects are taken in these conferences.

(f) *Central Literature* : Hundreds of books, pamphlets, manuals, reports, reviews, posters, folders, etc., concerning state subjects are brought out by the centre and are sent to the states for information and guidance. Such literature do influence thinking and course of actions of the state governments.

REFERENCES

1. Santhanam, K., *Union-State Relations in India* (Bombay : Asia Publishing House, 1960), p. 44.
2. Hicks, Ursula K., *Federalism : Failure and Success–A Comparative Study* (London: The Macmillan Press Ltd., 1978), p. 108.
3. Sinha, R.K., *Fiscal Federalism in India* (New Delhi: South Asian Publishers Pvt. Ltd., 1980), p. 82.
4. Asok Chandra, *Institutional Base of Centre-State Relations* in B.L. Maheshwari (ed.), *Centre-State Relations in Seventies* (Calcutta : Minerva Association, 1973), p. 139.
5. Santhanam, K., *Union-State Relations in India* (Bombay : Asia Publishing House, 1960), p. 45.
6. *Ibid.*, p. 47.
7. Jha, A.N., "Planning, The Federal Principle and Parliamentary Democracy", *The Indian Journal of Public Administration,* Vol. XI, No. 2, April-June 1965 (New Delhi : I.I.P.A., 1965), p. 169.
8. Ramachandran, G., *Union-State Relations in Finance and Planning,* The Indian Journal of Public Administration, Vol. XII, No. 3, July-September 1966 (New Delhi : I.I.P.A., 1966), p. 380.
9. Rao, V.K.R.V., *Key Note Address in Seminar on Centre-State Relations,* Bangalore, August 5-7, 1983, organised by the Economic and Planning Council, Government of Karnataka, in Association with the Institute for Social and Economic Change, Bangalore and the Centre for Policy Research, New Delhi (Bangalore : Government Press, Government of Karnataka, 1983), p. 25.
10. *Report of the Centre-State Relations Inquiry Committee* (Popularly known as Rajamannar Report) (Madras : Government of Tamil Nadu, 1971), p.106.
11. Paranjape, H.K., *Centre-State Relations in Planning* (New Delhi : The Indian Institute of Public Administration, 1970), p. 37.
12. *Gopal, B., Dynamics of Centre-State Relations : Experience of Andhra Pradesh Since 1983,* The Indian Journal of Political Science, Vol. L, No.3, July-September 1989 (Madras : The Indian Political Science Association, 1989). pp. 365-66.
13. Deole, D.R., *Central Assistance for Planned Economic Development of the States With Special Reference to Madhya Pradesh* (Unpublished thesis; Thesis submitted to Vikram University, Ujjain, 1977), p. 57.
14. Lakdawala, D.T., *Planning and Centre-State Relations* in H.V.R. Athre (ed.), *Union-State Relations* (Bangalore : The Mysore Economic Review, 1986), pp. 137-38.
15. Dandekar, V.M., *Unitary Elements in a Federal Constitution,* Economic and Political Weekly, Vol. XXII, No. 44, October 31, 1987 (Bombay : Sameeksha Trust Publication, 1987), p. 1869.
16. *Report, Commission on Centre-State Relations* (Popularly known as Sarkaria

Commission), Part I (Nasik : Printed by the General Manager, Government of India Press, 1988), pp. 366 and 367.

17. Rao, V.K.R.V., *Centre-State Financial Relations in India* (Bangalore : Institute for Social and Economic Change, 1973), pp.7 and 8.

18. George, K.K. and Gulati, I.S., *Central Inroads into State Subjects : An Analysis of Economic Services,* Economic and Political Weekly, Vol. XX, No. 14, April 6, 1985 (Bombay : A Sameeksha Trust Publication, 1985), p. 600.

19. Report, Administrative Reforms Commission, Referred by George, K.K. and Gulati, I.S., *Centre-State Resource Transfers : An Appraisal,* Economic and Political Weekly, Vol. XX, No.7, February 16, 1985 (Bombay : A Sameeksha Trust Publication, 1985), p. 293.

20. Santhanam, K., *Union-State Relations in India* (Bombay : Asia Publishing House, 1960), pp. 40-41.

21. *Report of the (Fourth) Finance Commission* (Delhi : The Manager of Publications, Government of India, 1965), pp. 90-92.

22. Thimmaiah, G., *Federal Fiscal Systems of Australia and India : A Study in Comparative Relevance* (New Delhi : Associated Publishing House, 1976), p. 274.

23. ——, *"Plan Grants in India : A Critical Evaluation", The Indian Journal of Public Adminstration,* Vol. XXIII, No. 2, April-June 1976 (New Delhi : I.I.P.A., 1976)

24. ——, *Burning Issues in Centre-State Relations* (New Delhi : Ashish Publishing House, 1985), p.113.

25. *Report of the Third Finance Commission* (New Delhi : The Manager of Publications, Government of India, 1962), p. 56 Quoted by G.Thimmaiah, *Burning Issues in Centre-State Relations* (New Delhi : Ashish Publishing House, 1985), p. 98.

26. George, K.K., *Centre-State Financial Flows and Inter-State Disparities in India* (Unpublished thesis; Thesis submitted to the University of Cochin for Ph. D. Degree, 1983), p. 165.

27. *Report, Commission on Centre-State Relations* (Popularly known as Sarkaria Commission), Part II (Nasik : Printed by the General Manager, Government of India Press, 1987), p. 57.

28. George, K.K., *Discretionary Budgetary Transfers – A Review,* in I.S. Gulati (ed.), *Centre-State Budgetary Transfers* (Bombay : Published for Sameeksha Trust by Oxford University Press, 1987), p. 148.

29. Sharma, N.K., "Evolving Programmatic Centre-State Financial Relations", *Yojna,* Vol. 30, No. 6, April 1-15, 1986, (New Delhi : Director, Publications Division, Government of India, 1986). p. 12.

30. Gopal, B., "Dynamics of Centre-State Relations : Experience of Andhra Pradesh Since 1983", *The Indian Journal of Political Science,* Vol. L, No. 3, July-September, 1989 (Madras : The Indian Political Science Association 1989), p. 367.

31. *Administrative Reforms Commission; Report on Machinery for Planning* (New Delhi : Cyclostyled copy in the library of the Central Planning Commission, 1968), p. 53.

32. Sarkar, R.C.S., *Union-State Relations in India* (New Delhi : National Publishing House, 1986), p. 123.

33. *Centrally Sponsored Schemes : An Instrument for Centralization in Planning* (Bangalore: Special Studies Division, Planning Department, Government of Karnataka, 1988), pp. 4 and 5.

34. Lakdawala, D.T., *Planning and Centre-State Relations* in H.V.R. Athre (ed.), *Union and State Relations* (Bangalore : The Mysore Economic Review, 1986), p.140.
35. *Ibid.*, p.140.
36. Dandekar, V.M., "Unitary Elements in Federal Constitution", *Economic and Political Weekly*, Vol. XXII, No. 44, October 31, 1987 (Bombay : Sameeksha Trust Publication, 1987), p. 1869.
37. *Centrally Sponsored Schemes : An Instrument for Centralisation in Planning* (Bangalore : Special Studies Division, Planning Department, Government of Karnataka, 1988), p.10.
38. *Report, Commission on Centre-State Relations,* Part I (Popularly known as Sarkaria Commission) (Nasik : Printed by the General Manager, Government of India Press, 1988), p. 375.
39. *The Tribune,* November 8, 1982, p. 4. Quoted by Chandra Pal, *Greater Fiscal Autonomy : A Justified Demand of States,* Cochin University Law Review 7(3), September, 1983 (Cochin : University of Cochin, 1983), p. 243.
40. Santhanam, K., *Union-State Relations in India* (Bombay : Asia Publishing House, 1960), p. 54.
41. Asok Chandra, *Federalism in India : A Study of Union-State Relations* (London : George Allen and Unwin Ltd., 1965), p. 283.
42. Dubhashi, P.R., "Unitary Trends in a Federal System", *The Indian Journal of Public Administration,* Vol. VI, No. 3, 1960, p. 250 ; Quoted by Raman Bombwall, *Federal Financial Relations in India* (Meerut : Meenakshi Prakashan, 1968), p. 53.
43. Kolandaivelu, P., *Financial and Economic Issues in Centre-State Relations,* Paper presented at Seminar on Centre-State Relations, 5-8 January, 1984, organised by Tamil Nadu Academy of Political Science, Madras, p.10 (Papers are in cyclostyled form and are available in Madras Institute of Development Studies, Madras).
44. Jha, A.N., "Planning, The Federal Principle and Parliamentary Democracy", The Indian Journal of Public Adminístation, Vol. XI, No. 2, April-June 1965 (New Delhi : I.I.P.A., 1965), p. 165.
45. Dubhashi P.R., "Unitary Trends in a Federal System", *The Indian Journal of Public Administration,* Vol. VI, No. 3, July-September 1960 (New Delhi : I.P.P.A., 1960), p. 254.

CHAPTER VII

AREAS OF PENETRATION BY THE CENTRE

I. INTRODUCTION

A large part of central expenditure on plan projects in the state sector is concerned with schemes relating to education, agriculture, co-operation, village and small scale industries, community development, panchayat raj institutions, health, etc. Centre's penetration into state and concurrent subjects is both direct and indirect. Its direct penetration is through expenditure incurred by its departments and agencies and indirect penetration is through plan and non-plan schemes.

The centre has some ministries like agriculture, health, education, etc., which correspond with the state ministries. Over the years the central ministries have come to perform staff functions and the state ministries have come to perform line functions.[1] The former have come to depend on the latter for implementation of plan projects relating to state subjects. Such dependence is sustained by central financial assistance to the states.

2. REASONS FOR PENETRATION

There are several reasons why the centre has penetrated into state fields through the central grants and loans. Among these several reasons, three important reasons are listed here and references to other reasons are made elsewhere in this study.

(i) *Planning*: With the introduction of planning in India, the scheme of distribution of taxes between the centre and the states has created problem of imbalance between resources and functions at the state level. The framers of the Indian Constitution relied more on shared taxes than on grants and loans for reducing financial deficit of the states. The actual developments have gone beyond the expectations of the framers of the Indian Constitution. Consequently the role of the Finance Commission as an umpire in the centre-state financial relations has been reduced to great extent by the operation of five year plans. The planning process has helped the centre to penetrate into state fields through plan grants and loans.

(ii) *Imbalance between Resources and Functions* : There is imbalance between the resources and function of the states. The states are put in charge of socio-economic services with inelastic resources while the centre is entrusted with elastic resources without jurisdiction over welfare activities. Such imbalance has compelled the states to depend on the central grants and loans to implement various socio-economic programmes. Memorandum submitted by the United Left Front Government of Kerala to the National Development Council explains why the central grants have become inevitable to the states : "Under the division of functions envisaged in the constitution, the responsibility for providing social and econommic overheads for development is that of the states, but the power to raise main resources vests with the union government. Within a few years of coming into force of the constitution it was found that resources of considerable magnitude had to be transferred to the states to enable them to implement the plans. It was found that the device of sharing taxes under article 268 to 272 was totally inadequate to meet the new demands, and substantial grants-in-aid had to be given under both articles 275 and 282 of the Constitution"[2] The central grants under article 282 have enabled the centre to penetrate into state fields in various forms.

(iii) *Unwillingness to Levy More Taxes* : One of the reasons for central penetration into the exclusive sphere of state jurisdiction is unwillingness of the states to tap their own tax resources with sufficient vigour. The states would like to depend on the Finance Commission to recommend greater devolution of central resources and grants-in-aid to them. The report of the third Finance Commission thus comments on the states' dependence on its recommendations and unwillingness to tap tax resources in the rural sector: "Secure in the knowledge that the annual budgetary gap would be fully covered by devolution of union resources and grants-in-aid, the states are tending to develop an allergy to tap resources in the rural sector on many considerations and also a disinclination to make up the leeway in others."[3] Many states have not made serious attempts to levy taxes in rural area but have abolished land revenues of marginal and small land-holders. Though at one time land revenue was the backbone of the provincial revenues, its importance has declined due to many factors. The rural rich are not adequately taxed. As the states have not sufficiently developed their own resources, they have to depend on the central grants and loans. The centre does not provide grants and loans without conditions.

3. AREAS OF PENETRATION

The centre has made penetration into many fields of states. However, a few state fields like education, agriculture, co-operation, village and small scale industries, community development, panchayat raj institutions, health, etc., are taken up in this study to point out how the centre has penetrated into state fields.

(a) *Education* : Though the Constitution has divided education between the centre and the states, education mainly belongs to the states. Education under all stages including university education is given to the states under entry 11 of the state list subject to the provisions of the Constitution like entries 63, 64, 65 and 66 of the cental list and entry 25 of the concurrent list. Under entry 63, institutions of national importance are to be run by the centre. Under entry 64, institutions of scientific or technical education financed by the centre and declared by the Parliament to be of national importance are under the control of the centre. Under entry 65, research bodies, professional and vocational institutions are under the control of the centre. Entry 66 entrusts co-operation and determination of standards of higher education and research and technical institutions to the centre. Entry 25 in the concurrent list deals with vocational and technical training for labour. In 1976 through 42nd amendment to the Constitution, education is put under concurrent list. Still major and vast activities of education are carried on by the states.

Between 1950 and 1976 education had informally become concurrent subject for the following reasons : (a) The Congress has been in power in the centre and in many states for a number of years. It was responsible for uniform policy of education for the whole country. (b) Charismatic leadership of Pt. Jawaharlal Nehru and Smt. Indira Gandhi did not allow the states to raise the question of state autunomy in the field of education. (c) Large quantity of financial assistance was made available to the states on the advice of the Planning Commission for development of education.

Education which had been informally concurrent subject from 1950–1976 was formally and officially put into concurrent list in 1976 through 42nd amendment. The amendment was the result of the Sawarn Singh Committee. The committee had opined that education is a subject of great national importance to achieve socio-economic changes. Moreover, the constitutional commitments could not be fulfilled by the states alone. As the centre did not have much hold on education, the committee recommended that education might be placed under concurrent list.

Central penetration in the field of state education can be studied with reference to three aspects of education – policy formulation, administration and finance.

Educational planning originates from the centre. The central ministry of education (now called Human Resources Development) formulates national policy and determines priorities. The bureau of planning in the central ministry of education works in close collaboration with the education division in the Planning Commission. The latter prepares guidelines for forthcoming plan in advance. The guidelines are sent to the educational ministries of the centre and the states. These ministries prepare the educational plans. After scrutiny by the Planning Commission, these educational plans are incorporated in the central and state plans. The centre plays an important role in planning educational policies. The Seventh Five Year Plan explains the role of the centre in the field of education : "The provision for education is mainly in the state's sector. The centre will play a co-ordinating role and provide leadership and guidance for new and innovotive programmes."[4] The list of policy programmes contained in the booklet, 'National Policy on Education', published by the central ministry of Human Resources Development clearly indicates that the educational policy will be comprehensive, uniform and standardised in order to achieve certain national goals :[5] (i) early childhood care and education, (ii) elementary education, non-formal education and operation blackboard, (iii) secondary education and navodaya vidyalayas, (iv) vocalization of education, (v) higher education, (vi) open university and distance education, (vii) rural universities and institutes, (viii) technical and management education, (ix) making the system work, (x) delinking degrees from jobs and manpower planning, (xi) research and development, (xii) education for women's equality, (xiii) education of scheduled castes/scheduled tribes, and other backward sections, (xiv) minorities' education, (xv) education of the handicapped, (xvi) adult education, (xvii) content and process of school education, (xviii) evaluation process and examination reforms, (xix) youth and sports, (xx) language development, (xxi) cultural perspective, (xxii) media and educational technology (including use of computer in education), (xxiii) teachers and their training, and (xxiv) management education. The list of these items clearly indicates that the centre makes policy decisions in regard to nature, scope, relevance, and framework of education from early childhood education to university education, from adult education to distance education, and from vocational education to technical and professional education. Though the states are consulted in planning these programmes, yet overall responsibility for preparation of new education system is taken over by the centre. The states have to implement these programmes because the centre provides financial assistance to many of these programmes.

The central ministry of education evaluates the performance of implementation of various educational programmes prepared by it. It also makes suggestions in the light of its evaluation of programmes. It convenes the meeting of the educational ministries and secretaries of the states from time to time to review the educational programmes and projects.

As the constitution has vested elastic and growing financial resources in the centre, the states have to depend on central financial assistance for effective implementation of national education programmes. The centre wants to give conditional grants while the states insist on unconditional grants. Shri J.P. Naik, an eminent educationist, explains controversy between centre and states and views of educationists in this respect : "The major problem here is whether the grants given by the centre to the states be tied to certain educational objectives or not. The state governments naturally prefer to have grants which are not tied up to any programme, including education. On the other hand, the centre may prefer – and in this it has the support of the vast majority of educators to give tied grants for educational development."[6] In all the five year plans tied grants have been given by the centre to the states for educational purposes. Through the financial assistance the centre has been able to penetrate into state education.

In the modern scientific age, the Indian higher education has expanded rapidly and has put severe strain on the traditional resources of the states. Expansion and research in university education is not possible without grants from the centre. The academic community in higher education has not rejected the central aid for expansion and research but has been demanding more and more central aid for various purposes. The state governments cannot ignore the demands of the academic community and are compelled to accept the central aid. Though fear of central control persists, yet the state governments have not refused the central aid.

University Grants Commission, a central institution, provides development grants, but not block grant, to the universities. It prescribed conditions for grants to be used for specific purposes. Grants are provided for appointment of staff, purchase of books, journals and equipments, construction of buildings, examination reforms, faculty improvement programmes, introduction of new courses, research programmes, leadership projects, seminars, conferences, etc. Proposals from the universities must be based on the guidelines issued by the U.G.C. and are to be sent for the approval of the latter. The U.G.C. also sends committees of experts to examine the needs and standards of the university departments. On the basis of recommendations of the committees, the U.G.C. allocates funds. The universities which do not comply with the recommendations of the committees of the experts and the guidelines issued by the U.G.C. will not get grants.

When the programmes of U.G.C. are accepted by the universities and the state governments, some matching contributions are to be made by the state governments. The U.G.C. provides grants for development but not for maintenance. Many development schemes come under maintenance provision after a stipulated period. The state governments have to provide grants to the universities to maintain these schemes and projects. With the financial assistance from U.G.C., both the central control and expenditure of the states on higher education will increase.

Similarly U.G.C. assistance to the colleges is generally on sharing basis and is subject to certain conditions prescribed by the former. If the colleges are to receive financial assistance from the U.G.C., they must be recognised by U.G.C. The U.G.C. has prescribed certain terms and conditions like minimum students enrolment, faculty strength, etc., to receive grants. It has set up College Development Councils (C.D.C) in the universities to co-ordinate the development of colleges. It provides funds for College Science Improvement Programme (COSIP) and College Humanities and Social Sciences Improvement Programme (COHSSIP). It also provides funds for women, scheduled castes and scheduled tribes for higher education.

Thus the centre penetrates into the higher education through the University Grants Commission. The U.G.C. determines and maintains standards of teaching, examination and research in the universities and colleges by allocating distributing grants among them.

(b) *Agriculture* : Agriculture has been placed as entry 14 in the state list along with some ancillary matters while some agriculture related items have been placed in the concurrent list and central list. However, agriculture is primarily the responsiblility of the states because substantial matters relating to agriculture are placed in the state list. They include all aspects of agriculture, animal husbandry, irrigation, land records, land revenue, agricultural income tax, etc. Entry dealing with agriculture in the concurrent list is 33. It deals with trade and commerce, production, supply and distribution of some goods, foodstuff, edible oil seeds, oils, cattle fodder, oilcakes, raw cotton, raw jute, etc. The centre derives its powers over agriculture through indirect means like price control, produciton and distribution of food-stuffs including edible oil, raw cotton, raw jute, inter-state rivers, labour relations, commerce and industry, finance and taxations, banking and insurance, etc.

Since the Second World War the centre's interest in agriculture has been increasing due to crisis in food supply. It has taken initiative in modernising agriculture in order to feed ever growing population of India. Since the adoption of five year plan in 1951 it has taken a lead role in agricultural development. Its leading role in agricultural development is in part the result of its greater command over financial resources needed to make discretionary grants to the states for implementation of plan projects relating to agriculture. A very large share of the central aid flows to the agricultural sector. Irrigation and flood control projects are largely dependent on central financial assistance.

The centre plays an important role in policy-making, determining priorities for various crops and finding out resources to achieve the targets in the agricultural sector. "The pattern of development of cash crops and state research programmes have also been influenced by central aid."[7] The Planning Commission provides broad framework of agricultural policies for the state plans. It determines broad priorities for food and cash crops keeping in view the position of balance of payments. It also indicates the total resources including foreign exchange available for agricultural development. It also suggests land reforms for socio-economic purposes. The centre decides the size of food reserves to be built at the national level. Even the Directorate of Economics and Statistics of Ministry of Agriculture at the centre plays an important role as an expert agency in planning agricultural production and policy. Its advice is based

TABLE I

Central Assistance to States under different heads of development under Second and Third Plans

(Rs. in crores)

Sl. No.	Head of Development	Second Plan			Third Pland		
		Loan	Grant	Total	Loan	Grant	Total
	1	2	3	4	5	6	7
1.	Agricultural programmes*	112.70	47.00	159.00	289.04	113.81	402.85
2.	Community Development and Panchayats	48.00	63.00	111.00	82.77	126.50	209.27
3.	Co-operation	12.00	7.00	19.00	17.64	12.32	29.96
	Total of 2 & 3	60.00	70.00	130.00	100.41	138.82	239.23
	Total of 1 to 3	172.00	117.00	289.00	389.45	252.63	642.08
4.	Irrigation (Major & Medium)	380.00	-	380.00	580.00	-	580.00
5.	Flood control, drainage and anti-water logging schemes	48.00	-	48.00	87.00	-	87.00
	Total of 4 & 5	428.00	-	428.00	667.00	-	667.00
	Total of 1 to 5	600.00	117.00	717.00	1,056.45	252.63	1,309.08
	Total Central assistance for all programmes			1,058.00			2,515.30

*Including Minor Irrigation, Animal Husbandry, Dairying and Milk Supply, Fisheries, Forests, Soil Conservation and Warehousing and Marketing.

Note : Figures are only approximate. These, however, do not include Union Territories. Centrally Sponsored Schemes are covered.

Source : Plan documents relating to Second Plan, Annual Report, Ministry of Irrigation & Power, 1969-70, pp. 38 & 46, Annual Reports for Department of Community Development for 1962-63 to 1966-67, and Reviews of Cooperative Movement, R.B.I.

on "data collected by it regarding crops estimates, price behaviour, cost of production of various crops, farm management studies, etc."[8] Thus the central government and the Planning Commission play a vital role in the agricultural sector. The states have been unable to influence the size and contents of agriculture policies in any substantial way.

The centre has been providing financial assistance in the form of grants and loans to the states for agricultural development since the first five year plan. The table I shows the central assistance to agriculture, community development, etc., during the Second and the Third Five Year Plan.[9]

What is true of these plans is also true of subsequent plans. The trends in the increase of central assistance to agriculture and allied subjects has continued in the subsequent plans with variations.

The centre penetrates into the state field of agriculture through its expenditure on agriculture and allied subjects. Through entry 33 of the concurrent list, it covers trade, commerce, production, supply and distribution of food-stuffs including edible oil and oil seeds. "Of the total budgetary expenditure on food, the centre's involvement amounts to 96 per cent. In fact this head is the largest single head of expenditure of the centre within the group, agriculture and allied services, accounting for 43 per cent of the total. It is to be noted, however, that 92 per cent of the centre's expenditure under this head was on food subsidies. It will be appropriate to note here that funds required for procurement, storage and distribution are raised by the central agency responsible for their administration, *viz.*, Food Corporation of India, from the commercial banking system. Food credit amounted to Rs. 3000 crores at the end of June 1979 and formed 16 per cent of the total credit of the banking system."[10]

The centre has been spending huge amount on various agricultural items like major and minor irrigation, soil and water conservation, area development, food, animal husbandry, dairy development, fisheries, forests, manures, fertilizers, agricultural research, schemes for small farmers, marginal farmers and agricultural labourers, cattle, sheep and wool development, etc. Out of total expenditure on agriclutre, the centre's expenditure on this head directly and indirectly account for two-thirds.[11] Though agriculture is substantially state subject under entry 14 of the state list, yet the central expenditure on agriculture is substantially very heavy.

Two commissions appointed by the government of India have noted central penetration in the state field of agriculture. The Setalvad Study Group on Centre-State Relationships of the Administrative Reforms Commission (1969) has noted that the centre has been spending huge amount directly and indirectly on agriculture through plan and non-plan schemes. The Sarkaria Commission (1988) opined that the centre has made deep inroads into state agriculture by introducing a number of centrally sponsored schemes: "It is a matter of concern that in an area which is primarily the responsibility of the states, the number of centrally sponsored schemes keeps on increasing unduly and along with it the concomitant union direction and control."[12]

(c) *Co-operation* : Though co-operative societies come under the state list (entry 32), yet the central budget includes expenditure on co-operation. The centre also depends on many central and centrally sponsored schemes relating to co-operation. In addition to these direct and indirect budgetary roles, the central financial institutions like the Reserve Bank of India, Life Insurance Corporation of India, Agricultural Refinance and Development Corporation, National Co-operative Development Corporation, Commercial banks, etc., play and important role in the field of co-operation. These institutions are the major sources of finance to the co-operative institutions in the states.

(d) *Village and Small Scale Industries* : The centre has also penetrated into the field of village and small scale industries. Though these industries are in the state list, yet the centre has made penetration through grants, loans, subsidies, etc. The following table indicates the central involvement in these industries.[13]

(*E*) *C.D. and P.R.I.* : The centre has made penetration into the state fields like Community Development (C.D.) and Panchayat Raj Institutions (P.R.I.). Earlier the community development was a major programme of the states. The centre had a separate ministry called Ministry of Community Development. It was providing financial assistance to the states for community development. Later on the various activities of the community development were entrusted to the panchayat raj institutions. Now attempts are made to strengthen the panchayat raj institutions.

The community development programmes were conceived and evolved by the central government, though these were within the exclusive jurisdiction of the states. The programmes were evolved to speed up the

TABLE 2

The following table indicates the central involvement in village and small scale industries in comparison with the states during 1978-79

(Rs. In lakhs)

Name of Item	Union	States	Total	Scheme-wise central loans and grants to states	Share of scheme-wise central transfers in states expenditure	Adjusted expenditure of share in total adjusted expenditure			
						Union (1+4)	States (2–7)	Union (6/3)	States (7/3)
	1	2	3	4	5	6	7	8	9
Village and small scale industries	11894	13596	25490	4604	33.9	16498	8992	64.7	35.3

progress of villages, to increase the production of agriculture and to provide basic facilities to the villagers. The centre had worked out the details regarding the size of the block, staffing pattern including extension officers and village level workers, etc. Shri A.N. Jha, an eminent ex-civil servant of government of India, explained how the centre controlled even ordinary matters connected with the community development : "The central Ministry of Community Development lays down what salaries will be paid to the Village Level of Worker and the Block Development Officer and how they will work along with other Extension Officers. That, one would think, would be a matter very much in the state field, but it is all regulated by Delhi."[14] The centre controlled even training of the personnel of the community development programme. Shri P.R. Dubhashi who had worked in the community development programme explains how the centre controlled the pattern and contents of training institutions meant for personnel of the community development : "But in the training of the personnel, the union has taken either direct responsibility or has decisively influenced the pattern of the training institutions as well as the contents of the training. The expenditure on these training schemes and institutions is debited to the Central Exchequer."[15] Another means of central penetration into the community development programme was programme evaluation. The centre evaluated the programmes for which it had given financial assistance. "The evaluation of C.D. blocks in all states is done by the Programme Evaluation Organisation under the Planning Commission whose annual reports influence state administration of the Community Development Programme."[16] Thus the centre penetrated into the field of community development through various means. Shri K. Santhanam, a prominent member of the Indian constituent assembly and an authority on centre-state relations, thus concludes : "In some respects, the Community Development Programme was an even greater inroad into state autonomy than national planning."[17]

After discontinuation of community development programmes, the panchayat raj institutions were strengthened. Certain central programmes like water supply scheme, literacy programme, family planning, dryland development, rural integrated programme, Jawahar Rozagar Yojana, etc., are entrusted to the panchayat raj institutions. The centre under the prime ministership of Shri Rajiv Gandhi wanted to directly control panchayat raj institutions by amending the constitution and by providing grants to them. Delivering the valedictory address at the two day Panchayat Raj Sammelan (conference) of four southern states and two union territories at Bangalore in April 1989, Shri Rajiv Gandhi, then Prime Minister of India, said, "The panchayat raj institutions should become a fulcrum for implementation of plans at the district, taluk and village levels. We must have a revolution for maximum devolution of powers and maximum democracy and the institutions should have better financial discipline and fiscal responsibility. It was not a centre-state issue, but a joint responsibility of both."[18] Thus the centre under Shri Rajiv Gandhi wanted to share power with the states and control panchayat raj institutions by amending the Constitution. The Constitution amendment for panchayat raj institutions moved by the Congress government was defeated in Rajya Sabha in 1989. With this, the attempt of the centre to have direct control over the Panchayat raj institutions was frustrated temporarily. The Congress government under Shri P.V. Narasimha Rao has amended the constitution in this respect.

(f) *Jawahar Rozagar Yojana* : Among the central programmes the Jawahar Rozagar Yojana has assumed an important role in centre-state relations in recent years. It is centrally sponsored scheme. It is explained here to illustrate how the centrally sponsored schemes penetrate into state fields at various levels and how the states remain only as instrument of executive.

The centre determines the following in respect of J.R.Y. (Jawahar Rozagar Yojana) : (i) objectives, (ii) criteria and procedure for allocation of resources, (iii) earmarking and utilization of resources, (iv) works to be undertaken, (v) planning and execution of works, (vi) monitoring and evaluation of works undertaken, (vii) training of personnel, monthly progress report, and quarterly progress report. [19] The states have accepted these guidelines because they get handsome financial assistance from the centre. The resources for J.RY. are shared in the ratio of 80:20 between the centre and the states. Eighty per cent of the funds allocated to each district should be distributed among gram panchayats or mandal panchayats in the district. The remaining twenty per cent of funds is to be utilized at the district level for works. However, diversion of funds from one district to another is not permissible. But two or more districts or gram panchayats may pool their resources. In the first week of June 1989, the central government released Rs. 610.66 crores to the District Rural Development

Agencies (DRDA)/Zilla Parishads for the Jawahar Rozagar Yojana as the first part of the first instalment of its share for 1989-90.[20] Thereafterwards funds are regularly released from the centre.

Out of the seven cetegory of guidelines listed by manual, Jawahar Rozagar Yojana, published by the government of India, Ministry of Agriclutre and Rural Development, in 1989, a few of them may be explained to some extent in order to find out how J.R.Y. penetrates into state field and leaves no initiative and options for the states : (i) The objectives of J.R.Y. are determined by the centre. The primary objective is to generate additional gainful employment for the unemployed and underemployed men and women in rural areas. The second objective is creation of productive community assets which can strengthen rural social and economic infrastructure. (ii) Criteria and procedure for allocation of resources are spelt out in detail. Even minor details are not left out for the state governments to work out. (iii) Earmarking and utilization of resources are prescribed for administrative expenditure, provision for incurring training expenses, provision for maintenance of assets, utilization of interest earned on deposits of J.R.Y. The state governments have no options but to follow the instructions strictly. (iv) The manual of J.R.Y. further explains the types of works to be undertaken by the state governments. The works relate to land development, social forestry, house construction under Indira Awas Yojana, wells for irrigations, etc. It also prescribes wage and non-wage components of the works. (v) It explains how the zilla parishad should prepare annual plan action. (vi) It describes monitoring and evaluation of works and explains how the officers at the state level and district level should inspect the execution of works. (vii) It prescribes how the monthly, quarterly and annual reports are to be submitted by the states to the centre. These reports enable the central authorities to keep close watch on quality and trend of implementation and take corrective measures in time. (viii) The manual states how to keep the records of assets created, disposal of gunny bags used for foodgrains, etc. These guidelines clearly prove that how the centre maintains control over policy and programme formulation of J.R.Y. and exercises supervisory functions over execution of these programmes.

(g) *Health* : The Planning Commission determines national health policy. The states have to take national health policy into consideration while they prepare their plan for health. Centre provides financial assistance to the states for certain health programmes. The states have to follow the guidelines for these programmes if they want central financial assistance. Sometimes the central directions become too detailed and trifle. Rejamannar report (Centre-State Relations Inquiry Committee, Tamil Nadu) refers to such incident: "An official of the government of one of the states refers to an instance where the Central Ministry of Health suggested a reduction in the height of rooms of a proposed medical college and intimated that grants would be given only for the dimensions prescribed by them."[21]

4. IMPACT OF PENETRATION ON STATE AUTONOMY

Central penetration through voluntary grants and loans has affected state autonomy in many respects:

The states have come to depend on central financial assistance due to implementation of five year plans, growing social welfare measures of the states and inelastic nature of their own resources. They have come to depend more on central discretionary grants provided under article 282 than on the statutory grants provided under article 275. The former grants are made by the centre on the advice of the Planning Commission while the latter grants are made by the centre to the states on the advice of the Finance Commission. Quantum of former grants has increased by many folds in course of time. The Lok Sabha Secretariat Study says, "All capital grants to the states for implementing their respective shares of the five year plans are made in the form of these discretionary grants which have been much larger in quantum than the grants given under article 275."[22] Thus the states have come to depend more on the non-statutory grants. The states' dependence on the central discretionary grants has been increased many times due to the enormous increase in their revenue expenditure and decrease in their revenue collection : "The share of the states in the total expenditure on revenue account has always been higher than the central government and has been fluctuating from year to year. After a rise in the second half of 1950s, it fell to 52.2% in 1965-66, but again rose to 56% in 1973-74 but since then it is hovering around 51%. Thus, while the share of revenues collected by the states had been falling over the years and their share in expenditure was as high as 51%."[23] In his welcome address to the ninth Finance Commission, Shri S.R. Bommai, then Chief Minister of Karnataka, stated in 1989 : "The states' share in total plan outlay has been steadily declining. In the First Five Year Plan, the expenditure of the states covered 73 per cent of the total plan. In 1984-85 this had come down to only 40 per cent."[24] Financial dependence of the states on central voluntary grants and loans has paved the way for erosion of state autonomy.

When the centre provides voluntary grants and loans to the states for plan and non-plan purpose, it insists on common policies and common pattern of staff structure for centrally sponsored and centrally assisted programmes and projects. The states accept these central directions in order to receive central financial assistance even though these policies and pattern of staff structure may not be suitable to them. Shri G. Ramachandran, an ex-administrator, gives an example for unsuitability of common staff structure from the department of Community Development which existed in the past. He says : "Many states knew, for example, that there was no adequate work for Extension Officer (Industries) in every block. But even so, because of the prescription of a uniform pattern, the states had to fall in line."[25]

As the centre provides grants and loans and prescribes priorities, policies and common staffing pattern for certain programmes, the states have no freedom in choosing their priorities. The states have been helplessly complaining that the Planning Commission overlooks regional dissimilarities and needs and imposes priorities which have no relevance to the local conditions. Shri A.K.Chanda, a former Comptrolier and Auditor-General of India and the chairman of the third Finance Commission, explains gap between central priorities and local needs by taking an example from West Bengal: "Dr. B.C. Roy (Chief Minister of West Bengal) told me that the Planning Commission had allotted a large sum of money to his state for the eradication of filaria. He said that there was hardly any filaria in his state, but tuberculosis was rampt; yet he was unable to divert the proposed grant for controlling tuberculosis."[26] Thus the regional requirements of the states receive set back. When the states have to provide matching grants to the centrally approved programmes, they may not be in a position to finance their own non-aided but essential regional programmes.[27] Thus, the states are not free to choose their own regional priorities in view of attraction of central voluntary grants and of their own limited resources.

When the state governments strictly adhere to patterns of schemes financially assisted by the centre, initiative and enterprise of the state governments are stifled. Thus, there is loss of initiative in socio-economic policies of the states. As a result of this, the states are not developing innovative in both policy formulation and administration of new programmes and projects. They should have been centres of experiments in new socio-economic policies and programmes under a federal system. The federal system visualizes plurality and not uniformity in socio-economic development in a country like India with vast diversities and pressing local needs.

The net result of penetration of central voluntary grants and loans into state fields like education, agriculture, co-operation, village and small scale industries, community development and panchayat raj institutions, health, etc., through means like Planning Commission, centrally sponsored and centrally assisted schemes, relief measures, etc., is reduction in state autonomy.

REFERENCES

1. Dubhashi, P.R., "Unitary Trends in a Federal System", *The Indian Journal of Public Administration*, Vol. VI, No. 3, July-September, 1960 (New Delhi : I.I.P.A., 1960), p. 250.
2. Text of the Memorandum submitted by the United Left Front Government of Kerala in 1967 to the National Development Council in Anirudh Prasad's book, *Centre-State Relations in India* (New Delhi : Deep and Deep Publications, 1985), p. 705.
3. *Report of the Third Finance Commission* (Delhi : Manager of Publications, Government of India, 1962), p. 38. Quoted by Bombwall Raman, *Federal Financial Relations in India* (Meerut : Meenakshi Prakashan, 1968).
4. *The Seventh Five Year Plan–1985-90* (Delhi : The Controller of Publication, Government of India, 1985), p. 264.
5. *National Policy on Education, 1986* (New Delhi : Ministry of Human Resource Development, Dept. of Education, Government of India, 1986).
6. Naik, J.P., *Union-State Relations in Education : Their Implications for Educational Administration* in T.N. Chaturvedi (series editor) and Abhijit Datta's (volume editor) book, *Union-State Relations* (Delhi : Indian Institute of Public Administration, 1984), p. 254.
7. Singh, S.P., *Centre-State Relations in Agricultural Development* (Delhi : Vikas Publishing House, Pvt. Ltd., 1973), p. 132.
8. *Ibid.*, p. 61.
9. *Ibid.*, p. 368.
10. George, K.K., and Gulati, I.S., 'Central Inroads into State Subjects, An Analysis of Economic Services', *Economic and Political Weekly*, Vol. XX, No. 14, April 6, 1985 (Bombay : A Sameeksha Trust Publication, 1985), p. 598.
11. *Ibid.*, p. 597.
12. *Report, Commission on Centre-State Relations* (Popularly known as Sarkaria

Commission), Part I (Nasik : Printed by the General Manager, Government of India Press, 1988), p. 442.

13. Government of India, *Combined Finance and Revenue Accounts of the Union and State Governments in India* (1978-79, Delhi, 1983), Quoted by George, K.K. and Gulati, I.S. in "Central Inroads into State Subjects", An Analysis of Economic Services, *Economics and Political Weekly*, Vol. XX, No. 14, April 6, 1985 (Bombay : A Sameeksha Trust Publication, 1985), p. 597.
14. Jha, A.N., "Planning, The Federal Principle and Parliamentary Democracy", *The Indian Journal of Public Administration*, Vol. XI, No. 2, April-June 1965 (New Delhi : I.I.P.A., 1965), p.165.
15. Dubhashi, P.R., "Unitary Trends in a Federal System", *The Indian Journal of Public Administration*, Vol. VI, No. 3, July-September 1960 (New Delhi: I.I.P.A., 1960), p. 252.
16. *Ibid.*, p. 254.
17. Santhanam, K., "The Changing Pattern of Union-State Relations in India", *The Indian Journal of Public Administration*, Vol. IX, No. 3, July-September 1963 (New Delhi: I.I.P.A., 1963), p. 463.
18. *The Hindu*, Daily National English Newspaper 30.4.1989 (Madras : Messrs Kasturi and Sons, 1989), p.1.
19. *Jawahar Rozagar Yojana : Manual* (New Delhi : Government of India, Ministry of Agriculture, Department of Rural Development, 1989), pp. iii and iv.
20. *The Hindu*, Daily National English Newspaper 4.6.1989 (Madras : Messrs Kasturi and Sons, 1989), p. 1.
21. Referred by Markandan, K.C., *Centre-State Relations : The Perspective* (Jalandhar : ABS Publications, 1986), p. 181.
22. *Union-State Relations : A Study* (New Delhi : Lok Sabha Secretariat, 1970), p. 41.
23. Sinha, R.K., *Centre-State Relations : Present Status of Debate* in H.V.R. Athre's (ed.), "Union-State Relations", (Bangalore : *The Mysore Economic Review*, 1986), p. 263.
24. Speech of Shri S.R. Bommai, Chief Minister, at the discussion with the Ninth Finance Commission during their visit to Karnataka on 13th January, 1989 (Bangalore: Government Press, Government of Karnataka, 1989), p. 9.
25. Ramachandran, G., "Union-State Relations in Finance and Planning", *The Indian Journal of Public Administration*, Vol. XII, No. 3, July-September, 1966 (New Delhi : I.I.P.A., 1966), p. 385.
26. Chanda, A.K., *Federal Finance in India* in A.G. Noorani's (ed.), *Centre-State Relations in India*, Proceedings of a Seminar held in Agra, March 1972 (Bombay: Leslie Sawhny Programme of Training for Democracy, 1972), p. 110.
27. Doss, Veda, *Impact of Planning on Centre-State Financial Relations in India* (New Delhi : National Publishing House, 1978), p. 36.

CHAPTER VIII

TRENDS IN CENTRALIZING TENDENCIES OF GRANTS

The central voluntary grants have penetrated into various state fields. This has been demonstrated through (a) increase in the quantum of central grants to the states, (b) greater role for the Planning Commission and other central financial institutions, (c) increase in the number of centrally sponsored schemes, (d) growing dependence of the states on central voluntary grants, statutory grants and shared taxes, (e) increasing dependence of the states on central loans, (f) attempts of the centre to provide central grants to local self-governing institutions, (g) growing central guidelines for certain state subjects, (h) politicisation of grants, (i) increase in central supervision and control over certain state programmes receiving central aid, and (j) movement towards concurrent subjects from the state subjects.

(a) *Increase in the Quantum of Central Grants* : In terms of percentage, non-statutory transfers (voluntary grants and loans) from the centre to the states for plan and non-plan purposes exceed statutory transfers (grants-in-aid, etc.) provided by the centre to the states. The statutory transfers amounted to 40 per cent while non-statutory transfers amounted to 60 per cent (plan assistance 41% and non-plan assistance 19%) between 1951 and 1985. The report of the Sarkaria Commission has brought out this comparative picture : "Statutory transfers – Transfers effected on the recommendation of the Finance Commission (called by some statutory transfers) – are normally determined for a period of five years. Bulk of these transfers are unconditional and have a built in buoyancy with respect to the growth of the concerned tax receipts. In the totality of resource transfers, those on the recommendations of the Finance Commissions account for 40 per cent during the period 1951–85. Central Plan Assistance : A substantial part of the transfers in the second category are by way of assistance for the execution of the state plans. These accounted for 31 per cent of the total resource transfers from the union to the states during the period 1951–85. If to these transfers are added those on account of central and centrally sponsored schemes, the totality of plan transfers during the period 1951–85 works out to about 41 per cent of the total transfers. The central assistance for the plan is based on the recommendations of the Planning Commission. It includes both loans and grants .... A larger part of the central assistance for the state plans is allocated on the basis of the modified Gadgil Formula and other predetermined conditions .... Other transfers : Besides the transfers effected on the recommendations of the Finance Commission and on plan account, the union government gives grants and loans for various other purposes, like relief of natural calamities, improvement of roads, upgrading the salaries of teachers, relief and rehabilitation of displaced persons, etc. These comprise the third category. During the period 1951–85 such transfers accounted for about 19 per cent of the total transfers."[1]

The following table gives a comparative picture of statutory, plan and discretionary transfers from the centre to the states for plan and non-plan purposes during the period 1951–84.[2]

TABLE 1

(Amount in crores of rupees)

Plan period	Statutory Transfers	Plan transfers	Discretionary Transfers	Total
1951–56	447 (31.2)	350 (24.5)	634 (44.3)	1431
1956–61	918 (32.0)	1058 (36.9)	892 (31.1)	2868
1961–66	1590 (28.4)	2515 (44.9)	1495 (26.7)	5600
1966–69	1782 (33.3)	1767 (33.1)	1798 (33.6)	5347
1969–74	5421 (35.9)	3535 (23.4)	6145 (40.7)	15101
1974–79	11168 (44.2)	7757 (30.7)	6357 (25.1)	25282
1979–84	22757 (43.1)	15808 (30.0)	14203 (26.9)	52768
Total (1951–84)	44083 (40.7)	32790 (30.2)	31524 (29.1)	108397

The table clearly indicates that non-statutory transfers (plan and non-plan discretionary transfers) exceed statutory transfers. With increase in non-statutory transfers, the control of the central government and the Planning Commission has increased over the state subjects for which grants and loans are provided.

Various commissions and experts have noted centralizing tendencies of central non-statutory transfers in general and voluntary grants in particular. The third Finance Commission in its report noted that discretionary grants accounted for a substantial part of total assistance to the states.[3] An ex-central civil servant, Shri G. Ramachandran, explains the consquences of states' dependence on central discretionary transfers to the former : "The increasing reliance of states on discretionary central grants has naturally led to a situation in which the constitutional division of functions between the centre and the states is getting blurred, and the centre is able, increasingly through the mechanism of grants, to influence state government's policies and even decisions of administrative nature in fields such as education and public health."[4] The Report of the Administrative Reforms Commission on machinery for planning observed growing quantity of central voluntary grants and loans and decreasing role of the Finance Commission in centre-state financial relations.[5] Recently the report of the Sarkaria Commission has also noted centralizing tendencies of central non-statutory transfers to the states for plan and non-plan purposes.

(b) *Greater Role for P.C. and Others :* New centralizing trends in Indian federal finance have been set in motion by the establishment of the Planning Commission as a major agency for canalizing resources for financing the state plans. This is very clear from the table 1. During the first plan period (1951–56) plan transfers (grants and loans) from the centre to the states were Rs. 350 crores but during the sixth plan period (1979–84) they were Rs. 32790 crores.

The centre has control over various financial institutions like Reserve Bank of India, Life Insurance Corporation of India, National Co-operative Development Corporation, Central Social Welfare Board, Indian Dairy Corporation, etc. The states have to depend on these institutions for a number of purposes. Institutional finance is available to the states through these central financing and refinancing institutions.

(c) *Increase in C.S.S.* : There has been increase in the number of centrally sponsored schemes which mainly cover the state subjects. The report of the Sarkaria Commission gives a picture of expanding centrally sponsored schemes:[6] In 1979, on the recommendation of the National Development Council, the centre transferred 72 centrally sponsored schemes to the state sector and retained only 75 schemes. During the sixth plan period, these schemes increased by many folds. During 1984-85 their number stood at 201. Financial outlay on these schemes has also increased enormously. The following (Table 2) gives a picture of growing quantum of central assistance for centrally sponsored schemes and their growing numbers from 1969-70 to 1987-88. The table is prepared by the government of Karnataka.[7]

TABLE 2

Assistance for State Plan and Centrally Sponsored Scheme

(Rs. in crores)

Year	Karnataka: Assistance for: Centrally Sponsored Schemes	Karnataka: Assistance for: State Plan	Karnataka: Col. 2 as % of Col. 3	All States: Assistance for: Centrally Sponsored Schemes	All States: Assistance for: State Plan Schemes	All States: Col. 5 as % of Col. 6
1	2	3	4	5	6	7
1969-70	6.36	30.11	21.1	76.57	497.20	15.4
1973-74	18.40	35.46	51.9	261.74	610.19	42.9
1977-78	32.42	87.50	37.0	585.48	1882.86	31.1
1979-80	40.61	97.77	41.5	722.49	2241.51	32.2
1984-85	142.18	150.15	94.7	2166.90	4961.84	43.7
1987-88 (B.E.)	203.56	196.94	103.4	3075.15	5804.37	53.0

(d) *Growing Dependence on Central Grants*: Inadequate resources have compelled the states to seek both statutory and non-statutory grants in bigger quantity from the centre. Dr. R.J. Chellaiah, a leading economist of India, says, "Since the gap between the sates' expenditure and revenues is to be filled by shared taxes and grants from the centre, the proportion of shared taxes and grants to the total revenues of the states may be taken as another measure of dependence. This proportion has increased from 36.5 per cent in 1961-62 to 44.5 per cent in 1980-81."[8] Thus the states are increasingly dependent on both statutory grants and shared taxes. The taxes collected by the states amounted to only just about 33 per cent of total taxes.[9] Increasing dependence of the states on the statutory grants and shared taxes speaks of their inadequate financial position to meet ever growing socio-economic welfare measures. To meet the growing needs of the states, the central voluntary grants and loans step in. Plan and discretionary transfers were Rs. 984 crores during the first plan period (1951–56) and they rose to Rs. 64314 crores during the sixth plan period (1979–84). As they are discretionary in nature, they affect the autonomy of the states by prescribing targets, policy guidelines, staffing pattern, supervision, submission of periodical reports, etc., in respect of the programmes accepted by the states.

(e) *Increasing Dependence on Central Loans* : Loan content has been more than grant content in the total plan assistance given to the non-special category states by the centre. Consequently loans from the centre to the states constitute a major portion of the states' public debt. A huge amount of debt repayment reverses flow of financial resources from the states to the centre, reduces financial stability and autonomy of the states and increases their dependence on central voluntary grants.

Central loans were Rs.13,473 crores in 1978-79 and were Rs. 27,059 in 1983-84.[10] Increase in the states' indebtedness indicates that the states are unable to finance their five year plans with their own resources. However, they have to implement plan schemes with central voluntary grants and loans. They prefer grants to loans. Therefore, they are very eager to accept those central schemes which carry more grant component and less loan component. They jump to seize those central schemes which carry hundred per cent central grants. Poor financial position of the states has compelled them to accept all central schemes carrying central aid with all sorts of central guidelines.

(f) *Attempts to Provide Grants to L.S.G.I.* : The centre under the prime ministership of Rajiv Gandhi in 1989 made attempts to amend the constitution in order to provide grants to the local self-governing institutions which are under the jurisdiction of the states. The non-Congress state governments and the opposition parties severely criticised the move of the Congress government to directly provide grants to the local self-governing institutions. The amendment was defeated in the Rajya Sabha. The opposition parties viewed the central grants to the local self-governing institutions as a device to penetrate into state field and to establish direct central control over these institutions of the states. The central attempts in this direction speak of growing role of central voluntary grants in centre-state relations and of centralizing tendencies of these grants. In 1991 the Congress government under Shri P. V. Narasimha Rao intended to amend the constitution in this respect. It has already done it.

(g) *Growing Central Guidelines* : When the centre provides voluntary grants to the states for plan and non-plan purposes, it insists on common policies, guidelines, common staffing pattern, etc., in respect of those schemes which receive central aid. Such insistence has curtailed the autonomy of the states. Such common policies, guidelines, common staffing pattern, etc., are on increase from one plan period to another.

(h) *Politiasation of Grants :* The central voluntary grants have political teeth with which they can bite autonomy of the states. They can smile at the states with which the centre has good relations. They can manipulate state policies and centre-state relations. The following two examples illustrate this point: (1) In 1974 the centre was not happy with the Gujarat government headed by Chimanbhai Patel (who also belonged to the same Congress party). When the state was facing shortage of foodgrains, flow of foodgrains suddenly declined. The scarcity led to dissatisfaction among the people. There were disturbances in the state which resulted in the death of many people. Consequently Shri Chimanbhai Patel resigned and flow of foodgrains quickly increased. When the resources of the states are committed to the five year plans and other activities, the states cannot suddenly meet emergencies arising out of floods, earthquakes, famines, etc., with their own limited resources. Under such conditions, they can face these situations only with the central assistance. "It is widely believed that the grants of this assistance to some extent is treated as a matter of political favour. The statements made by central leaders on occasions like elections, emphasizing when making likely to be useful in ensuring better development of the state, provides an inevitable foundation for such suspicions."[11] (ii) The centre under the Congress was not generally and always happy with the D.M.K. government in the past. Under the National Front government in 1990 the centre was happy with the D.M.K. government in Tamil Nadu because of close political alliance between the Janata Dal and the D.M.K. "The financially weak Tamil Nadu found a 'friend-in-need' in the V.P. Singh government. It could secure a significant increase in the state plan and also ensure larger allocations in the central budget for the Mass Rapid Transit System (in Madras) and other railway projects in Tamil Nadu which the state had been pressing for. The centre also took a few concrete steps to help minimise the problem of coal linkages for power generation in the state. The latest is the sanctioning of Rs.1300 crore aromatic plant."[12] Many such examples can be given to point out discriminatory tendencies of the central voluntary grants.

(i) *Increase in Supervision and Control :* Since most of the plan grants are purpose grants, the central ministries concerned have considerable control over the execution of purpose grants in terms of inspection, supervision and periodical reports. As there has been increase in the number of schemes receiving central grants, there has been increase in central supervision and control over the schemes.

(j) *State list to Concurrent list :* There is no conflict between the centre and the states in the central fields like foreign affairs, defence, etc. It is only in the state and concurrent fields where there are conflicts between the centre and the states. The states have been complaining that the centre has been increasingly encroaching on the state spheres and has been playing a dominant role in the concurrent sphere through its financial assistance.

A major part of education subject belongs to the state list. It is only subject to the provisions of entries 63, 64. 65 and 66 of the central list. These entries mainly deal with central universities, scientific and technical education, etc. Through 42nd amendment to the Indian Constitution in 1976 education was placed in the concurrent list and is added to entry No. 25. Though education was formally put in the concurrent list in 1976, it was informally treated as concurrent subject before 1976. The central Planning Commission has been determining national policies pertaining to primary, secondary, university, technical and professional education. The state governments have to frame their educational policies in conformity with the national policies. Various centrally assisted and centrally sponsored schemes covering state education field have been prepared by the centre. The central Ministry of Education (now Ministry of Human Resources Development) has been co-ordinating the educational programmes of the states. It convenes the meetings of the state education ministers and secretaries to discuss various aspects of educational policies and programmes. The centre accomplishes this task through its financial assistance. Without the financial assistance from the centre, the state governments are not in a position to meet the growing needs of ever expanding higher education. For example, they cannot implement new U.G.C. pay scales for college and university teachers without the substantial aid from the centre. U.G.C. recommends implementation of new pay scales subject to certain conditions which the state governments must fulfil if the latter want financial assistance from the centre.

Agriculture has also informally become concurrent subject. From the very beginning the central government has taken keen interest in agriculture in view of food shortage in the country. The central Planning Commission has been determining policies and targets in respect of food production, cropping pattern, research, etc. It has introduced several centrally assisted and centrally sponsored schemes covering vast area of agriculture. The central budget has been allocating substantial amount for agricultural development. Production potentialities are harnessed irrespective of administrative democration between the centre and the states. The centre also supervises implementation of various agricultural programmes.

Summing up : Reasons for continuation of centralizing tendencies of the central voluntary grants may be summed up: The states have inadequate financial resources to meet their ever growing developmental responsibilities. Consequently they have to depend on the centre for plan and non-plan grants and loans. The centre has relatively elastic financial resources. The central taxes are elastic and can grow with economic development in the country. The centre has control or influence over central financial institutions whose resources can be utilized under special circumstances. Further it can make use of foreign aid and can resort to deficit financing to a considerable extent. Consequently it has ability to provide grants and loans to the states for plan and non-plan purposes. These grants and loans have centralizing tendencies and have curtailed autonomy of the states by prescribing certain policies, programmes, guidelines, etc., and by insisting on central supervision, staffing pattern, periodical reports from the states about implementation of centrally assisted and centrally sponsored schemes, etc. Centralizing tendencies of the central voluntary grants are revealed through increasing quantum of central grants to the states, increase in centrally assisted and centrally sponsored schemes, increase in central supervision and control, increase in the number of uniform policies, attempts to provide grants to the local self-governing institutions, political consideration in providing certain types of grants, etc. Trends in centralizing tendencies of the central voluntary grants are on increasing scale.

REFERENCES

1. *Report, Commission on Centre-State Relations* (Popularly known as Sarkaria Commission), Part I (Nasik : Printed by the General Manager, Government of India Press, 1988), p. 277.

2. George, K.K. and Gulati, I.S., "Centre-State Resource Transfers, 1951__84 : An Appraisal", *Economic and Political Weekly*, Vol. XX, No. 7, February 16, 1985 (Bombay : A Sameeksha Trust Publication, 1985), p. 290.
3. *Report of the (Third) Finance Commission* (Delhi : The Manager of Publications, Government of India, 1962), p. 40.
4. Ramachandran, G., "Union-State Relations in Finance and Planning", *The Indian Journal of Public Administration*, Vol. XII, No. 3, July-September, 1966 (New Delhi : I.I.P.A., 1966), p. 379.
5. *Report of the Administrative Reforms Commission on Machinary for Planning* (Cyclostyled copy is available in the library of the Central Planning Commission, New Delhi, 1968), pp. 47-48.
6. *Report, Commission on Centre-State Relations* (Popularly known as Sarkaria Commission), Part I (Nasik : Printed by the General Manager, Government of India Press, 1988), p. 375.
7. *Centrally Sponsored Schemes An Instrument for Centralization in Planning* (Bangalore : Special Studies Division, Planning Department, Government of Karnataka, 1988), p. 3.
8. Chellaiah, R.J., *The Economic and Equity Aspects of the Distribution of Financial Resources between Centre and State in India,* Seminar on Centre-State Relations, Bangalore, August 5-7, 1983, organised by the Economic and Planning Council, Government of Karnataka, in association with the Institute for Social and Economic Change, Bangalore, and the Centre for Policy Research, New Delhi (Bangalore : Government Press, Government of Karnataka, 1983), p. 79.
9. *Ibid.*, p. 80
10. *Report of the (Eighth) Finance Commission,* 1984 (Delhi : Printed by the Ministry of Finance Press), p. 98, Quoted by Sinha, R.K., *Fiscal Federalism in India* (New Delhi : Sterling Publishers Pvt. Ltd., 1987), p. 284.
11. Paranjape, H.K., *Centre-State Relations in the Indian Union,* Seminar on Centre-State Relations, August, 5-7, 1983 (Bangalore : Government Press, Government of Karnataka, 1983), p. 263.
12. *The Hindu,* A National Daily English Newspaper, 4.11.1990 (Madras : S. Rangarajan, 1990).

CHAPTER IX

REACTIONS TO THE CENTRALIZING TENDENCIES OF GRANTS

1. INTRODUCTION

Between 1947 and 1967 there was one party of dominance of the Congress at the centre and in many states. This period was marked by the process of strengthening the centripetal forces. The Planning Commission was established to formulate common socio-economic schemes for the centre and the states. There was increasing demand for central grants for economic development and social change in the states. National priorities of the plans blurred the federal distinction between the central and state spheres. The central departments and agencies came to acquire a commanding role in constitutionally reserved areas of the states. "Consequently, the territorially horizontal federation conceived by the makers (of the Indian Constitution) was transformed into a functionally vertical one."[1] The dominant position of the Congress party and charismatic personality of Prime Minister Pt. Jawaharlal Nehru facilitated and sustained the unitary process of planning. Though there were regional pressures, pulls and murmurs after reorganisation of the states on linguistic basis, yet they were kept within the bonds by the Congress high command. However, the powerful chief ministers usually got away with whatever they wanted and the centre was able to subdue others. Murmurs were generally about inadequacy of financial assistance from the centre to the states than about the centralizing tendencies of the grants.

Since the fourth general elections in 1967, non-Congress parties have come into power in many states. There have been complaints against inadequacy of financial resources of the states and discretionary grants made by the centre to the states. The non-Congress governments in Tamil Nadu, Kerala and West Bengal took a leading role in criticising centralizing tendencies of the central voluntary grants. Later on other non-Congress governments followed them. The non-Congress chief ministers and the non-Congress leaders have been demanding redistribution of financial resources between the centre and the states with a view to meet the growing financial needs of the states. Shri C.N. Annadorai, a powerful regional leader and Chief Minister of Tamil Nadu "complained that in the existing constitutional framework the sharing of responsibilities was federal, but the power to raise resources was unitary."[2] The D.M.K. government in Tamil Nadu appointed an expert committee (popularly known as Rajamannar Committee) in 1969 to examine the centre-state relations. Similarly the centre appointed two commissions – Administrative Reforms Commission in 1969 and Sarkaria Commission in 1983 – to examine the centre-state relations including financial relations. Since 1983 the combined opposition has taken up this issue at various forums.

Since 1967 diversity in political composition of state governments has become normal feature of Indian federal system. Under such federal system, it is natural for federal units with divergent political, linguistic, cultural and ethnic composition to demand greater autonomy for states and complain against centralizing institutions like central ruling party, office of Governor, Planning Commission, voluntary grants, etc. This has profound impact on the institutional pattern of centre-state relations. Tension has acquired new dimensions and has been affecting the unity of India. The non-Congress governments are over-jealous about state autonomy and are extremely articulate and vocal.

However, reactions to the centralizing tendencies of the central voluntary grants depend on political alliance or hostility between the centre and the states. If there is one party rule at the centre and in some states, one party ruled states do not openly react against the centralizing tendencies of the central voluntary grants. The centre-state conflicts are resolved at the party level. If there are different parties at the centre and in some states, these opposition party ruled states do openly react against the centralizing tendencies of the central voluntary grants. These protests become vocal when such state parties are supported by regional forces like language, culture, ethnicity, religion, etc. When sub-nationalism is very strong, protest against the centre is vocal and frequent. These parties want to survive and succeed on such issues. A demand for state autonomy and redistribution of financial resources between the centre and the states has been motivated by aggressive cultural separatism (as in the case of Tamil Nadu), by religious separatism (as in the case of Punjab and Jammu and

Kashmir), by ethnic consideration (as in the case of Nagaland, Mizoram, etc.), and by political consideration (as in the case of non-Congress national and regional parties like Janata Dal, Telagu Desham, Asom Gana Parishad, Communist parties, etc.). Nature of reactions to the centralizing tendencies of the central voluntary grants and to the central institutions associated with such grants is not uniform. It has changed from time to time and from party to party.

2. REACTIONS AGAINST CENTRALIZING TENDENCIES OF GRANTS

Reactions against the centralizing tendencies of the central voluntary grants are examined here:

(a) **State Governments :** Before the implementation of the Fourth Five Year Plan, the central grants were schematic and tied and were not given according to any formula. To great extent they were discretionary in nature. A non-Congress state government like Kerala openly questioned such grants. A memorandum submitted by the United Left Front Government of Kerala to the National Development Council in 1967 sharply reacted to the centralizing tendencies of the central voluntary grants given to the states for plan purposes: "In the matter of assistance for the plan, there have been complaints that all the states did not get a fair and equitable treatment. During the second plan period, for instance, the central assistance given to Kerala for the plan was not only inadequate but was far lower than the assistance given to other states, more or less similarly placed. There is a strong criticism that 'politics much more than economics influences the flow of plan assistance.' "[3] The memorandum further stated that under such conditions the centre becomes a financial Leviathan and such actions of the centre eat into the very vitals of the federal structure. It further pleaded that the states should be given freedom to decide priorities for individual schemes within the state sectors relating to education, health, etc. It opined that planning has resulted in centralization. It suggested that the trends should be reversed. The Kerala legislative assembly passed a resolution on 3rd March 1978 urging a complete overhauling of the centre-state relations through constitutional amendments.[4]

The West Bengal Left Front Government strongly reacted to the guidelines issued by the Planning Commission to the states for formulation of state plans to and the letter sent by the Prime Minister regarding performance of family planning programme.[5] It pleaded for greater autonomy for the states and revision of centre-state financial relations.

Shri P. Kolandaivelu, a minister of Tamil Nadu, explained, at a seminar in 1984, how the centre has interfered in the state subjects through the instruments of central grants and loans. "Even a superficial examination of the role of the central government in economic matters will reveal that as years passed the process of centralization assumed dangerous proportion. At present, almost every vital decision is taken by the centre, quite often neglecting the genuine protests of the states. The centre exercises unilateral control in regard to industrial, commercial and monetary policy including licencing of industries, location of industrial units, export-import policy, ... and interest rates. The interference of the central government in these functional areas is underpinned by the powers it has in making grants and loans to the states, the financial and other institutions it controls, the direct investments it makes, its control over the borrowings of the states and its command over foreign exchange, foreign aid and foreign loans."[6] The minister further said that the quantum of grants under article 282 from the centre to the states has been increasing over the years and has exceeded the statutory grants recommended by the Finance Commission.

The government of Karnataka under the Janata Party sharply reacted to the increase in the central expenditure on state subjects: "Again, over the years, there has been an alarming increase in central government expenditure on state subjects which according to the constitution fall within the states' jurisdiction. Apart from causing avoidable multiplicity and distortion in developmental and non-developmental expenditures, this has eroded the authority as well as effectiveness of state administration in several areas."[7] Further the government of Karnataka in its memorandum submitted to the Sarkaria Commission stated that there had been more transfers of discretionary resources from the centre to the states: "Progressively more and more resource transfers from the centre have become discretionary, resulting in discretionary treatment of states on political considerations."[8]

It its replies to the questionnaire of the Sarkaria Commission, the Assam government under the Asom Gana Parishad complained that the states have lost marginal decision-making power in their own fields due to financial assistance from the centre: "Owing to their poor finances and due to inadequate planning machinery, the states are landed in a situation where they can take a few terminal decisions on the development of their own states. Irrigation, power, education and health scheme are conceived, planned, financed and implemented by the state governments. Requirement that the schemes conform to national schemes of priority takes away the marginal decision-making power from the states. When, as have been mentioned earlier, finance of the state is in a bad shape, involvement of the centre is complete. The sectors mentioned above, though essentially state subjects, by their very nature need huge capital outlay compelling the states to look to the centre for finance and materials resulting in increasing central encroachment on state subjects.''[9]

Many state governments have expressed that the centrally sponsored schemes have encroached upon the jurisdiction of the states. They have further complained that these schemes have curtailed their limited decision-making power and have helped the centralization process. The government of Andhra Pradesh under the Telgu Desham Party has opined that the centrally sponsored schemes have converted the states into executive machineries of the centre: ''The centrally sponsored schemes are conceived and formulated in detail by the concerned ministries and the states are left with the task of execution only. Most of the schemes like soil and water conservation, minor fishing ports, DPAP, etc., are in the areas of states' constitutional responsibilities but are encroached upon by the central ministries.''[10] Similarly the government of Assam under Asom Gana Parishad Party expressed similar views to the questionnaire sent by the Sarkaria Commission regarding centrally sponsored schemes: ''Most of the centrally sponsored schemes are conceived, formulated and sponsored by the centre. Schemes of this category, coming under primary education, public health and social welfare, constitute a part of the state plan. The states are obliged to implement them even if such schemes do not get integrated with the rest of the state plan and remain attached as appendages. The centre may consider these schemes necessary from the national point of view while the states are tempted by the inducement of central assistance in the initial stages.''[11] The government of Jammu and Kashmir also expressed similar views in reply to the questionnaire sent by the Sarkaria Commission regarding centrally sponsored schemes. It stated that these schemes have eroded the autonomy of the states. The government of Rajasthan also maintained in its reply to the Sarkaria Commission that the centrally sponsored schemes do not take the specific needs of the states and that the expenditure of such schemes becomes committed expenditure for the states after a stipulated period. The government of Karnataka under the Janata Party in its replies to the questionnaire sent by the Sarkaria Commission explained how agricultural policy of the state government is influenced by the central Ministry of Agriculture and the centrally sponsored schemes: "We agree the observations of the Study Team of the Administrative Reforms Commission on Centre-State Relations. The position has, in fact, worsened since 1967 and the control exercised by the union ministry of agriculture in determining agricultural policy at the state level has greatly multiplied; such control is in large measure also exercised through the central resource transfers to states on centrally sponsored schemes."[12] In his preface to the booklet, Centrally Sponsored Schemes, An Instrument for Centralisation in Planning, the Director, Special Studies Division, Planning Department, Government of Karnataka, says, "Karnataka had taken a stand that assistance for these schemes (centrally sponsored schemes) was of tied nature; they contribute to centralisation and inflexibility in planning; and often they distort state priorities and immobilise the state resources."[13] Further the booklet opined that process of formulation of centrally sponsored schemes by the central ministries is not adequate. Many a time such schemes are introduced in sudden response to changes in policy emphasis of the central government. Details of the schemes are worked out without consultation with the state governments. Thus the government of Karnataka expressed its unhappiness over formulation and centralizing tendencies of the centrally sponsored schemes.

(b) **Political Parties :** Though the political parties aired their general views on centre-state relations in broad terms after 1967, they have taken up the specific issues of centre-state financial relations after 1980. They have criticised the Planning Commission, discretionary nature of voluntary grants, etc. The paper presented at the three day conclave of opposition parties at Srinagar in October 1983 stated that the states have no role in formulating and determining priorities and in shaping implementation strategies of the five year plans: "Equally, the states have virtually no role in formulating the five year plans, determining the priorities and shaping the implementation strategies. The Planning Commission, although a non-statutory and extra-constitutional body, enjoys wide powers and authority, administrative and otherwise in all matters relating to planning from formulation to execution. The National Development Council has become a deliberate body and its occasional meet at the behest of the Prime Minister is a ritual. Nor is the National Development Council a product of the Constitution. It is the executive of the central government which is its creator and naturally it works at its behest.''[14] The states have accepted priorities of plans and strategies for implementing plan programmes because they cannot take up socio-economic schemes without the central assistance. As the major share of their revenues are taken away by the civil service and service sectors, they are left with no substantial revenues for economic development. Consequently they cannot carry on developmental activities without the central assistance in the form of grants and loans. Further the leaders of opposition parties at the Srinagar conclave demanded that all discretionary transfers from the Planning Commission and the central Ministry of Finance should be drastically curtailed and that all financial transfers should be made through the statutory body like the Finance Commission: ''The present authority of the Planning Commission and the Union Ministry of Finance to offer discretionary grants to the states must be drastically curtailed. Such discretionary transfers now account for more than 70 per cent of the total transfers to the states and constitute a major source of arbitrary behaviour on the part of the centre. All financial transfers should belong to the jurisdiction of the Finance Commission. The President should consult the states on the composition and terms of reference of this commission.''[15] The leaders of the opposition parties further insisted that the central plan loans should be converted into plan grants.

A memorandum submitted by the Janata Party to the Sarkaria Commission opined that the states suffer from inadequacy of financial resources and consequently the autonomy of the states faces constraints. The memorandum demanded reconsideration of centre-state financial relations.[16]

The Bharatiya Janata Party in its replies to the questionnaire sent by the Sarkaria Commission demanded that the resources of the states should be increased so that they can discharge their expanding responsibilities in the context of ambitious developmental plans and can overcome their inelastic resources.[17]

In its memorandum to the Sarkaria Commission, the Communist Party of India stated how the centre influences the policies of the state governments through its discretionary grants: "It is the discretionary grants, not assured assistance under the Constitution, which has begun to predominate and constitutes the major share of the total aid, giving the central government a powerful leverage for unjustly pressurising and influencing the policies of the states in many fields of the latter's activity. Occasionally this is used as an instrument even of political pressure on the states. This has caused much resentment in the states, although under the monopoly of one party power, such resentment has been silenced at the official level."[18] Further the Communist Party of India repeated that both the central voluntary grants and the Planning Commission have become instruments of centralization in the hands of the central governments.

(c) **Civil Servants and Academicians :** Shri Asok Chanda, a former Comptroller and Auditor-General of India and the chairmain of the Third Finance Commission, opines that the central government influences priorities of the state sectors through the voluntary grants and the states are tempted to accept such grants.[19] He suggests to limit the role of article 282 which enables the centre to provide voluntary grants to the states. He says: "The questionable use of article 282 of the Constitution to channel assistance, much larger than that afforded by the Finance Commission, should be abandoned."[20]

Dr.V.K.R.V. Rao, a leading economist of India, explained how the centre has penetrated into the state and concurrent fields on the strength of its sound financial position: "The grievance of the states has been that the centre has been increasingly encroaching on the sphere exclusively allotted to them under the Constitution in the list 2 of the seventh schedule and tending to play a dominant role in the sphere allotted to them for concurrent jurisdiction under the list 3 of the same schedule; and this they trace in the last analysis to the dominant power of the centre in the financial sphere and the lack of sufficient fiscal resources on the part of the states for fulfilment of their constitutional functions. The major problem for review in centre-state relations thus turns out to be financial sphere of these relations."[21]

Shri Asok Mitra, an eminent economist, in his foreword to the book, *Essays in Federal Financial Relations,* criticises discretionary nature of grants under article 282 and opines that such grants have put the states in subservient position: "The so-called discretionary transfers, sanctified by article 282, now threaten to constitute as much as two-thirds of the total. This is where the prejudices and predilections of the union government have come into full play, converting the supposedly companionship relationship of a federal policy into almost a master servitor one.''[22] Further Shri Asok Mitra explains how the plan grants under the Gadgil formula have assumed the nature of discretionary grants in indirect manner: "The so-called plan assistance to the states, advanced on the recommendations of the Planning Commission, is assumed to be in the nature of non-discretionary transfers. But this is rarely the case. True, for the past two decades, the basic criteria for deciding plan assistance to the states are as set down in the so-called Gadgil formula, minimising the scope of subjective allocation. Determining the magnitude of the total sum to be transferred to the states each year under plan assistance nonetheless remains the prerogative of the union government. The Planning Commission may vary the amount to be made available in a particular year to a particular state, but the total amount earmarked for the states for the five year plan period is subject to the union government's discretion.... In the more recent period, the Planning Commission itself has been rendered indistinguishable from any central ministry; it cannot be any longer expected that its judgement and decisions will not be covered by the union government's overall and specific attitude. In that sense, plan assistance has been reduced to a category determined at the central discretion.''[23] Shri Asok Mitra states that discretionary element enters into plan assistance given even according to the Gadgil formula in three ways: (i) It is the prerogative of the central government to determine the magnitude of the total amount to be transferred to the states each year as central plan assistance. (ii) The Planning Commission can vary the amount to a particular state in a particular year. (iii) The Planning Commission is influenced by the attitude of the central government.

Two economists from Kerala, Drs. I.S. Gulati and K.K. George maintain that the centralizing tendencies in the centre-state relations are due to imbalance in the distribution of resources between the centre and the states, centralized planning and centralization in political process.[24] The centralizing tendencies of the central voluntary grants are the byproducts of the factors listed by these two economists.

(d) **Reports :** Reports of the commissions like Finance Commission, Administrative Reforms Commission, Rajamannar Commission, Sarkaria Commission, etc., have also noted the centralizing tendencies of the central voluntary grants :

(i) Finance Commission : The Finance Commissions have also pointed out centralizing tendencies of the central voluntary grants. The Third Finance Commission observed that voluntary grants provided under article 282 exceeded statutory grants provided under article 275 of the Indian Constitution.[25] Dr. P.V. Rajamannar, the chairman of the Fourth Finance Commission, in his separate minute, had strongly reacted to the present use of article 282. He opined that use of article 282 to provide central voluntary grants to the states has blurred functional demarcation between the centre and state spheres and that the centre has acquired spending power over the state subjects under this article without legislative power.[26] The report of the Sixth Finance Commission noted that there has been increase in the transfer of resources from the centre to the states.[27]

(ii) A.R.C. : The Administrative Reforms Commission was appointed by the centre to study centre-state relations. When the study teams of A.R.C. were studying various aspects of centre-state relations, the centre was providing schematic grants to the states for various purposes. These schematic grants provided a greater degree of discretion to the centre and had centralizing tendencies. The Report of the Study Team on Centre-State Relationship recommended measures to lessen the centralizing tendencies of the central voluntary grants.[28] The Report of the Administrative Reforms Commission echoed the dissatisfaction of the states with respect to the procedure evolved in giving grants to the states under article 282 and recommended simplification of procedure to give a greater measure of autonomy to the states.[29]

(iii) Rajamannar Report : D.M.K. (Dravid Munetra Kazagam) which stated as a protest movement against the dominance of the upper castes has been an advocate of state autonomy. It came to power in Tamil Nadu in 1967. At the same time a number of non-Congress parties came to power in several states. The Congress, at the centre, became very weak. In order to reinforce its demand for greater autonomy for states, in 1969 the D.M.K. government appointed a three man committee to go into centre-state relations and to recommend the powers to be transferred from the centre to the states. This committee (The Centre-State Relations Inquiry Committee) consisted of Shri P.V. Rajamannar, a former Chief Justice of Madras High Court, Dr. A. Lakshamanaswami Mudaliar, a former Vice-Chancellor of Madras University, and Shri Ramachandra, a

former Chief Justice of Andhra Pradesh High Court. Shri P.V. Rajamannar was the chairman of this committee. The advocates of state autonomy give much importance to the recommendations of this committee. The Rajamannar committee started its inquiry on the basis of K.C. Wheare's concept of federal system in which both sets of governments (centre and states) are independent within their allotted fields. It prepared questionnaire to secure a model type of federal system. The recommendations were also based on such conception. The report of the committee (1971) explains how the discretionary grants under article 282 have curtailed the freedom of the states in formulating plans according to individual needs : "Practically, all grants for plan schemes are discretionary grants under article 282. These discretionary grants have outstripped those recommended by the Finance Commission and placed the states in the position of supplicants for central assistance. Moreover, grants are conditional and circumscribe the freedom of the states in the matter of formulating plans according to individual needs. It is a disturbing trend to be taken note of that the non-statutory grants or discretionary grants have completely eclipsed the statutory grants. Discretionary grants constituted 71.3 per cent of the total grants paid by the centre to the states in the third plan period .... The predominance of discretionary grants has given the central government a powerful leverage in influencing policies and programmes of the state governments even in spheres such as education, medical and public health which are constitutionally within the competence of the states."[30]

(iv) Sarkaria Commission : The Sarkaria Commission (officially known as Commission on Centre-State Relations) was set up by the centre in June 1983 to examine and review the centre-state relations and to recommend suitable measures. The commission consisted of Justice R.S. Sarkaria (chairman), Shri B. Shivaraman (member) and Dr. S.R. Sen (member). Its report (1988) states that the centre has penetrated into state fields through Planning Commission and planned grants: "Centralised planning through the Planning Commission is conspicuous example of how, through an executive process, the role of the union has extended into areas, such as agriculture, fisheries, soil and conservation, minor irrigation, area development, rural reconstruction and housing, etc., which lie within the exclusive state field."[31] Many states have complained that the Planning Commission has become a part of central government and has ceased to be an advisory body serving the central and state governments.

Further it is alleged that the Planning Commission has been used to get the states to fall in line with the thinking of the central ministries. The Sarkaria Commission has given a summary of such complaints against the central government and the Planning Commission: "The main criticism voiced by several state governments and experts is that over the years the Planning Commission has come to function as a limb of the union government, a far cry from the original concept of an expert advisory body serving both the union and the states 'free from the burden of day-to-day administration'. This criticism is based on the salient or vocal premise that the union government has assumed too dominant role in the formulation of plans, even in areas which are very much a part of states' responsibilities. ..... It has also been alleged that sometimes the union ministries and departments seek to use the Planning Commission as an instrument to get the states to fall in line with their own thinking. Frequent change in the composition of the Planning Commission and insecurity of tenure of its members is seen to be attempts by the union government at securing conformity."[32]

The Sarkaria Commission has summed up the reactions of the state governments towards centrally sponsored schemes which have penetrated into the autonomy of the states in one way or another way: "The states have, by and large, criticised the centrally sponsored schemes on the following grounds – (a) Lack of consultation with them before they are introduced; (b) arbitrariness or discretion introduced in the transfer of resources on this account; (c) examination of even the minutest detail by the union government instead of leaving the detailed formulation to the states within broad guidelines; (d) distortions introduced in the state plans on account of the matching principles. The lure of 50 per cent of central assistance induces the states to accept some of the schemes even though they themselves do not give high priority to them; (e) union ministries build their own empires supported by the concerned departments of the state governments, in opposition to those responsible for co-ordination of planning and finding resources for the accepted plan; (f) the uniform approach and contents generally followed in the case of centrally sponsored schemes do not take into account the wide diversity in the local situations."[33]

The Sarkaria Commission recalls the reactions of the state governments to the special problems grants: "Another criticism is that the formula-assistance allocated on the basis of 'special problems' (10 per cent) carries an element of discretion.''[34]

3. REACTIONS IN FAVOUR OF CENTRALIZING TENDENCIES OF GRANTS

Centralizing tendencies of central voluntary grants are expressed through the Planning Commission and other central agencies. Among these agencies the planning is important. Pt. Jawaharlal Nehru, the Prime Minister of India from 1947–1964, had visualised that planning would definitely lead to centralization and he had accepted such tendency in the overall interest of the country: ''Planning is cent per cent centralization and nothing else. The centralized authority responsible for planning might be big and there might be joint planning by all states for the whole of India. But decisions by such an authority should be taken in an overall way and given effect jointly. The central government and state government should be looked on as a part of the same living organism which had a duty to look after the country as a whole.''[35]

Shri G. Ramachandran, a former civil servant, has defended the beneficial effects of central discretionary grants and central planning process: ''In so far as the plan seeks to promote certain national priorities and objectives, some sacrifice of independence of action on the part of the states cannot be helped. One should in fairness also concede that planning, while limiting the freedom of action of the states, has helped to promote uniform policies calculated to aid economic growth and has imposed a measure of discipline on the states in regard to control of non-planned non-developmental expenditure. The states have also been persuaded to undertake various measures for mobilisation of resources on a scale which, left to themselves, they may not have undertaken. To this extent, the powerful control exercised by the Planning Commission through discretionary central assistance for economic development has helped to raise the rate of capital formation in the country. Discretionary grants-in-aid within the framework of the plan have been a mechanism through which resources have been diverted to comparatively backward states and have thus helped to bring about a measure of equalization in standards of social services and economic development.''[36] Shri G. Ramachandran has emphasized the importance of central control over state plans and discretionary grants.

Dr. Malcom S. Adiseshiah, an academician, maintains that increase in the powers and functions of the central government is inevitable: "Over the three decades, there has been a move towards expanding and strengthening the union government's power and functions. To some extent, this was indispensable. The overriding priority objective of abolishing poverty, of establishing a minimum needs programme, the special attention to be paid to the scheduled castes and scheduled tribes, the rapid industrialization of the country and movement towards self-sufficiency in foodgrains production initially involved initiative action, monitoring and co-ordination from the union government. And what is to be regretted is that in most of these areas, a few initiatives have come from or interest shown by the states."[37]

The Indian National Congress (I) in its replies to the questionnaire sent by the Sarkaria Commission defended the present centre-state financial arrangements and was not in favour of further transfer of resources from the centre to the states: "The existing provisions of the Constitution have proved to be satisfactory over the last 35 years since the Constitution makers had taken the various socio-economic and regional factors into account while incorporating these provisions. They do not seem to require any alteration. Any alteration is likely to create imbalance leading to weakening of the national fabric.... The basic issue for consideration at this stage is whether there is scope for larger transfer of resources from the centre to the states. This would have to be viewed with reference to the obligations of the centre in the fields of defence and external affairs as well as the plan priorities that have a bearing on the national economy as a whole. It is equally important to assess whether the states can mobilise additional resources within the areas earmarked for them by the Constitution."[38]

Dr. G. Thimmaiah, an academician, has defended plan grants under article 282 in order to bring about co-ordination among the programmes of the states over which the centre has no constitutional control and which have national importance and relevance: "Plan grants under article 282 are meant for effecting some sort of co-ordination among the state programmes in areas over which the central government has no other constitutional control. Agriculture is a major economic activity over which the central government has no constitutional power for regulation or co-ordination. Such regulation and co-ordination as there has been, has been achieved by means of financial strings."[39]

4. SUMMING UP

Reactions of state governments, political parties, civil servants, academicians, leaders and reports of three commissions can be classified into four categories on the basis of some theoretical considerations.

(i) *Classical Theory of Federalism* : Some have reacted to the centralizing tendencies of the central voluntary grants on the basis of classical theory of federalism. The report of Rajamannar Committee (Report of the Centre-State Relations Enquiry Committee) prepared its questionnaire on the basis of model federalism as explained by K.C.Wheare. Its recommendations were also made in the light of such theoretical considerations. To some extent the reports of Administrative Reforms Commission and Sarkaria Commission are influenced by the classical model of federalism. However, these two reports are also concerned with the problems of national unity. Reactions of some academicians and civil servants are also guided by the classical model of federalism.

(ii) *Origin Theory of Federalism* : Reactions of D.M.K. Party and its leaders are based on consideration for linguistic and cultural autonomy for the states. Reactions of Akali Dal are influenced by religious considerations. Other regional parties and leaders are motivated by regional considerations in their reactions to the centralizing tendencies of the central voluntary grants. They believe that federalism in multi-religious, multi-lingual and multi-racial state has its origin in the implicit consent of the regional units. According to them, these regional units must have substantial autonomy and the centre should have limited powers.

(iii) *Organic Theory of Federalism* : The national party like the Indian National Congress (I) is silent on centralizing tendencies of the central voluntary grants and is in favour of *status quo* in respect of centre-state financial relations. It is in favour of strong centre. Reactions of some academicians and civil servants are influenced by organic theory of federalism. They believe that the federal theory is an organic theory. The centre-state relations including financial relations are to be readjusted from time to time by keeping a margin for emergence of strong centre in the evolution of federalism.

(iv) *Developmental Model of Federalism* : A maker of modern India like Pt. Jawaharlal Nehru gave importance to economic development and social change of the country as a whole without much caring for autonomy of states. He looked at theory and practice of Indian federalism within the developmental model.

REFERENCES

1. Ray Amal, *Tension Areas in India's Federal System* (Calcutta : The World Press Pvt. Ltd., 1970), p. 36.
2. *Ibid.*, p. 43.
3. Memorandum submitted by the United Left Front Government of Kerala to the National Development Council. Text of the memorandum is given in Prasad Anirudh, *Centre-State Relations in India* (New Delhi : Deep and Deep Publications, 1985), p.706.
4. *Centre-State Financial Relations in India,* Prepared by Birla Institute of Scientific Research and Economic Research Division (New Delhi : Abhinav Publications, 1979), p.10.
5. Patel Himmat, ''Centre-State Financial Relations'', *The Indian Journal of Political Science*, Vol. XXXXI, No. 4, October-December, 1980 (Chandigarh : The Indian Political Sciencc Association, 1980), p. 654.
6. Kolandaivelu P., *Financial and Economic Issues in Centre-State Relations,* Paper presented at the Seminar on Centre-State Relations, 5-8 January, 1984, organised by Tamil Nadu Academy of Political Science, Madras, p. 10 (Papers are in cyclostyled form and are available in Madras Institute of Development Studies, Madras).
7. *Report, Commission on Centre-State Relations* (Popularly known as Sarkaria Commission), Part II (Nasik : Printed by the General Manager, Government of India Press, 1987), p. 253.
8. *Ibid.*, p. 253.
9. *Ibid.*, p. 83.
10. *Ibid.*, p. 56.
11. *Ibid.*, pp. 84 and 85.
12. *Ibid.*, p. 241.
13. *Centrally Sponsored Schemes : An Instrument for Centralisation in Planning* (Bangalore : Special Studies Division, Planning Department, Government of Karnataka, 1988), p. nil.
14. *A Text of the Paper* presented at the three day Conclave of Opposition Parties at Srinagar in October 1983 and includes in Sahani Sati (ed.), *Centre-State Relations* (New Delhi : Vikas Publishing House Pvt. Ltd.,1984), p. 168.
15. Statement on Centre-State Relations released by opposition parties at Srinagar in October 1983 and published in the *Journal of Constitutional and Parliamentary Studies*, Vol. 20 (1-4), Jan.-December, 1986 (New Delhi : Director, Institute of Constitutional and Parliamentary Studies, 1986), pp. 415 and 416.
16. Memorandum on Centre-State Relations, *Janata*, Vol. XXXX, Vol. 11, Independence Number, 1985 (Bombay : G.B.S. Choudhari, 1985), pp. 19-23.
17. *Report, Commission on Centre-State Relations* (Popularly known as Sarkaria Commission), Part II (Nasik : Printed by the General Manager, Government of India Press, 1987), p. 620.
18. *Ibid.*, p. 623.
19. Chanda, Asok, *Federalism in India : A Study of Union-State Relations* (London : George Allen and Unwin Ltd., 1965), pp. 284 and 285.

20. ——, *Federal Finance in India* in A.G. Noorani's (ed.) Centre-State Relations in India, Proceedings of a Seminar held in Agra, March 1972 (Bombay : Leslie Sawhny Programme of Training for Democracy, 1972), p.111.
21. Rao, V.K.R.V., *Centre-State Financial Relations in India* (Bangalore : Institute for Social and Economic Change, 1973), p. 3.
22. Gulati, I.S. and George, K.K., *Essays in Federal Financial Relations* (New Delhi : Oxford and IBH Publishing Co. Pvt. Ltd., and Trivandrum : Centre for Development Studies, 1988), p. IX.
23. *Ibid.*, p. IX.
24. *Ibid.*, p. I.
25. *Report of the (Third) Finance Commission* (Delhi : Manager of Publications, Government of India, 1962), p. 40.
26. *Report of the (Fourth) Finance Commission* (Delhi : The Manager of Publications, Government of India, 1965), pp. 90 and 91.
27. *Report of the (Sixth) Finance Commission* (New Delhi : Government of India, 1973), p. 6.
28. *Report of the Study Team on Centre-State Relationships,* Vol. I, submitted to the Administrative Reforms Commission in October 1967 (Typed copy is available in the Library of the Planning Commission, New Delhi), pp.184-185.
29. *Report, Administrative Reforms Commission on Centre-State Relations* (Delhi : The Manager of Publications, Government of India, 1969), pp.10 and 11.
30. *Report of the Centre-State Relations Inquiry Committee* (Popularly known as Rajamannar Report) (Madras : Government of Tamil Nadu, 1971), pp. 93 and 94.
31. *Report, Commission on Centre-State Relations* (Popularly known as Sarkaria Commission), Part I (Nasik: Printed by the General Manager, Government of India Press, 1988), p. 14.
32. *Ibid.*, pp. 376-377.
33. *Ibid.*, p. 375.
34. *Ibid.*, p. 372.
35. Quoted in Institute of Inter-governmental Relations, Queen's University, Report: *Inter-governmental Liaison on Fiscal and Economic Matters*, Queen's Printer, Ottawa, 1969, p.379, requoted by R.K. Sinha, *Fiscal Federalism in India* (New Delhi : South Asian Publishers Pvt. Ltd., 1980), p. 85.
36. Ramachandran, G., "Union-State Relations in Finance and Planning", *The Indian Journal of Public Administration,* Vol. XII, No. 3, July-September, 1966 (New Delhi : I.I.P.A., 1966), p. 379.
37. Malcom, S. Adiseshiah, *Union-State Relations in the Economic and Fiscal Areas,* Paper presented at the Seminar on Centre-State Relations, 5-8 January, 1984, Madras. It was organised by Tamil Nadu Academy of Political Science, Madras (The papers are in cyclostyled form, p. 4. They are available in Madras Institute of Development Studies, Madras).
38. *Report, Commission on Centre-State Relations* (Popularly known as Sarkaria Commission), Part II (Nasik: Printed by the General Manager, Government of India Press, 1987), p. 671.
39. Thimmaiah, G., "Centre-State Financial Relations", *Economic and Political Weekly,* Vol.V, No. 42, October 17, 1970 (Bombay : A Sameeksha Trust Publications, 1970), p. 1751.

CHAPTER X

CONCLUSIONS AND SUGGESTIONS

1. CONCLUSIONS

The first six conclusions that are made in this study relate to six factors (six intervening variables) which have influenced the relation between the independent variable (central voluntary grants) and dependent variable (autonomy of the states). These are specific conclusions and the last two are general conclusions but are generally connected with the six factors (six intervening variables).

Ideologies like socialism and democracy, concept like welfare state, welfare provisions of Indian Constitution, planning process, emphasis on certain services like education, health, agriculture and social service, political compulsions like one party domination at the centre and in many states for a longer period, electoral promises, new class of elites, etc., have contributed to the growth in the functions of the states. Comprehensive planning, rapid economic development and social justice for weaker sections on a uniform basis have become inevitable. The states with their limited resources cannot carry out their functions and new responsibilities imposed by new conditions without the central assistance. It is not only these new programmes which have compelled the states to depend on central voluntary grants but also difference in the growth of resources between the centre and the states has also contributed to the dependence of the states on the central financial assistance. The central resources are elastic and buoyant and have grown with economic development of the country. The resources of the states are not elastic and have not grown rapidly. Consequently there has been wide gap between the resources and the functions of the states. The budgetary deficits of the states grew by twenty-times between-1961–1982 but those of the centre grew only by thirteen times during the same period. Thus the states are forced to depend on central voluntary grants on account of growing programmes in the state sector and of inelastic nature of their resources to meet the growing responsibilities. This has affected the autonomy of the states.

The central grants are provided by three agencies – Finance Commission, Planning Commission and central ministries to the states. The grants provided by the first agency are unconditional and do not penetrate into state autonomy. The grants provided by the last two agencies are conditional and have penetrated into state autonomy through various means. The Planning Commission penetrates into state fields through central voluntary grants and loans. The states have to prepare their plan proposals in accordance with the national plan priorities determined by the Planning Commission. In order to get central grants and loans they submit their plan proposals to the Planning Commission for its approval. The various working groups in the Planning Commission make detailed scrutiny of all the individual sectoral schemes of the state plan proposals and suggest modifications. The state governments are tolerating such detailed scrutiny of state plan proposals because they are dependent on central voluntary grants and loans. The Planning Commission controls formulation, outlay and implementation of state plans through various means including central voluntary grants. It has become the main instrument for transferring the central grants to the states for developmental needs of the latter. Though the constitution has provided power structure only for centre and states, new extra constitutional power structure has emerged in the form of Planning Commission. The Planning Commission has tilted the balance of power in favour of central power structure and has affected the autonomy of the states. In addition to the Planning Commission, the central ministries also play an important role in providing grants to the states. The central ministries and departments also participate in the process of formulating state plan schemes and provide grants to the states. They have control over state departments through policy formulation, evaluation of performance of aid receiving programmes and utilization of financial assistance. Thus they have penetrated into state autonomy through their voluntary grants and loans.

The centre has provided grants to the states by making use of various means like Planning Commission, advisory boards, central financial institutions, relief assistance, one party domination, office of Prime Minister, central ministries, Central Secretariat, conferences and seminars convened by the centre, centrally sponsored schemes, etc. The centre has penetrated into state fields through these means. Among these means the centrally sponsored schemes have become effective means of penetration into state autonomy. They have penetrated into state fields on four accounts : (a) They mainly cover popular state subjects like education, agriculture, public health, etc. (b) The states have no effective voice in the formulation of these schemes. (c) The states have no freedom to work out the details of these schemes in the light of local conditions and needs. (d) Rigid conditions are attached to these schemes for implementation. The centrally sponsored schemes which have affected the state autonomy have been accepted by the state governments due to the lure of financial assistance from the centre.

The centre has made inroads into state subjects like education, agriculture, co-operation, village and small scale industries, community development and panchayat raj institutions, etc., through central voluntary grants and loans. The analysis of the budgetary involvement of the centre in the state subjects clearly indicates that the centre has made massive inroads into state subjects. Separation between central subjects and state subjects is becoming less and less clear. A major state subjects like agriculture has been transferred into concurrent subject in reality. The centre has become a senior partner in state fields through central voluntary grants and loans. For many programmes relating to state subjects, the central ministries lay down policies and norms for implementation. They establish training institutions for the personnel of the state governments and conduct periodical seminars and conferences for state officials. They produce relevant literature for state governments for their guidance in implementing the programmes. Consequently the states have lost a certain degree of legislative initiative because of central guidelines and uniform policies relating to state subjects. They have quietly accepted this loss of legislative initiative in certain fields because they are lured by central voluntary grants and loans.

Flow of resources from the centre to the states has not only increased but has also made the latter more dependent on the former. It is followed by uniform central policies, supervision and control relating to certain state subjects. Inadequate resources of the states, statutory grants and shared taxes have sharpened the centralizing tendencies of the central voluntary grants. Acceptance of central voluntary grants in increasing measure by the states has prompted the centre to make attempts to penetrate even into local self-governing institutions.

The reactions against the centralization of the central voluntary grants are more than the reactions for centralizing tendencies of such grants. The former reactions have highlighted loss of initiative in policy formulation, of financial autonomy, etc., of the states. Such loss of state autonomy is leading neither to unitary type of government nor to very weak state system. In spite of loss of financial autonomy, the states still maintain their political independence because they are organised on very powerful and emotional bases like language, religion, culture, ethnicity, etc. The reorganisation of states has resulted in the emotional consolidation of areas. The states thus organised on the basis of language/religion/culture/ethnicity have become more homogeneous units and have been demanding greater autonomy. Though the central voluntary grants have reduced the autonomy of the states, yet they cannot wipe out separate identities of the states which are sustained by emotional forces.

Relation between central voluntary grants (first variable) and state autonomy (second variable) is influenced by many factors. In this study it is proved that the first variable (central voluntary grants) influences the second variable (state autonomy) with the help of intervening variables like (a) growing socio-economic programmes, (b) commanding position of central Planning Commission, central ministries, central financial institutions, etc., (c) powerful central means of penetration like centrally sponsored schemes, one party domination at the centre for a longer period, etc., (d) ever growing areas like education, agriculture, health, etc., in need of central financial assistance, (e) increase in the quantum of central voluntary grants, central supervision, etc., and (f) emergence of regional parties, regional groups and regional elites and their reactions against centralizing tendencies of the central voluntary grants. The first five intervening variables help the process of centralization and affect the state autonomy. The last intervening variable reacts against the centralizing tendencies of the central voluntary grants (independent variable) and demands strengthening of the state autonomy (dependent variable). It is an emotional intervening variable and may swing the pendulum in favour of dependent variable.

2. SUGGESTIONS

The suggestions that are made in this chapter are guided by two criteria/factors : (i) A model classical federal system is kept in mind. In such set up centre and states are to be independent within their allotted fields including finances. Both sets of governments should have power to raise financial resources necessary to perform their exclusive functions.

If the Indian state governments have to depend substantially on the central voluntary grants, they will be deprived of their autonomy. The autonomy of the states is to be maintained for historical, linguistic, religious and ethnic compulsions. (ii) This study, at the same time, takes note of reality of centralizing tendencies in a modern federal system including Indian federal system.

Suggestions in this study relate to five areas : (i) sufficient resources for the states, (ii) central institutions connected with statutory and non-statutory grants, (iii) functional aspect of centre-state relations with reference to some programmes, (iv) need for state autonomy, and (v) need for maintaining balance of power between the centre and the states.

In order to strengthen the financial autonomy of the states and to enable them to discharge their growing socio-economic functions without much dependence on central voluntary grants, the following measures may be taken up : (A) The states must make serious attempts to increase their own resources by various means: (i) They can increase the tax-paying capacity of the people by improving agriculture, by expanding the areas of medium scale, small scale and cottage industries and by running public undertakings efficiently. With the improvement in the tax-paying capacity of the people, they can enhance rate of tax on agriculture, sales of goods, professions, etc. They should also levy agricultural income tax on rich farmers. (ii) They should take up vigorous measures to prevent tax evasion, tax avoidance and loan avoidance. (iii) They should avoid wasteful expenditure on cheap vote-catching programmes. They should concentrate on productive measures for weaker sections and make serious attempts to provide employment and self-employment opportunities for these sections of society,who can be economically self-reliant and will eventually contribute to the economic development, social change and wider political participation. (B) As a number of central tax items cannot be transferred to the states in view of their inter-state nature, some other means may be adopted to increase the resources of the states : (i) The first course is to increase the share of the states in the existing divisible taxes like income tax, union excise, etc. (ii) The second course is to allow the states to have share in the non-divisible taxes like corporation tax, customs, surcharge on income tax, etc. These additional shares of the states should be brought within the purview of the Finance Commission and should become statutory resources. (C) Grant component of central plan assistance should be increased while loan component of central plan assistance should be decreased. (D) The total quantum of loans sanctioned by the World Bank to the state projects should be passed on to the respective states on the same terms and conditions without charging service charges by the centre. (E) The concerned states should be given power to raise state royalties on major minerals periodically. Such provisions will help some states to increase their resources. (F) Though the central voluntary grants have become a permanent feature of the federal financial system, their role is to be reduced from time to time. (G) Grant component of the central assistance for drought and flood relief should be more than the loan component.

Some suggestions relating to composition and functioning of some central institutions like Planning Commission, National Development Council, Finance Commission and state planning boards are made here to strengthen the state autonomy: (A) The Planning Commission which plays an important role in recommending plan grants to the states and in scrutinizing and giving approval to state plans requires modifications in its composition and functioning. At present it has been functioning as a part of the central government in exercising its control over the state governments. It should work like a true federal institution. If it has to work as an independent and impartial expert federal body, both the centre and the states should have a voice in the appointment and removal of its members. Security of tenure of the members should be ensured. National Development Council should have full control in such matters. The Planning Commission should remain, to a great extent, a high level advisory body with experts from different and relevant fields. It should be broad-based and federal in character with political executives from the centre and from the groups of states. Its political and non-political members should be appointed by the President on the advice of N.D.C. They should be removed by the President on the advice of N.D.C. The Planning Commission should be given statutory status and should work under the guidance and control of N.D.C All policy matters and targets of the national plan should be decided by N.D.C. The Planning Commission should confine itself to giving broad guidelines in the interest of balanced economic development and should coordinate plan activities in the country. Distinction should be made between national planning and regional planning. The programmes which require all India uniformity should be entrusted to the national Planning Commission. The programmes which require disversity and local initiative and are in accordance with local needs should be entrusted to the state planning boards. The Planning Commission should not scrutinise in detail all the individual sector schemes of the state plan proposals but should concentrate on key sectors which have large outlays, inter-state or national interests and foreign exchange component. (B) The National Development Council should have a constitutional status and authority. There should be a committee of advisers drawn from the states and the centre to assist N.D.C. Duration of its meetings should be longer and should meet frequently. It should have continuous control and influence over Planning Commission. It should remain the highest policy making body on socio-economic issues concerning planning. (C) The Finance Commission which is a statutory and independent body should be a permanent body. It can reduce the scope of the central government to make discretionary grants to the states. It can continuously advise on fiscal matters in view of changing economic conditions. It can deal with devolution of divisible taxes and statutory grants frequently. (D) As India is a multi-racial, multi-religious and multi-lingual country, the state planning boards must have greater freedom and autonomy in state planning. With increased resources, the state planning boards can play an effective role in economic development of the states. They can assess their own material, human and financial resources and prepare a viable plan for themselves. Thus they can maintain state autonomy, to a great extent, in plan formulation and plan implementation. The state plan proposals may be sent to the central Planning Commission for some kind of broad and general co-ordination in order to keep step with the national priorities. There should be no control and influence from the central government or the central Planning Commission with regard to the details of the state plan proposals.

Suggestions here relate to functional aspects of centre-state relations with respect to some programmes : (A) There should be no duplication and overlapping of functions by the centre and the states in respect of some state subjects like agriculture, public health, co-operation, education, etc. The role of the centre should be confined to co-ordination of certain functions/services which require minimum national uniformity. It is wasteful to run parallel organisations by both the centre and the states to provide the same services to the people. (B) As the centrally sponsored schemes cover the state subjects, the state governments should be taken into confidence. Before these schemes are formulated the centre should consult the states. The centre can prepare only broad guidelines for these schemes and should leave the details to be worked by the states in the light of local conditions and compulsions. These schemes should be selective and demonstrative and should not cover the vast areas of the states through the lure of the central voluntary grants.

In terms of origin theory of federalism, Indian federalism is the result of social, economic and political conditions prevalent before and during the framing of the Indian federalism. In the course of the present study it is found out that religious, linguistic, regional and political groups and parties have resented the centralizing tendencies of the central voluntary grants. Therefore, it is imperative on the part of the leaders of India to maintain the autonomy of the states in order to preserve separate religious, cultural, linguistic and ethnic identities of the various groups which are territorially organised into states. Consequently the states must be free to frame their own policies and strategies for their own socio-economic development within the national framework. Through the central voluntary grants and loans, the centre should not curb state autonomy in many matters. The financial autonomy of the states can be maintained by reducing the quantum of central voluntary grants, by increasing the resources of the states by various means and by allowing the states to have more shares in the central divisible taxes. Such measures alone preserve legislative, administrative and financial autonomy of the states. Autonomy of federating units is the very essence of federalism.

Federalism is a solution to maintain balance between centripetal and centrifugal forces. It is a unifying device in a country like India with vast diversity in religion, language, culture, ethnicity, etc. India is a democratic plural society in which certain forces have separatist tendencies. Therefore, the centre should be strong in matters of all India concern and interest. At the same time the states should have sufficient resources to carry on developmental and welfare activities for the people and should have sufficient autonomy to preserve their racial, ethnic, religious, linguistic and cultural identities. Thus, the balance between the centre and the states should be maintained.

3. CONTRIBUTION TO FEDERAL THEORY

This study intends to contribute to the theories and practice of federalism. The contribution is with reference to classical theory of federalism, origin theory of federalism and theory of co-operative federalism.

The classical theory of federalism works evenly when both sets of governments have sufficient resources to maintain their autonomy. Theoretically under such arrangements there is no process of centralization or decentralization. But in practice there is movement either towards centralization or towards decentralization or towards secession. Usually the process is towards centralization. This study indicates that semi-classical model of Indian federalism with strong centre and with dominant role of central voluntary grants has moved towards centralized federalism. It also reveals that under the present conditions and compulsions it is difficult to retain even semi-classical federalism as it was visualised by the makers of the Indian Constitution. In practice Indian federalism has become a centralized federalism under the impact of planning, central voluntary grants, one party domination at the centre for a longer period, etc.

Origin theory of federalism takes into account factors responsible for emergence of federalism in a particular country. It is explained by three sub-theories – sociological theory, multiple factor theory and political theory. (a) Sociological theory explains how certain social factors are responsible for emergence of federalism. Indian federalism is the result of such sociological factors like race, religion, language, culture, ethnicity, etc. The central voluntary grants have adversely affected these sociological factors. The Indian states organised on various sociological factors have strongly reacted to the centralizing tendencies of various central devices and forces including the central voluntary grants. They demand financial autonomy for states in order to maintain their social autonomy in terms of race, ethnicity, religion, language, culture, etc. The study reveals that the sociological factors which were responsible for creation of Indian federalism are also responsible for preserving it. These social factors have not yielded to the centralizing tendencies of the central voluntary grants. They have emotional appeal to retain separate identities through demand for greater autonomy for the states. (b) Multiple factor theory of federalism states that a federalism is also the result of non-sociological factors like regional economic interests, historical legacy of past existence of states, etc. The Indian federalism is also the result of these factors. The centralizing tendencies of the central voluntary grants have affected regional economic interests, autonomy of the states, etc. The states have reacted to these centralizing tendencies. The multiple factors which are responsible for creation of Indian federalism are also responsible for preserving it. However, these factors are not so powerful and emotional as those of sociological factors. (c) Indian federalism is also the result of political factors like past political reforms, political leaders, etc. It is an outcome of past political reforms (Acts passed in 1909, 1919 and 1935) and compromise made between national leaders and regional leaders. The national leadership is generally in favour of centralization while the regional leadership is usually in favour of greater autonomy for states. The present study reveals that the national parties like the Congress and the Bharatiya Janata Party have nothing against the centralizing tendencies of the central voluntary grants but the regional parties and the regional leaders who are in favour of state autonomy have strongly protested against the centralizing tendencies of the central voluntary grants. The regional leadership wants more resources for the states to carry out its promises made to the electorates and to sustain itself in power on the basis of regional considerations. After a long period of centralization of power, the opposite trend has set in motion in recent years. Contents of compromise between national leadership and the regional leadership may change from time to time but the spirit of compromise is to be retained in a plural society like India.

When the functions of the governments were minimum, the central and state governments under the federal set up followed independent course of action within their allotted fields. Since the industrial revolution and introduction of welfare state, the functions of the governments have been increasing. In order to cope with new challenges, the older federations like U.S.A., Canada and Australia have developed extra-constitutional devices like central voluntary grants, administrative co-operation, etc. They have moved towards co-operative federalism which means promotion of common welfare of the people with minimum conflicts between the centre and the states. The co-operative federalism is meant to encourage mass production, mass consumption, uniformity of policies with regard to certain state subjects, common benefits, common services to the people, etc. In order to achieve these targets both the centre and the states have been working together. Consequently there has been partnership between the centre and the states in this common venture. Indian constitution, in the light of past experiences of older federations, has adopted provisions for co-operative federalism. There is a concurrent list for both the centre and the states to have common programmes. Pt. Jawaharlal Nehru, the first Prime Minister of independent India, believed in co-operative federalism and introduced planning on that basis. The centralizing tendencies of central institutions and forces including central voluntary grants were tolerated by the regional forces and the regional leaders during Pt. Nehru's regime. After the death of Pt. Nehru and after emergence of regional parties, various socio-cultural regional groups and regional leaders, theory of co-operative federalism is being questioned. These regional parties, groups and leaders are questioning the centralizing tendencies of the various central institutions and forces including the central voluntary grants. The present study reveals that it is difficult to operate co-operative federalism in multi-religious, multi-racial, multi-lingual and multi-cultural country like India. Co-operative federalism can work well in homogeneous countries like U.S.A., Australia, etc. Ideal of common welfare of the people compels the Indian federalism to move towards co-operative federalism but regional compulsions indicate move towards classical federalism. India has to strike a balance between the traditional classical federalism and the modern co-operative federalism in the light of Indian conditions and compulsions.

This study also contributes something to the federal concept in a limited manner. The federal concept is not a static concept because it represents changing relationship between centrifugal and centripetal forces under everchanging socio-economic and political conditions. Consequently definition of federalism will continue to change and addition of adjectival modifiers of federalism is a part of such changing process. The following adjectives/metaphors can be used to describe Indian federalism in the light of centralizing tendencies of central voluntary grants:

(i) *Centralized Federalism* : Under the impact of planning and central voluntary grants, the Indian quasi-federal system has moved towards centralized federalism. This type of federalism will continue in future for two reasons. As long as the centre continues to provide voluntary grants and loans to the states on massive scale to meet the growing plan needs of the states and as long as the central Planning Commission continues to be a creature of the centre, the Indian federalism will continue to be centralised federalism.

(ii) *Cliental Federalism* : Indian federalism is a cliental federalism because the states have to depend on the centre for voluntary grants and loans on a massive scale in order to undertake welfare measures.

(iii) *Separatist Federalism* : Indian federalism can also be called a separatist federalism because one state or another at one time or other has been demanding secession. One of the reasons for such secession is inadequate financial resources of the states under the present financial arrangements between the centre and the states.

(iv) *Other adjectives/metaphors* like democratic socialist federalism, welfare federalism, multi-dimensional federalism, bamboo fence federalism, etc., can be applied to the Indian federalism on the basis of various conditions, compulsions, ideology, legal framework, etc. As these adjectives are beyond the purview of centralizing tendencies of the central voluntary grants, they are not explained here.

4. AREAS FOR FURTHER RESEARCH

The following areas for further research are indicated on the basis of the present study. Some of the topics suggested here have direct bearing with the present study and some of them have indirect bearing. The list of topics suggested here is not exhaustive but is only suggestive:

(i) One Party Dominant System and Centre-State Financial Relations : A Case Study of the Indian National Congress and Federal Finances.

(ii) One Party Dominant System and Central Voluntary Grants in Federalism: A Case Study of the Indian National Congress at the Centre.

(iii) Central Planning and Federal Process.

(iv) Central Plan Grants and State Autonomy.

(v) Demand for Redistribution of Statutory Resources in Plural and Homogeneous Societies: A Comparative Study of India and U.S.A. or A comparative Study of India and Australia.

(vi) Emergence of New Class of Elites and Demand for More Resources for States: Case Studies of some elites groups in some states can be made.

(vii) Central Financial Penetration is more in Developmental Departments than in Regulatory Departments of States : A Comparative study of some departments like Health and Police or Agriculture and Police can be made.

(viii) Under the impact of Central Voluntary Grants, the State Subjects are becoming concurrent subjects in reality : Some case studies can be taken up.

(ix) Central Expenditure on State Subjects and Centre-State Relations.

(x) U.G.C. Grants and State Autonomy in Higher Education.

(xi) Centralizing Tendencies of Central Financial Institutions and State Autonomy.

(xii) Centralizing Tendencies of Centrally Sponsored Schemes : Case Studies of several centrally sponsored schemes can be taken up individually.

BIBLIOGRAPHY

PRIMARY SOURCES

Constitutent Assembly Debates

Constituent Assembly Debates, Vol. V, No. 4. (New Delhi : The Manager of Publications, Government of India, 1956)

Constituent Assembly Debates, Vol. VII, No. 1 (New Delhi : The Manager of Publiations, Government of India, n.d.).

Constituent Assembly Debates, Vol. VIII, No. 23. (New Delhi : The Manager of Publications, Government of India, n.d.).

Constituent Assembly Debates, Vol. IX, No. 6 (New Delhi : The Manager of Publications, Government of India, n.d.).

Constituent Assembly Debates, Vol. XI, No. 11 (New Delhi : The Manager of Publications, Government of India, n.d.).

General

Adult Education Components in the Development Schemes of Government of India, A Compendium (New Delhi : Director, Directorate of Adult Education, Ministry of Education and Culture, Government of India, 1984).

Centrally Sponsored Schemes : An Instrument for Centralization in Planning (Bangalore : Special Studies Division, Planning Department, Government of Karnataka, 1988).

Challenge of Education : A Policy Perspective (New Delhi : Ministry of Education, Government of India, 1985).

Finance Accounts, Union Government of India (Number of Financial Accounts consulted – 1965-66, 1974-75, 1975-76, 1976-77, 1977-78, 1978-79, 1979-80, 1980-81, 1981-82, 1984-85, 1985-86).

The Government of India Act, 1935 (New Delhi : The Manager of Publications, Government of India, 1935).

Inter-State Economic Indicators (Bangalore : Special Studies Division, Planning Department, Government of Karnataka, 1988).

Jawahar Rozgar Yojana: Manual (New Delhi : Government of India, Ministry of Agriculture, Department of Rural Development, 1989).

Memorandum of Centre-State Relations, Janata, 40(11), Independence Number 1985 (Bombay : G.B.S. Choudhari, 1985).

Memorandum to the Ninth Finance Commission, Vol. I, Submitted by the Government of Karnataka, 1988 (Bangalore : Government Press, Government of Karnataka, 1988).

National Policy on Education, 1986 Programme of Action (New Delhi : Ministry of Human Resource Development, Department of Education, 1986).

Proceedings of the Conference of State Ministers, Srinagar, June 7, 1965 (New Delhi : Planning Commission, 1965).

Proceedings of the Meeting with the Eighth Finance Commission, held on 10th August 1983 (Bangalore : Government Press, Government of Karnataka, 1983).

Speech of Shri Ramakrishna Hegde, Chief Minister, Discussion with the Eighth Finance Commission, August 10-12, 1983 (Bangalore : Government Press, Government of Karnataka, 1983).

Speech of Shri S.R. Bommai, Chief Minister, at the Discussion with the Ninth Finance Commission during their visit to Karnataka, 13th January, 1989 (Bangalore : Government Press, Government of Karnataka, 1989).

Statement on Centre-State Relations, Released by Opposition Parties, Srinagar, October 1983 [Published in Journal of Constitutional and Parliamentary Studies, Vol. 20 (1-4), January-December 1986; New Delhi : Director, Institute of Constitutional and Parliamentary Studies, 1986].

West Bengal Memoradnum on Centre-State Relations (Adopted by the West Bengal Cabinet at its meeting held on December 1, 1977), [Published in Journal of Constitutional and Parliamentary Studies, Vol. 20 (1-4), January-December 1986; New Delhi: Director, Institute of Constitutional and Parliamentary Studies, 1986].

Five Year Plans

First Five Year Plan (New Delhi : Government of India, Planning Commission, n.d.).

Second Five Year Plan (New Delhi : Government of India, Planning Commission, n.d.).

Third Five Year Plan (New Delhi : The Manager of Publications, Government of Idnia, 1961).

Fourth Five Year Plan, 1969-74 (New Delhi : Government of India, Planning Commission, n.d.).

Draft Fifth Five Year Plan, 1974-79, Vol. I (New Delhi : Government of India, Planning Commission, n.d.).

Draft Fifth Five Year Plan, 1974-79, Vol. II (New Delhi : Government of India, Planning Commission, n.d.).

Draft Sixth Five Year Plan, 1978-83 (Revised) (New Delhi : Government of India, Planning Commission, n.d.).

Seventh Five Year Plan, 1985-90 (New Delhi : The Controller of Publications, Government of India, 1985).

Reports

Administrative Reforms Commission – Report on Machinery for Planning (Cyclostyled copy is available in the library of Planning Commission, New Delhi, 1968).

Administrative Reforms Commission – Report on Centre-State Relationships (Delhi : The Manager of Publications, Government of India, 1969).

Report of (First) Finance Commission, 1952 (Delhi : The Manager of Publications, Government of India, 1953).

Report of the (Second) Finance Commission, 1957 (New Delhi : Printed in India by the General Manager, Government of India Press, 1957).

Report of the (Third) Finance Commission, 1961 (Delhi : The Manager of Publications, Government of India, 1962).

Report of the (Fourth) Finance Commission, 1965 (Delhi : The Manager of Publications, Government of India, 1965).

Interim Report of the (Fifth) Finance Commission, 1968 (New Delhi : Printed by the Manager, Government of India Press, 1968).

Report of the (Fifth) Finance Commission, 1969 (Delhi : The Manager of Publications, Government of India, 1969).

Report of the (Sixth) Finance Commission, 1973 (Delhi : The Government of India, 1973).

Report of the (Seventh) Finance Commission, 1978 (Delhi : The Controller of Publications, 1979).

Report of the (Eighth) Finance Commission, 1984 (Delhi : Printed by the Ministry of Finance Press, n.d.).

Report of the Study Team on Centre-State Relations, Vol. I (Submitted to the Administrative Reforms Commission on 9th October 1967; Typed copy is available in the library of the Planning Commission, New Delhi).

Report of the Centre-State Relations Inquiry Committee (Popularly known as Rajamannar Report) (Madras : Government of Tamil Nadu, 1971).

(Report) Evaluation of Centrally Sponsored Scheme for Rehabilitation of Bonded Labour (New Delhi: Planning Commission, 1984).

Report of the Group of Officials on Centrally Sponsored Schemes (New Delhi : Planning Commission, 1987).

Report, Commission on Centre-State Relations, Part I (Popularly known as Sarkaria Commission) (Nasik : Printed by the General Manager, Government of India Press, 1988).

Report, Commission on Centre-State Relations, Part II (Popularly known as Sarkaria Commission) (Nasik : Printed by the General Manager, Government of India Press, 1987).

SECONDARY SOURCES

Agarwal, P.P., *The System of Grants-in-Aid in India* (Bombay : Asia Publishing House, 1959).

Aiyar, S.P. and Mehta Usha (eds.), *Essays on Indian Federalism* (Bombay : Allied Publishers, Pvt. Ltd., 1965).

Athre, H.V.R., *Union and State Relations* (Bangalore: The Mysore Economic Review, 1986).

Baker, Abu, *The Union and the States in Education : A Study in Educational Finance and Planning* (New Delhi : Shabd Sanchar, 1976).

Bhargava, Madhuri, *Inter-Governmental Financial Relations in India Since Independence* (Unpublished thesis; thesis submitted for the degree of Ph.D. in Economics to Banaras Hindu University in 1971).

Birla Institute of Scientific Research and Economic Research Division, *Centre-State Financial Relations in India* (New Delhi : Abhinav Publications, 1979).

Bombwall, K.R., *The Foundations of Indian Federalism* (Bombay : Asia Publishing House, 1967).

——, *National Power and State Autonomy* (Meerut : Meenakshi Prakashan. 1968).

Bombwall, Raman, *Federal Financial Relations in India* (Meerut : Meenakshi Prakashan, 1968).

Centre-State Financial Relations, Papers Read at the Indian Economic Conference, Bodh Gaya, 1972 (Bombay : Popular Prakashan, 1974).

Chanda, Asok, *Federalism in India : A study of Union-State Relations* (London : George Allen and Unwin Ltd., 1965).

Chatterji, Amiya, *The Central Financing of State Plans in the Indian Federation* (Calcuta : Firma, K.L. Mukhopadhyaya, 1971).

Chaturvedi, T.N. (Series Ed.) and Datta Abhijit (Volume Ed.), *Union-State Relations* (Delhi : Indian Institute of Public Administration, 1984).

Deole, D.R., *Central Assistance for Planned Economic Development of the States with Special Reference to Madhya Pradesh* (Unpublished thesis; thesis submitted to Vikram University, Ujjain, for the award of Ph.D. degree in 1977).

Diwan, Paras, *Union-State Fiscal Relations – An Overview* (New Delhi : Light and Life Publishers, 1981).

Doss, Veda, *Impact of Planning on Centre-State Relations in India* (New Delhi : National Publishing House, 1978).

Elazar, Daniel J., *American Federalism – A View from the States* (Third edition; New York : Harper and Row Publishers, 1984).

Fadia, Babulal, *State Politics in India,* Vol. I, (New Delhi : Radiant Publishers, 1984).

George, K.K., *Centre-State Financial Flows and Inter-State Disparities in India* (Unpublished thesis; thesis submitted to University of Cochin in 1982 for the award of Ph.D. degree).

Gulati, I.S. (ed.), *Centre-State Budgetary Transfers* (Bombay : Published for Sameeksha Trust by Oxford University Press, 1987).

Gulati, I.S. and George, K.K., *Essays on Federal Financial Relations* (New Delhi : Oxford and IBH Publishing Co., Pvt., Ltd., and Trivandrum : Centre for Development Studies, 1988).

Haqqi, S.A.H. (ed.), *Union-State Relations in India* (Meerut : Meenakshi Prakashan, 1967).

Hicks, Ursula, *Federal Finance in a Developing Economy* (New Delhi : Indian Institute of Public Administration, 1971).

——, *Federalism: Failure and Success,* A Comparative Study (London : Macmillan, 1978).

Jain, S.N., Kashyap, S.C., Srinivasan, N., and Shah, M.C. (eds.), *Union and the States* (New Delhi : National Publishing House, Published under the auspices of the Indian Law Institute, the Indian Institute of Public Administration and the Institute of Constitutional and Parliamentary Studies, 1972).

Jha, Prabodhkumar, *Federal Finance in Developing India* (Delhi : Capital Publishing House, 1983).

Kurian, Mathew K. and Varughes, P.N. (eds), *Centre-State Relations* (Delhi : Macmillan India Limited, 1981).

Lakadwala, D.T., *Union-State Financial Relations* (Bombay : Lalvani Publishing House, 1967).

Lionel Curtis, *Dyarchy* (London : Oxford University Press, 1920).

Maheshwari, B.L. (ed.), *Centre-State Relations in the Seventies* (Calcutta : Minerva Associates, 1973).

Markhandan, K.C., *Centre-State Relations, The Perspective* (Jalandhar : ABS Publications, 1986).

Mehtab, Giri, *Centre-State Relations in Educational Planning and Administration with Reference to the State of Andhra Pradesh* (Unpublished thesis; thesis submitted to Osmania University and Ph.D. degree was awarded in 1986).

Mukherjee, Subhra, *Centre-State Administrative (Educational) Relations in India 1950-1968* (Unpublished thesis; thesis submitted for the degree of Ph.D. in political science to Banaras Hindu University in 1972).

Nanjundappa, D.M., *Inter-Governmental Financial Relations in India* (New Delhi : Sterling Publishers Private Limited, 1974).

Nataraj, V.K. and Sastry, N.N. (eds.), *New Perspectives in Centre-State Relations in India* (Mysore : The Director, Prasaranga, University of Mysore, 1975).

National Institute of Public Finance and Policy, *Trends and Issues in Indian Federal Finance* (New Delhi : Allied Publishers Private Limited, 1981).

Noorani, A.G. (ed.), *Centre-State Relations in India,* Proceedings of a Seminar held in Agra, March 1972 (Bombay : Leslie Sawhny Programme of Training for Democracy, 1972).

Pal, Chandra, *Centre-State Relations and Co-operative Federalism,* (New Delhi : Deep and Deep Publications, 1983).

——, *State Autonomy in Indian Federation, Emerging Trends* (New Delhi : Deep and Deep Publications, 1984).

Panigrahi, D.D., *Centre-State Financial Relations in India* (New Delhi : Vikas Publishing House Pvt. Ltd., 1985).

Panwar, R.D., *Economic Federalism* (Delhi : Pragati Publications, 1980).

Paranjape, H.K., *Centre-State Relations in Planning* (New Delhi : I.I.P.A, 1970).

Prasad, Anirudh, *Centre and State Powers Under Indian Federalism* (New Delhi : Deep and Deep Publications, 1981).

——, *Centre-State Relations in India* (New Delhi : Deep and Deep Publications, 1985).

Rao, Hemlata, *Centre-State Financial Relations* (New Delhi : Allied Publishers Private Limited, 1981).

Rao, N.R., *Union-State Financial Relations in India* (Dharwad : Karnatak University, 1972).

Rao, V.K.R.V., *Centre-State Financial Relations in India* (Bangalore : The Institute for Social and Economic Change, 1973).

Rath, Sharada, *Centre-State Relations in the Field of Social Services in the United States of America, Australia and India 1950-1970* (Unpublished thesis; thesis submitted to Utkal University for the degree of Ph.D. in Political Science, 1975).

Ray, Amal, *Inter-Governmental Relations in India : A Study of Indian Federalism* (Bombay : Asia Publishing House, 1966).

Ray, Amal, *Tension Areas in India's Federal System* (Calcutta : World Press Pvt. Ltd., 1970).

Sahni, Sati (ed)., *Centre-State Relations* (New Delhi : Vikas Publishing House Pvt. Ltd., 1984).

Santhanam, K., *Union-State Relations in India* (Bombay : Asia Publishing House, 1960).

——, *Democratic Planning : Problems and Pitfalls* (Bombay : Asia Publishing House, 1961).

Sarkar, R.C.S., *Union-State Relations in India* (New Delhi : National Publishing House, 1986).

Sastry, M.L. and Reddy, G.R., *Centre-State Financial Relations, A Study in Levels of Development of States* (Hyderabad: Centre for Economic and Social Studies and New Delhi : Concept Publishing Company, 1988).

Satyamurthy, T.V., *India Since Independence : Studies in the Development of the Power of the State,* Vol. I, *Centre-State Relations : The Case Study of Kerala* (New Delhi : Ajanta Publications, 1985).

Seminar on Centre-State Relations, Bangalore, August 5-7, 1983 (Papers, Group Reports and Conclusions), Organised by the Economic and Planning Council, Government of Karnataka, in association with the Institute for Social and Economic Change, Bangalore, and the Centre for Policy Research, New Delhi) (Bangalore : Government Press, Government of Karnataka, 1983).

Seminar on Centre-State Relations, 5-8 January 1984 (It was organised by Tamil Nadu Academy of Political Science) (Papers are in cyclostyled form and are available in Madras Institute of Development Studies, Madras).

Seminar on Union-State Relations in India, Conducted by Indian Institute of Advanced Studies, Simla, May 18-31, 1969 (Cyclostyled copy is available in I.I.P.A., New Delhi).

Setalved, M.C., *Union and State Relations Under the Indian Constitution* (Calcutta : Eastern Law House, 1974).

Singh, S.P., *Centre-State Relations in Agricultural Development* (New Delhi : Vikas Publishing House Pvt. Ltd., 1973).

Singhvi, L.M., (Chairman, Editorial Board), *Union-State Relations in India* (New Delhi : The Institute of Constitutional and Parliamentary Studies, 1969).

, (ed)., *Federal Financial Relations in India* (New Delhi : The Institute of Constitutional and Parliamentary Studies, 1974).

Sinha, R.K., *Fiscal Federalism in India* (New Delhi : South Asian Publishers, Pvt. Ltd., 1980).

Sinha, R.K., *Fiscal Federalism in India* (New Delhi : Sterling Publishers Pvt. Ltd., 1987).

Subrahmanya, K.N. and Sreekantaradhya, B.S. (eds.), *Taxation and Centre-State Financial Relations* (New Delhi : Deep and Deep Publications, 1983).

Thimmaiah, G., *Federal Fiscal Systems of Australia and India : A Study in Comparative Relevance* (New Delhi : Associated Publishing House, 1976).

Thimmaiah G., *Burning Issues in Centre-State Relations* (New Delhi : Ashish Publishing House, 1985).

Tilak, B.G. Jandhyala, *Centre-State Relations in Financing Education in India* (New Delhi : National Institute of Educational Planning and Administration, 1984).

Tripathy, R.N., *Federal Finance in a Developing Economy* (Calcutta : The World Press Private Limited, 1960).

Union-State Relations (A Study) (New Delhi : Lok Sabha Secretariat, 1970).

Wheare, K.C., *Federal Government* (Third edition; London : Oxford University Press, 1953).

Journals and Periodicals

Bhargava P.K., *Rationalising Allocation of Resources,* Mainstream, Vol. XXI, No. 48, July 30, 1983 (New Delhi : Perspective Publications Pvt. Ltd., 1983).

Chaube, S.K., *Towards an Analysis of Social Bases of Federalism,* The Indian Journal of Political Science, Vol. XXXIX, No.4, October-December 1978 (Bhagalpur : The Indian Political Science Association, 1978).

Dandekar, V.M., *Unitary Elements in a Federal Constitution,* Economic and Political Weekly, Vol. XXII, No. 44, October 31, 1987 (Bombay : A Sameeksha Trust Publication, 1987).

Dubhashi, P.R., *Unitary Trends in a Federal System,* The Indian Journal of Public Administration, Vol. VII, No. 3, July-September 1960 (New Delhi : Indian Institute of Public Administration, 1960).

George, K.K. and Gulati, I.S., *Centre-State Resource Transfers, 1951-84, An Appraisal,* Economic and Political Weekly, Vol. XX, No. 7, February 16, 1985 (Bombay : A Sameeksha Trust Publication, 1985).

——, *Central Inroads into State Subjects : An Analysis of Economic Services,* Economic and Political Weekly, Vol. XX, No.14, April 6, 1985 (Bombay : A Sameeksha Trust Publication, 1985).

Gopal, B., *Dynamics of Centre-State Relations : Experience of Andhra Pradesh Since 1983,* The Indian Journal of Political Science, Vol. 2, No. 3, July-September, 1989 (Madras : The Indian Political Science Association, 1989).

Jha, A.N., *Planning, The Federal Principle and Parliamentary Democracy,*

The Indian Journal of Public Administration, Vol. XI, No. 2, April-June 1965 (New Delhi : Indian Institute of Public Administration, 1965).

Lakdawala, D.T., *Evolution of Union-State Financial Relations,* Commerce, Vol.125, No. 3198, August 19, 1972.

Mukherjee, A.K., *Rethinking on Federal Finance,* Indian Finance, Vol. 83, No. 14, 5 April 1969 (Calcutta : Indian Financial Journal Private Ltd., 1969).

Nambiar, K.V., *Criteria for Federal Resource Transfers : Review Article*, Economic and Political Weekly, Vol. XXII, No. 22, 28 May 1983, (Bombay: A Sameeksha Trust Publication, 1983).

Pal Chandra, *Greater Fiscal Autonomy – A Justified Demand of States*, Cochin University Law Review, 7(3) (Cochin : University of Cochin, 1983).

Pandya, B.P., *The Federal Idea in India,* Journal of Constitutional and Parliamentary Studies, 20(1-4), Jan.-December 1986 (New Delhi : Director, Institute of Constitutional and Parliamentary Studies, 1986).

Patel, Himat, *Centre-State Financial Relations,* The Indian Journal of Political Science, Vol. 41, No.4, December 1980 (Chandigarh : The Indian Political Science Association, 1980).

Phul Chand, *Centre-State Relations in the Sphere of Planning,* Journal of Constitutional and Parliamentary Studies, Vol. 20(1-4), Jan-December 1986 (New Delhi: Director, Institute of Constitutional and Parliamentary Studies, 1986).

Puri, S.S., *Union-State Relationship in Agricultural Administration,* The Indian Journal of Public Administration, Vol. XVI, No. 3, July-September, 1970 (New Delhi : Indian Institute of Public Administration, 1970).

Ramachandran, G., *Union-State Relations in Finance and Planning,* The Indian Journal of Public Administration, Vol. XII, No. 3, July-September 1966 (New Delhi : Indian Institute of Public Administration, 1966).

Rao, H. Seetharama, *Devolution of More Funds to States,* Yojana, Vol. 29, No. 6, 1st April, 1985.

Rao, R. Sudarsana, *Role of Grants-in-Aid in Indian Federation,* The Indian Journal of Public Administration Vol. XXXII, No. 1, Jan-

March, 1986 (New Delhi : Indian Institute of Public Administration, 1986).

Rath, Sharda, *Federalism : A Conceptual Analysis,* The Indian Journal of Political Science, Vol. 39, No. 4 October-December 1978 (Bhagalpur: The Indian Political Science Association, 1978).

Santhanam, K., *The Changing Pattern of Union-State Relations in India,* The Indian Journal of Public Administration, Vol. IX, No. 3, July-September 1963 (New Delhi : Indian Institute of Public Administration, 1963).

Sharma, N.K., *Evolving Programmatic Centre-State Financial Relations,* Yojana, Vol. 30, No. 6, April 15, 1986.

Srinivasan, N., *Union-State Relations in Agricultural Development,* The Indian Journal of Public Administration, Vol. XII, No. 3, July-September 1966 (New Delhi : Indian Institute of Public Administration, 1966).

Stewart, William H., *Metaphors, Models and Development of Federal Theory,* Pubius, The Journal of Federalism, Vol.12, No. 2, Spring 1982 (Philadelphia, Pennsylvania : The Centre for the Study of Federalism, Temple University, 1982).

Thimmaiah G., *Centre-State Financial Relations,* Economic and Political Weekly, Vol.V, No. 42, October 17, 1970 (Bombay : A Sameeksha Trust Publication, 1970).

——, *Plan Grants in India – A Critical Evaluation,* The Indian Journal of Public Administration, Vol. XXII, No. 2, April-June 1976 (New Delhi : Indian Institute of Public Administration, 1976).

Zaidi Naseem A., "Fiscal Transfers Should Help to Remove Dispartries", *Yojana*, 30(12), Ist July 1986.

Newspapers

The Hindu, India's National Newspaper in English (Madras : S. Rangarajan, 1988-1991).

Samyukta Karnataka, Regional Newspaper in Kannada (Hubli : Lok Shikshan Trust, 1988-1991).

EBH